You're Entitled
To An Opinion...

You're Entitled To An Opinion...

The high times and many lives of Tony Wilson, Factory Records and The Haçienda

DAVID NOLAN

JOHN BLAKE

Published by John Blake Publishing Ltd,
3 Bramber Court, 2 Bramber Road,
London W14 9PB, England

www.johnblakepublishing.co.uk

First published in hardback in 2009

ISBN: 978-1-84454-863-7

British Library Cataloguing-in-Publication Data:
A catalogue record for this book is available from the British Library.

Design by www.envydesign.co.uk

Printed in the UK by CPI William Clowes Beccles NR34 7TL

1 3 5 7 9 10 8 6 4 2

Papers used by John Blake Publishing are natural, recyclable products
made from wood grown in sustainable forests. The manufacturing processes
conform to the environmental regulations of the country of origin.

Every attempt has been made to contact the relevant copyright-holders,
but some were unobtainable. We would be grateful if the
appropriate people could contact us.

Photographs courtesy BBC, Sebastian Cody/Open Media, Anthony Crook, Pat
Dilibero, Granada TV, Bob Greaves, Tadeusz Kasa, Yvette Livesey, Katherine
Macfarlane (www.shesnaps.co.uk), James Nice and Aidan O'Rourke
(www.aidan.co.uk). Manchester Mind Map by Elliot Eastwick.

For my sister Margaret – *thick as thieves*

ABOUT THE AUTHOR

David Nolan is the author of *Bernard Sumner: Confusion*; *I Swear I Was There: The Gig that Changed the World* and co-author of *Damon Albarn: Blur, Gorillaz and Other Myths*. He has written for newspapers, magazines and radio, contributed to *The Virgin Book of Hit Singles* and produced 150 programmes for Granada Television (winning three Royal Television Society awards) including documentaries about the Sex Pistols, Echo and the Bunnymen and The Smiths. He lectures at Salford University and lives on the outskirts of Manchester.

David Nolan and John Blake Publishing are donating 25p from the sale of each copy of this book to the Christie charity. The Christie is one of Europe's leading cancer centres and an international leader in research, treating over 40,000 patients every year. To find out more visit www.christies.org

CONTENTS

ACKNOWLEDGEMENTS

The first time I met Tony Wilson, he didn't say, 'Hello' or 'How are you?' He said, 'I've just been to the most amazing museum space... *do you know New York?*'

One nil to Tony.

I then had to hand him a cheque to pay him for the television interview we were about to do, despite the fact we were both employees of the company who were going to broadcast it – Granada Television in Manchester. Tony was in a row about money with Granada and was insisting on being paid up front before he held forth on any subject, even if it was for a colleague.

In the space of a few moments I got a small insight into Tony's world: intellectual pretention, argy-bargy and problems with money. Not a bad introduction to his many lives in just two minutes.

Like many people, I felt like I already knew him. This was the bouffant-haired newsreader who had provided me with the first glimpse of my about-to-be-favourite bands on TV. This was the man whose record company made singles that were often better to look at than they were to listen to. This was the man whose nightclub I'd begun visiting in its opening week in 1982. This was the man I was soon to be sharing an open-plan office with. *I felt like I knew him.*

Then I started work on this book. Turns out I didn't know him at all.

YOU'RE ENTITLED TO AN OPINION...

The following people definitely helped me know more about Tony Wilson. That there are musicians, DJs, journalists, TV executives, writers, actors, a former *Blue Peter* presenter, a doctor, a forensic scientist and a man with a papier-mâché head among them says a great deal about the rich palette of Tony's life. So my thanks to: Mark Alderton, Chris Batten, Peter Berry, Gordon Burns, Frank Cottrell Boyce, Larry Cassidy, Vin Cassidy, Sebastian Cody, Kieron Collins, Kevin Cummins, Pat Dilibero, Ray Fitzwalter, Bob Greaves, Dave Haslam, Professor Robert Hawkins, Alan Hempsall, Konnie Huq, Kathleen Houghton, Don Jones, Tadeusz Kasa, Howard Kingston, Geoff Knupfer, Chris Lee, David Liddiment, Michelle Mayman, Andy McCluskey, Rob McLoughlin, Peter McNamara, Bruce Mitchell, Martin Moscrop, Eamonn O'Neal, Steve Panter, Graeme Park, Craig Parkinson, Max Steinberg, Paul Ryder, Chris Sievey, Mike Spencer, Peter Trollope, Paul Welsh, Jenny Winstone and Dick Witts.

Thank you – only more so – to Tony's partner Yvette Livesey. Truly a Superstar DJ...

Also: Laura Baynam-Hughes, Polyanna Clayton-Stamm, John Cooper, Ian Cranna, Peter Davis, Simon Donohue, Bob Gallagher, Cerys Griffiths, John Jeffay, Ian Johnsen, Roger Platt, Paul Routledge, Lucian Randall, Lindsay Reade, Tom Smetham and Dave Woodward for their help in making things happen.

Oddly enough, just as I was finishing this book, I had a stroke. That was a funny day. So thank you to the staff at Stepping Hill Hospital, Stockport for looking after me.

Author interviews with Tony Wilson carried out in 1998, 2001 and 2006.

David Nolan – Manchester, England
August 2009

PREFACE

It's 2001 and a press conference is taking place to discuss the production of a film being shot in and around the city of Manchester, England. The film is called *24 Hour Party People*.

There are actors, producers and directors present. Some of them are in visible states of disrepair as some bright spark has decided to arrange this 'presser' for the morning after the filming of key scenes realistically recreating a Bacchanalian night at The Haçienda, the nightclub co-owned and co-founded by the person who acts as the film's central character: Anthony H Wilson.

Nobody calls him Anthony of course – or indeed mentions the H – they call him Tony. And the real Tony has decided to take charge of the press conference. 'Right, I'm doing my day job now,' he booms. 'I'm back on straightforward presenting duties. This is a press conference. Who wants to start? Who wants to start asking questions about this strange film?'

Tony is in his element. He is effing. He is jeffing. He is flinging his own queries in the direction of director Michael Winterbottom and producer Andrew Eaton, ones that are trickier than the ones being posed by the journalists. He is answering questions that are clearly aimed at the comic actor who is playing him in the film, Steve Coogan. He is making comments about people, places and businesses in and around the city of Manchester that the reporters present will be unable to reproduce because of the laws of libel in the UK. And his phone keeps going off. The others shout at Wilson to turn the offending mobile off. 'Fine,' he harrumphs. 'It's Yvette, my wife...'

Some of the reporters are doing what journalists have been doing to Wilson since the early 1970s. They're niggling him. Taking the piss. Hoping to get a rise. One in particular keeps returning to one of Wilson's favourite themes, that music and youth culture renew themselves every 13 years: Teddy Boys (1950), Beatles (1963), punk (1976) and acid house (1989). It's a neat piece of pop theory and if he's right there's another one due in a matter of months. As the PR person winds things up, the reporter tries one last time.

'Tony,' the journalist says forcefully, 'about your theory that there's a music revolution every 13 years. I would like to say that I disagree with that. I think it's a load of rubbish.'

Tony Wilson – television presenter, record label boss, nightclub entrepreneur and professional pop culture enthusiast – looks at the reporter with something approaching pity.

'You're entitled to an opinion,' he states. 'But your opinion is shit.'

ONE

RUINED

What does education do? It makes a straight-cut ditch of a free, meandering brook
– HENRY DAVID THOREAU

In an opening flourish of contrariness that would become a constant throughout his 57-and-a-half years, the man who became known as 'Mr Manchester' wasn't from Manchester at all. Anthony Howard Wilson was born in Hope Hospital, Salford on 20 February 1950. The fact that he was actually born in the city next door to the one with which he is associated was something he never tired of pointing out to those unfortunate enough to make the mistake. Leaning forward – surprisingly tall and broad – Wilson would fix you with a firm dose of eye contact across the top of the discreetly expensive glasses on the tip of his nose. 'Actually, darling... I'm from Salford.' In 1978 he introduced viewers of his regional arts slot on Granada Television to a new band. They were called Joy Division. He explained they were from Manchester, apart from the guitarist, who was from Salford: 'Very important difference.'

Plonked directly to the west of Manchester, Salford gets very uppity if you overlook the fact that it *is* a city. It's been one since 1926 yet in over 80 years no one has managed to provide it with a city centre. It's never had one and there are no plans to get one. It's a contrary place is Salford and it breeds contrary people.

Salford is a multi-skiller. Its many and varied districts offer a different facet of the city depending on which area you go to. There's the streetwise, unorthodox Ordsall and Weaste, the leafily genteel Worsley and Boothstown, and the shiny, envy-inducing Quays. Just looking at one and accepting it as being representative would not do the place justice. Today, as you cross the border into the city, gaudy pink signs erected by the council inform you that you are now 'IN SALFORD'. The signs manage the difficult trick of being informative, attention-grabbing, slightly incongruous and rather camp all at the same time.

Tony Wilson's forbears were busy folk; European of stock and shopkeepers by nature. 'My grandfather was German,' Tony told *Eyewitness in Manchester* in 1998. 'He came here in 1901. First he went to America, then came back to Salford. We're the great immigrant city – foreigners are welcomed, it's so hospitable to outsiders, they thrive and do so well, they become part of the city.'

Tony's grandfather, Herman Maximillian Knupfer, married four times after he arrived in Britain from Freiberg. Three times he was made a widower; he was in his late seventies when he married for the final time on the Isle of Man, where he'd moved for tax reasons. He had seven children through his life: Karl, Edgar, Doris, John, Lilly, Herman and Rose. The children of Herman's first and second marriages were to form the unusual family unit that surrounded the young Tony Wilson. Karl came from the first marriage and Edgar and Doris from the second.

Herman Knupfer was apprenticed to a Salford jeweller and watchmaker called Mr Ranks, with premises at 238 Regent Road, the main drag from Manchester city centre into Salford. When Ranks died, Herman got the money together to take over the business.

Salford wasn't such a welcoming city for German immigrants after the outbreak of World War I and the windows of Herman Knupfer's jewellery store were smashed in. Karl had joined the British army and a picture of him in uniform was swiftly displayed in the repaired window. The attacks stopped as quickly as they had begun.

The mini-business empire of the Knupfers expanded. To this day, the name is a familiar one to older Salford residents who recall the entrepreneurial family and the service they provided to the people of the city. Karl took over the shop and Edgar opened another jeweller's at nearby Cadishead before shifting nearer the other Knupfers to a shop at 80 Church Street, Eccles. Both stores were upmarket and they would answer phone calls to the shops with the words: 'Knupfer Brothers... Salford's *leading* jewellers...'

Doris was more than a match for the male Knupfers and opened up a tobacconist at 448 Regent Road. She'd married a man named Tom McNulty and the shop bore his surname. McNulty died – it's believed in a motorbike crash – and Doris was left a widow. By this stage, Karl had also lost his wife. Edgar would never marry.

The three decided to buy a house together at Sorrell Bank in Pendleton, a plan scuppered by Karl's decision to remarry. Doris also decided – in haste – that she too would remarry. The man in question was Sydney Wilson, more than 20 years her junior. The family knew only that he'd lived in India and had been part of ENSA (Entertainments National Services Association, the organisation set up to put on shows for the armed services during World War II). He had been married while overseas, but it was never spoken of. Shortly after he wed Doris, she became pregnant and gave birth at 46 to Tony. Or Anthony, as she insisted on calling him. The birth was traumatic – most likely due to Doris's age – and Sydney was taken to one side and told that there should be no more children.

Later described by Tony as a 'very good-looking failed actor', Sydney Wilson would always retain a raffish, theatrical swagger with his bow ties, waistcoats and plummy tones, but he put aside his dreams of a life in show business to work in the shop. He'd bristle when customers called him Mr McNulty, not unreasonable as the name of Doris's first husband stayed over the shop window. But there was another issue that caused consternation in the life of Sydney Wilson. He was gay.

'He was very, very theatrical,' remembers Geoff Knupfer, Tony's cousin and the son of Karl Knupfer. 'Charming guy, good fun to be with, the life and soul of the party – but as camp as Christmas. He loved amateur dramatics and was very good at it. He was always well turned out. Sydney always looked the dog's balls when you walked into the shop with the dickie bow and the waistcoat. Very, very extrovert. You weren't left in any great doubt. As kids we thought he was a hoot. Half-day closing was Wednesday in Salford in those days. Sydney always disappeared into Manchester on a Wednesday afternoon. You can draw whatever conclusion you wish to draw from that.'

Geoff Knupfer also paints a vivid picture of Tony's mother, Doris. 'She was sharp, to the point of being bad news. She wanted what she wanted and stuff the rest. She was a very strong personality. Mum ruled the roost. She made sure Tony got everything. She *ruined* him. So did Edgar. Spoilt him. He was never short of anything. Whatever he wanted he got. He was born to parents who were that bit older and were relatively affluent. The tobacconist's shop was quite a reasonable business and the brothers were doing quite well. You got this mix in Tony of Doris – who was a very calculating, very assertive, very shrewd woman – and Sydney, who was the theatrical. I think Tony had the combination of the two.'

'The family used to say, "Sydney's *theatrical*",' confirms Pat Dilibero, formerly Pat Knupfer, another of Tony's cousins. 'Sydney was lovely, so nice and kind. He adored Doris: the way he used to just sit and look at her. Sydney dressed her: hat, shoes and gloves that matched. You never saw her without hat and gloves. It was Sydney who chose all her clothes for her. Doris wasn't a likeable person. You wouldn't come away from meeting her thinking, Oh, what a lovely lady. She was very kind, a lovely person but a very strong woman. She would never be swayed. She had certain views and that was it.'

Sydney and Doris, along with Tony's bachelor uncle Edgar, lived above the Regent Street shop. Tony's childhood was filled

4

with the noise of the busy shopping street outside his window and the exotic smells from the shop; musky wafts of tobacco and snuff filled the air. He would retain vivid memories of seeing visiting seamen – some from Africa – in the shop, as the port of Manchester was nearby. He basked in the warmth of the adults' attention and like a seed serviced by three bright suns, his confidence grew. 'I am very much an only child,' he later told London's *Evening Standard*. 'Meaning I am self-reliant, egocentric, sociable. I had my mother, father and an uncle who lived with us, all doting on me. So I've got a lot of self-confidence. Badly placed, some might say.'

Not surprisingly, Tony's education was a priority. Monton House School was the first destination, chiefly because it was the pre-prep feeder school for Salford's premier educational establishment, De La Salle, a Catholic boys' grammar. But Doris was dissatisfied with living in the Salford flat. She wanted the best of both worlds: a fine education for her son but better surroundings to suit the family's social standing. So the Wilsons moved to Marple in Cheshire, some 17 miles away.

Marple sits southeast of Manchester. It's where the suburbs begin to spread out comfortably and rub up alongside the Peak District national park, the rolling hills of Derbyshire that have long been the favoured weekend destination for Salfordians and Mancunians. It's the sort of place that is often given the epithet 'leafy' and has become a byword for a certain brand of aspirant living – coasters and Hostess Trolleys, Jags and doilies. In fact it's a mixed community with fine town houses and pseudo-country residences as well as a fairly tasty housing estate. In 1955, the Wilsons and Edgar Knupfer moved to a brand new house on Ladythorn Avenue, a quiet cul-de-sac set back off Strines Road, the twisting route out of Marple that heads across the Derbyshire border. The house was given a German twist, named *Oberlinden* after Herman Knupfer's family home in the old country. Tucked into the corner, it had commanding views over the countryside that led to the villages of Marple Bridge and Mellor and on a clear day, the moorland plateau of Kinder Scout could be seen. The driveways are long on Ladythorn Avenue and have a reassuringly gravelly crunch when walked on. It's an avenue for the well-heeled, make no mistake.

The Wilsons soon settled into their new community. The fact that Edgar had moved with Sydney and Doris created an extra frisson of curiosity among the family. Flamboyant Sydney and bachelor Edgar under the same roof... well, people will talk. But the implication, that Sydney and Edgar were involved with each other, was never proven – nor was it openly discussed. Sydney became heavily involved with the local drama society based at the Carver Theatre and the family were connected with the local church.

'Doris was very religious,' says Pat Dilibero. 'They all went to mass every week. She was never frivolous. She was quite parsimonious. Very much so. Tony always had holes in his vest and she would darn them. He always had money, though. She lavished money on him but she never lavished praise. Sydney did, though. I can never remember her cuddling him. She wasn't the most affectionate person.'

The detached home was a marked difference from the flat in Salford and Tony revelled in the sights, sounds and smells of rural Marple. To the rear of the house was the icy tumble of the River Goyt, making its way from the edge of Buxton to the centre of Stockport to join the River Tame to form the Mersey. Alongside the river, the single-line railway track heading for Sheffield and beyond that, the moss-covered ruins of a nearby mill. 'A muddy forest of wonders,' Tony would later write, describing the sorties he and other boys made from the new housing development down to a playground of rubble and remains from an earlier age. 'Beneath the ferns and trees, the remnants of old stone buildings would lie, wet, lichen-covered, mossy and inviting to a curious bunch of pre-teens.' These were the remnants of Mellor Mill, built by industrial entrepreneur Samuel Oldknow in 1793. Next to them were the Roman lakes – actually built at the turn of the

19th century to service the mill. They became a popular attraction and they're still there today.

Despite their business interests taking them from Marple to Salford every day, the Wilsons thought that growing up in the countryside would be good for young Tony. 'All my relatives said this was a dreadful mistake,' Tony told *The Independent* in 2003. '"You've ruined his life! You've taken him away from a school that could have got him into De La Salle."'

Instead Tony went to St Mary's Catholic primary in neighbouring Marple Bridge, a community actually slightly leafier than Marple. There had been a school on the site since 1860 and had initially provided education for the children of Irish Catholics who'd moved to the North West to work on the railways and canals. Tony was one of 300 pupils, largely drawn from Marple, Mellor and Compstall. Doris and Sydney took a keen interest in Tony's education and were regular visitors, checking on their son's progress. But Tony didn't take to the school, later saying he didn't see eye to eye with the teachers.

He dawdled at seventh or eighth in class until his parents paid for a tutor to help him with his studies and to coach him towards passing the 11-plus examination, along with an additional entrance examination for De La Salle. It gave him the place his parents had yearned for and Wilson always took great pleasure in relating how he came first out of the thousand entrants in that year. It demonstrated to him something that would become a recurring theme in his life: not only was he clever but if he put his mind to it, he could be the cleverest person in the room.

The Wilsons were loath to up sticks and move back to Salford, so in 1961, aged 11, Anthony Howard Wilson began commuting twice a day – a round trip of some 35 miles. Looking slightly higgledy-piggledy in a bold red De La Salle blazer over mend-and-make-do clothes, he would be ready and on the platform by 7.30am to get the train into Manchester. Plenty of time to devour a book and admire the magnificent views from the Marple viaduct that carries the railway more than 120 feet over the River

Goyt, then on through Bredbury and Reddish towards Manchester. Then he would walk down Piccadilly Approach to Piccadilly Gardens to get a bus to De La Salle Catholic Grammar School for Boys.

'It was what you would call today a grant-maintained school,' recalls Tony's school friend Tadeusz Kasa. 'You passed your 11-plus, but then you still had to take an entrance exam before they let you in. Within our catchment area there were only three Catholic grammar schools and De La Salle was by far regarded as the most serious. And the most scary. We were sent there because it had high academic standards, but also strict discipline. It was considered a good school but it wouldn't be scary if you behaved. It had a fantastic reputation at that time – it was run by the De La Salle Christian Brothers who lived on site.'

The De La Salle teaching order, founded by St John Baptist De La Salle, was initially established as a means of helping and educating the children of the poor. By the 1960s the Salford school had become a byword for high standards of education and behaviour and was a beacon for parents with aspirations for their upper-working class and lower-middle class children. The De La Salle Christian Brothers are still going strong; they're often confused with the Edmund Rice Christian Brothers, though their Irish counterparts ran an even less liberal regime than the De La Salle order.

'There was a culture of discipline,' continues Tadeusz Kasa. 'The strap, the cane, the slipper. But most of the corporal punishment was carried out by the lay teachers. I don't think that excuses the order, because most of that stuff was carried out under their auspices. But it isn't right to say that the De La Salle order was made up of vicious individuals. Far from it. They were mostly decent blokes.'

Head teacher at the time was Brother Columba. His regime was a tough one with strict rules on everything down to the width of trousers and the length of pupils' hair. Brother Columba carried a cane in the sleeve of his cassock which he could produce, Derringer-like, to administer instant justice. In 1962 there was a change at the top and Brother Terrence took charge. Rules were relaxed. Slightly.

Another De La Salle pupil was Kevin Cummins, who went on to be the photographer-in-residence to the Manchester music scene. He had moved to Salford aged nine and went to the school on a scholarship. 'Nothing prepared me for it,' says Cummins. 'I didn't know we weren't allowed to play football. I didn't know we had to wear short trousers and caps until the fourth year. I didn't understand just how draconian the place was. We thought people must be stupid to pay to go to there. We had a religious knowledge teacher who was also a woodwork teacher. At the start of the woodwork lesson we had to make the sign of the cross. But we had to say "pencils, rulers, saws and squares" instead of "in the name of the Father..." and so on. I spent four years making a stool. It was like a borstal. I know it's fashionable to knock your old school, but I was terrified. The bullying came from the top. The teachers would choose people like themselves to be prefects and the prefects would then bully us. You just had to keep your head down.

'Tony was bright, but we were all bright. They hot-housed you for Oxbridge. If you weren't in the top five or six in class, they lost interest in you. You could be a swot or you could fuck about. Tony was older than me. We looked up to the older pupils but they didn't know who we were. It's a massive gap at that age – half a life away. I was an outsider. I was a Man City fan.'

In a conscious aping of public school rituals, rugby was De La Salle's game – and football was not on the syllabus. It was permitted in the school yard and Tony was an enthusiastic, albeit ungainly player, his loping gait getting in the way of any abilities he possessed.

Science was initially Tony's passion and he excelled at De La Salle. After being placed in the A stream – the top tier of his year – he would come top of his class for the first three terms. 'Tony didn't have a problem because he was academically brilliant, a high flyer,' says Tadeusz Kasa. 'He was young. He'd jumped a year and would eventually take his O Levels and A Levels a year earlier than anyone else. He didn't have a problem with that side of things. If he got into trouble it would be because the whole class would get in trouble and beaten. Sometimes 28 of us would get whacked for talking in the corridor. We'd all get slippered – the euphemism for being hit with a plimsoll. If he got into trouble it would be because he had a smirk on his face.'

'He was conspicuous because he was larger than life,' says Peter McNamara, another contemporary at De La Salle. 'Sweeping down the corridors, you'd notice him. He seemed a cut above. He had quite a posh voice – that probably came from Sydney. He was seen as a posh lad.

'He was well liked by the teachers, he worked hard and he was a conformist. I remember going into a classroom once before the teacher came in and Tony was testing the other lads on their Latin before the teacher arrived. I thought, what a swot! But he was a good lad. A high flyer. Flamboyant. Different. Extremely confident. Serious self-belief. I can't imagine him ever doubting himself unless he did that in privacy.'

The city that Tony walked through to get to his school was brash, noisy and in your face. Manchester would make a deep impression on him. He'd had a taste of what it had to offer through the frequent trips he'd make to Salford with his parents as they maintained their businesses interests. As he got older and his already considerable confidence grew, he began to linger after school, expanding his knowledge with heavy texts at the magnificent Central Library. He also got regular secondary whiffs of the heady glamour available in the city centre.

'I remember Manchester as a very groovy city, a club city,' he later recalled to writer and photographer Aidan O'Rourke. 'I remember my mum and dad coming home with the programme of *West Side Story*. We were the pre-run of the West End of London in those days. My mother used to go into Manchester, go for a coffee, meet friends, go to the Midland Hotel.'

Aged 14, Tony's scientific intentions were placed on the back Bunsen burner. A trip to Stratford-upon-Avon to see Peter Hall's production of *Hamlet* knocked him sideways. It starred Manchester-born David Warner in the title role and Glenda Jackson as Ophelia. Warner – then aged 24 – was the first rock'n'roll *Hamlet*. His prince was a louche, studenty radical with a studied air of fuck-you nonchalance. Despised by critics, Warner's Hamlet became highly attractive to youthful theatre audiences disenfranchised from Shakespeare as the 1960s began to swing oh-so-gently. During one performance, Warner gleefully incorporated audience heckles into the text. Water off a duck's back. Here was a man who didn't care what people said about him, he was going to do things his way. It made a deep impression on Tony and he decided there and then that he must read English at university.

His interests at De La Salle began to reflect his more artistic leanings. He took to strumming a guitar and wandering around school with lofty, impressive books. 'He would have been a target for piss-taking,' says Tadeusz Kasa, 'because he used to walk around with Chaucer and TS Eliot under his arm. I mean he *really did*. He did the drama and the theatre stuff. He was very noticeable to the macho crowd. Aesthetic is a good word for Wilson. That's exactly what he was. A sort of weakling aesthetic person. He would have been pushed around by the rugby crowd because he had a lot to say and he walked around with books under his arm and he was a target.' To the further annoyance of the rugger buggers, Tony's actorly leanings became pronounced too. He appeared in a De La Salle production –*The Lark* by Jean Anouilh and he played Autolycus in Shakespeare's *The Winter's Tale*.

'Looking back it's a bit typecast in a way,' says Peter McNamara. 'Playing the buffoon, the loud brash role.' When Sydney Wilson, actorly and fruity of voice, came to school to pick Tony up on one occasion, one pupil cried: 'Don't tell me – Wilson's dad!'

There was always a party after shows and the girls from the

nearby Adelphi school – who featured in the cast – went to these parties, providing a further reason for taking up the theatrical life. 'There was quite a lot of social life associated with it,' recalls Peter McNamara. 'The strong reasons for joining were being a thespian or that you were interested in meeting girls. We used to hire a hall in Worsley and we'd all pile in with wine and beer. And girls. And smoking. Although Tony was never a big drinker. He didn't seem to need it. When you were a kid you'd have a few pints to chat up girls to give you Dutch courage. Tony didn't need that. He had self-confidence. He wasn't shy with girls despite being in an all boys' school. Tony used to fall in love and write poems for girls. He used to see himself as a romantic. I think he *was* romantic.' His swooning *Variations On A Theme* was published in the school magazine *The LaSallian*:

> Does such gaiety evade
> Those who search for,
> This firm sensuality
> Has alloyed the golden ore
> To baser metal; enduring
> Steel; strength in a dual role.
> Like two burst dams, our lips pour
> Fluent libations of wine
> Into the fertile valley
> That narrows with each torrent
> Of passion, yet restoring
> Balance in the spirit, by
> Simple joys of the body.

With a Tiggerish enthusiasm familiar to those who knew him in later life, Tony scattered himself across a range of interests and activities. He was secretary of the English Society. He wrote loftily of the society in the school magazine: 'The great renaissance philosopher Pico Mirandola once said: "It profiteth a man more to discuss one hour with his equals than to study one day on his own."'

A fondness for an erudite quote was clearly well formed by this stage. He was also a leading light in the debating society, though even his own team mates admitted that his florid, bombastic style alienated audiences and judges alike when they entered debate competitions. The school magazine even noted that one problem the society had to contend with was 'Mr Wilson's proclivity for tabling provocative motions.' However, he did manage to curtail these to help the society win the Demosthenes trophy in the Salford public speaking competition of 1966. 'It's a great gift to be able to speak in public,' says Peter McNamara today. 'He was quite a presence. It certainly impressed me, having the balls to stand up and do that.'

Tony also became a master of ceremonies for school entertainments. There's a fascinating glimpse of the future in this aspect of his persona. Lunchtime and evening concerts were regular events at the school. Cheese and wine plus some discreet jazz. Tony's forte was to compere such events. Essentially he would take to the stage and tell people how utterly *fantastic* everything they were about to hear *really and truly* was. 'He was always the guy who came on and did the talking,' Tadeusz Kasa recalls. 'He never did any actual *playing*.' So Tony's favoured role at school was that of a ringmaster, hyping up expectation in the performances of others; the very thing he would essentially make a career of.

In January 1966, Karl Knupfer died. By the summer, Edgar Knupfer had also passed away. Doris drew Tony even closer to her. They even holidayed together in Paris, leaving Sydney literally minding the shop. All three, however, would regularly holiday together in Ireland. It was there that the teenage Tony picked up a habit that he would never shake off and one that would – nearly 40 years later – get him into big trouble: swearing. 'He was running round the house saying, "This is feckin' ridiculous" – feckin' this and feckin' that,' recalls Geoff Knupfer of Tony's return from one summer holiday in Ireland. 'Clearly done to impress. He'd picked it up in Ireland and obviously thought it sounded good. That was Tony to a T really. So he was feckin' everything. Doris and Sydney just let it happen.'

Doris and Sydney's relationship with their son remained one of barely-disguised indulgence and generosity. He was the centre of Doris's universe. But the gifts and the attention may have been a substitute for something more meaningful. This seeming gap in Tony's life is summed up by this memory from Geoff Knupfer of a Christmas morning when Tony stayed over at his cousin's house in Salford.

'Christmas morning he got up at our house,' says Geoff today. 'I was very close to my mum as my dad died when I was 17. Tony made some comment to his mother which got back to my mother about how warm and close we seemed and the wonderful way we celebrated Christmas – because I had lots of presents to unwrap. His parents just gave him money. It obviously hit home. They'd spoiled him but they just threw money at him. He was obviously quite shocked at the way we celebrated Christmas in our house as opposed to just throwing money at him, as they did at their house.'

As he entered his final terms at De La Salle, Tony expanded his socialising. He developed what turned into a lifelong love of flinging out quotations left, right and centre. He went to sixth-form parties, where he could play his beloved Beatles on a Dansette record player, but he didn't like nightclubs – places with names like The Twisted Wheel and The Oasis. Not Tony's thing. He also stayed away from Marple, keen on fraternising with the Salford locals and especially drinking in the Cross Keys pub in Eccles. A dimpled half-pint mug of bitter in one hand, Tony would hold forth on matters of art and literature, in an attempt to impress the girls from the Adelphi school.

'The Cross Keys was a favourite,' remembers Peter McNamara. 'It was olde worlde, but it was one of those places that would serve you if you were underage.'

The end result of his seven years at De La Salle would be eight O Levels – his lowest mark was a grade four in English – and three A Levels. His highest A Level mark was a grade A in English. Skipping a year meant Tony came out of De La Salle in

1968 with time on his hands before starting university. So he thought he'd try his hand at teaching.

Blue Coat School in Oldham was an imposing Church of England establishment with a firm religious brief; for many years it refused entry to non-Christians. During the spring and summer terms, 17-year-old Tony made the even longer trip from Marple to Oldham, approaching the task with a soon-to-be-familiar swagger. 'I thought I was God's gift to teaching,' he told the *Manchester Evening News* in 1976. 'I knew the other teachers didn't like me. I probably knew nothing.' He might have been saddened to learn that there is only one reference to him in the school records. In a summary of the 1967/68 Blue Coat academic year it reads: 'Mr Wilson, a student, arrived to help with English'. And that's it.

On his 18th birthday, Tony was given an impressive gift by his parents, an act of indulgence unheard of among his peers. 'His mother gave him a brand-spanking-new Sunbeam Stiletto,' says cousin Geoff. Tony took the car to show the regulars at the Cross Keys pub. The gift came at a time when his penchant for making bold pronouncements – and his taste for left wing politics – was coming to the fore. 'We were in the Cross Keys,' recalls Geoff, 'and Tony says, "I wish I had been born in a terraced slum down by the docks. So that I could experience it first hand."

'Someone said: "If you feel that strongly about it, Tony, why don't you give your Sunbeam Stiletto away?" He was a bit of a champagne-socialist type. He'd got older parents and an older uncle who all doted on him and he benefited from that. He was perceived as a bit of a prat in those days. He was very loud and he had views. He wasn't really one of the lads.'

After toying with Manchester University, Tony opted for Cambridge. How proud Doris must have been. 'She was over the moon,' remembers Geoff. 'She spoilt him even more.'

In an interview with journalist Jonathan Sale in 2003 about his educational life, Tony explained how he still felt torn about what to do with his academic abilities. 'In my first term I suddenly thought: all I want to be is a nuclear physicist. What am I doing reading English? What job will I do? I decided I would be a television journalist and joined the student paper.' In fact, by his second term Tony would be editing *Varsity*, putting in 40 hours a week. By his own admission, this would rise to 'something like 100' hours a week.

But as would happen again in the future, Tony found himself constantly drawn back to the North West. He attended social gatherings for De La Salle old boys. 'Tony was persuaded to perform in an old boys' troupe called the LaSallian players.' says Peter McNamara. It was at the insistence of flamboyant head of history Kevin Conroy, one of those teachers seemingly pulled from the pages of an Alan Bennett play. After a show he would invite current and former pupils round to his for drinkies. He was one of the few people who were louder and more more theatrical than Tony Wilson himself.

'We were round at Kevin Conroy's house in Eccles after one of these plays once, enjoying ourselves, having a few drinks. Kevin was a bit like Tony's dad. He fancied himself as quite the director. He liked to provoke Tony. He said, "Tony, how are you? Are you still in your International Marxist phase or is it some other radical grouping that you belong to?" He was setting Tony up for his punchline: "And tell me – how is your portfolio of investments?"

'Tony would respond with a, "Fuck off, Conroy..."'

Tony spread himself typically thin between return trips to home: *Varsity*, his studies at Jesus College and a new-found enthusiasm for dope-smoking and psychedelics. (He also contracted hepatitis in the second term of his third year.) He would later develop particular turns of phrase that he returned to virtually word for word whenever interviewed. A favourite which encapsulated growing up was: 'I'm very lucky. I was 13 in the school playground when The Beatles happened, I was 18 and went to university when the revolution in drugs happened, and I was 26 and a TV presenter with my own show when punk happened. And then it was when I was 38 that acid house happened. Because it's a 13 year cycle: 1950, 1963, 1976 and 1989. I was too young for the Teddy Boys in 1950. My big ambition is to be around for 2002 when the next thing happens.'

Tony's pride at having gone to Cambridge remained undimmed. He would mention it often. Then get cross if people mentioned that he'd mentioned it. He got a 2:2 in his finals, something that irked him for the rest of his days. 'Cambridge was a place I loved,' he later told Manchester writer Winn Walsh. "In the 60s it was the best university in Europe. It was the intellectual side of Cambridge which grabbed me rather than the bourgeois May Ball scene. It was the place to go for one's brain. I have always been very fond of my brain.'

Twenty-five years after he had left, Tony would show his daughter Isabel around Jesus College, hoping she too would feel what he felt. 'It was a big deal for me to get in,' Isabel told the *Manchester Evening News* in 2008. 'It was his dream for me as well. When I was 13 he took me round to take a look. He just said I would love you to come here. If you work hard enough you have got the brains to do it. It was his dream for me to follow in his footsteps.' A year after her father died, Isabel Wilson got four straight As in her A Levels and went to Cambridge to study medicine.

TWO
THE FUN FACTORY

Television has made dictatorship impossible, but democracy unbearable
– SHIMON PERES

For decades bright young things from Oxbridge have taken a route into television via graduate trainee schemes. Tony Wilson's television traineeship was at Independent Television News (ITN). He'd tried and failed to get on a scheme at the BBC. The same thing happened at the Reuters news agency. If he didn't get in at ITN, then it was looking like he was heading for a regional newspaper. Tony got lucky.

'At my interview they said, "Was there anything that we could have done better,"' he later remembered in an interview with *Q* magazine. 'I said that I didn't think much of their coverage of Jimi Hendrix's death. I said, "It might not matter much to you but from the culture I come from Hendrix is a very important person and it seems to me that you should be able to cover it with a little more insight and not treat it as something from the counter culture that means nothing to you." About four days later a telegram arrived at my room in Cambridge and I'd got the ITN job.'

ITN had broadcast its first bulletin on the first day of the new Independent Television (ITV) service on 22 September 1955. From the start ITV was seen as a somewhat gaudy upstart, and it was known in BBC circles as Cad's TV (because they felt it was run by ruffians, cads and bounders). At 10pm on its first night,

Christopher Chataway became the first ITN newscaster and the first person in Britain to read the news on television after an advertisement (for an electric razor, as it happens). ITN prided itself on being leaner and lighter on its feet as an alternative to the perceived stuffiness of the BBC.

The ITN that Tony Wilson arrived at nearly 20 years later was an edgy, combative place, full of larger-than-life characters. His editor was Nigel Ryan, a pinstripe-suited Oxford graduate with a reputation for getting what he wanted from and for his reporters. Wilson's era at ITN saw the birthplace of a concept that has since become familiar: newsreaders as TV personalities. It also had a notoriously boozy atmosphere. After the flagship *News at Ten* bulletin, reporters and newsreaders would ask: 'Who are we drinking against tonight?'

'I went to ITN, which had just reinvented TV news with *News at Ten*,' Tony later recalled in an interview with journalist Andy Fyfe in 2006. 'It didn't have people wearing bow ties and at that point in the early 1970s ITN was the second-best TV news organisation in the world behind CBS News New York, just. If you put yourself up there with CBS New York and its traditions and way of doing things it meant you felt you were the top of the pile. I learnt so much in those two years.'

The most high-profile card in the ITN pack when Tony arrived was Reginald Bosanquet. A toupee-topped Oxford graduate who lived, loved and drank beyond his means, Bosanquet was a lightning-fast interviewer who oozed mischief. Author Richard Lindlay, himself an ex-ITN man, described him in his biography of ITN, *And Finally...*: 'The whole point about Reggie was his unpredictability; it made him exciting to be with and as a viewer, exciting to see. But as the years went by his bosses increasingly watched him through their fingers, hearts in their mouths. "Vroom, vroom," he would shout stamping on an imaginary accelerator beneath the newscasters' desk as the *News at Ten* title music swelled. It was like watching a highly charged racing car about to leap from the grid. Everyone was waiting to see if the car made it round the circuit or came spinning off the track to crash spectacularly at some particularly tricky bend.'

There's no doubt that Bosanquet made an impression on Tony, if nothing else because Reggie gave the trainee reporter a tough time. Wilson would later tell colleagues at Granada how Reggie would thrust his news scripts back at him, telling how rubbish they were. Tony was learning at the feet of a true maverick. Impervious to all forms of man-management, Reggie did what he wanted, the way he wanted, when he wanted. His love life made tabloid editors rub their hands with glee; Reggie was the first newscasting personality who *had* personality and he was loved and lampooned in equal measure. Wilson's presenting career would follow a remarkably similar tack.

Not long after arriving in London, Tony was sent back up north, to the *Post & Echo* in Liverpool. Journalist Peter Trollope, a crime reporter on the paper, was assigned to look after him. 'ITN in their wisdom had a scheme where they sent their trainees to regional papers to learn how to be journalists. The *Post & Echo* was a place full of this breed of guys who still wore the hats and the coats – it was like *Life on Mars*. There was this fug of smoke, all these hard bastards, five pints at lunchtime, stagger back, do your last edition, back in the pub till 10.30, five days and nights a week. It was a goldmine of experience; guys who knocked the training into you... literally. There'd be fistfights going on, real blood on the tracks.'

On his first day, Tony was taken into the office of the editor George Gregeen, who had a routine he would go through to make it clear to new recruits just who was the toughest in the room. 'George's novelty was to put a flame under each bare arm to show he felt no pain,' says Peter Trollope. 'I could see him doing this to Tony, who was slightly bewildered by George's party trick. After George had set fire to himself, Tony was introduced to me. The first thing he said to me was, "Hi, I'm Tony Wilson. I'm going to be the next David Frost." He was cocky.'

Trollope recalls being impressed by Tony's long hair, his love of

West Coast American rock and the fact that he seemed to have five girlfriends on the go at the same time. Tony also got a taste for the Scouse versus Manc office banter, especially if it was football related and never missed a chance to stick up for Manchester United. 'There'd be big football debates – Liverpool were cocks of the north. He would always stick up for Manchester. He felt like he was in a foreign land. Here was this Manc in Scouseland.'

Tony became a regular gig goer and also got a taste for the free tickets that would come the newspapers' way. Peter Trollope: 'He knew he would never be a musician, but he loved the buzz of the musicians' world.'

One of the regular tasks was to take free copies of the papers to police stations, essentially an excuse to talk to the desk sergeants to see what was going on. On one visit to Hardman Street police station, Tony's recreational habits attracted the attention of a passing police dog. 'One of these ginormous Alsatians got away from its handler and leapt up at him,' says Trollope. 'This dog was a *beast*. It put its paws on his shoulders and backed him onto a wall. Tony went white. The handler managed to drag the dog away. We walked away and he pulled out an apple-sized lump of cannabis from his pocket. It was a *rock*.'

Tony was never cut out for newspapers and managed to not do a great deal of work in Liverpool. After three months he headed back to London with his hands still relatively clean. One of his girlfriends – an elfin, Irish girl named Eithme – went with him and moved into his groovy basement flat. He seemed to have it made. As ever he maintained his links with home and even received a delegation from De La Salle's drama players.

Peter McNamara: 'Myself, our teacher Kevin Conroy and a guy named Nick Dobson were down in London. It was decided that while we were down there we'd go and see Tony. He was living in a basement flat. We knocked on Tony's door and he was in bed. It was only about 10 o'clock. He let us in with a certain degree of reluctance. He had a fur coat on and nothing else. Kevin

Conroy was aware of Tony's predilection for smoking a joint. Kevin would have been in his thirties and he'd always wanted to smoke a joint. He insisted that Tony roll a joint – he put pressure on him. I was more into alcohol. Kevin was sitting there with his suit and tie on looking very straight. He kept saying, "This is having no fucking effect whatsoever. Fucking useless." But he got turned on, drawing on the joint: I could see a change in his behaviour. He started giggling. He was getting stoned as he was trying to convince us it was having no effect.'

Halfway through his ITN tenure, Wilson decided he'd had enough. There were too many faces ahead of him in the queue to be on TV – and by this stage, Tony *really* wanted to be onscreen. Seasoned ITN newsreader Gordon Honeycombe apparently informed Tony that the young trainee's appalling taste in ties would have to alter radically if he was to stand any chance of getting on television. 'I found it horrendous,' he later recalled in an interview with the *Manchester Evening News*. 'For 18 months I did nothing much more than writing news scripts. I wanted a bit of the action.'

He applied for a reporter's job at Granada Television in Manchester, the flagship operation within the independent network of companies. They were relaunching their regional teatime magazine show as *Granada Reports*. The Granada region – knowingly branded as Granadaland – was a geographically rum proposition, serving what's known as the North West of England. Afdter originally covering both sides of the Pennines, by 1968 it had pared down to a patch covering Manchester, Lancashire, Cheshire and Liverpool, but also taking in the lower half of the Cumbria, a bit of North Wales and small slices of Staffordshire and Derbyshire. This 'region' makes no sense until you realise that the North West is actually defined by nothing more scientific than the power of the Granada transmitter. When the analogue signal fades away, so does the idea of the North West. Granada defined the North West rather than the other way around.

Tony was interviewed for the job by David Plowright, the

former head of the station's current affairs flagship *World in Action* who had since become controller of programmes. Despite Wilson talking too much during the meeting, his looks and charm impressed sufficiently to win him the job. But Tony's mother took a dim view of his TV career. 'She thought television was frivolous and didn't really approve at all,' remembers Pat Dilibero. 'She thought he should get a proper job. Doris always used to have a go at Tony. She would never acknowledge how clever Tony was.'

Tony settled into Granada – and Granadaland – instantly. He became a big fish in a relatively small pond. It was something he could continue to be for the next 30 years. It seemed to be the way he liked it. Granada suited Tony and he would henceforth refer to himself as a 'Granada boy'.

'People called it The Fun Factory,' recalls Tony's colleague Bob Greaves, some 35 years after the two first met at Granada's first-floor newsroom overlooking Quay Street in Manchester. 'Eighty per cent of my working life was fun. I was there from the early 1960s to the turn of the century, by which time it was going downhill at a fair lick in terms of getting rid of people and cost-cutting. I'd been there through the halcyon years. I was one of the lucky ones in the sense that I went to Granada in 1963 as news editor and I was surrounded by people like Michael Parkinson, Bill Grundy, Peter Eckersley. My newsreaders were Brian Trueman and Peter Wheeler, both radio actors. David Plowright was running regional programmes. Then it turned into a journalist's paradise. They decided to get rid of actors and presenters reading the news and get journalists to do it. Which was very clever of them, because they got two jobs out of people for the price of one. I was news editor then I became the main news presenter. They were very clever with money.'

Tony's on and off screen persona – one part effete Oxbridge intellectual to one part groovy hipster – made him stand out. 'The cliché "a breath of fresh air" was the wrong way of looking at it,' says Bob Greaves. 'Gale is another way of looking at it. He was different to any others who were around. He stormed in – I don't mean angrily – he was like a tempest. It took all of us either a long time to get to know what he was really like, or we should have just *accepted* what he was like. He was a marvellous maverick. He spoke a different language. Literally, a different language. Apart from the Americanisms – "Hey, move ass man!" – You could sit with him in the canteen or in a newsroom conference and he would use high-flown phrases – all the 'ologies and 'osophies – most of which I'd never heard of. We used to hang on his every word because his language and his vocabulary was different to any of ours. Most of it wouldn't make sense to us, because he would use high-flown, fluttery phrases. He was eminently likeable.'

Belfast-born Gordon Burns joined the new-look magazine show as a reporter. With four years of reporting experience with Ulster Television under his belt, Burns had toughened up quickly reporting on The Troubles. The environment he found in Manchester couldn't have been more different. 'When I came to *Granada Reports* my jaw dropped,' he recalls. 'It was massive. They had umpteen researchers, directors and producers. If you were going out on a story you said to someone, "Get me a hire car." A hire car was duly delivered. Expenses were terrific. It was a huge operation and it was very exciting. The competition was fierce and I remember a lot of outstanding people came from that pot. Charles Sturridge came in as a researcher. He went on to do *Brideshead Revisited*. Anna Ford was there and went on to ITN. Paul Greengrass [later director of *The Bourne Supremacy*] was there as a sport researcher. It was massive, it was all happening. It was the best company to work for anywhere and what appealed to me was their absolute dedication to quality. Everything you did at Granada had to be quality.'

It seemed to Burns that Tony Wilson had the confidence of someone who had been in the newsroom much longer than he had. 'Tony was very competitive. Very young but an outgoing, loud, friendly warm guy who was a daily reporter. Whatever story he was sent on – no matter how boring it was – he always brought back a very watchable story. He always found a twist. But getting it on air was unbelievable – like a vaguely orchestrated crash.'

As Burns saw first-hand on many occasions, the strict running times required for television really didn't suit Tony's style. News was shot on 16mm film and those films had to be off to the Granada labs for developing by 4pm if the item was to be ready for the teatime news. Gaps were left on the soundtrack in between interviews to allow reporters to lay their commentaries down live. Running orders were chillingly precise as production assistants timed the items to the second to keep the half-hour show running smoothly.

'Tony and his stories just fell into the building,' recalls Burns. 'He was always late. He flung himself into the studio like a whirlwind. No one in the gallery had any idea what he'd be doing. Amazingly it always worked. Afterwards everyone jumped up and down and screamed and yelled and told him it must never happen again. But Tony was Tony. It was always meant to be that way. Because his stuff was so good he got away with it. He understood film-making.'

Tony also understood that he needed to stand out from the other reporters. One element in his work was certainly different: action. It was, after all, the very thing that he'd found lacking at ITN. He soon got it, settling into the rather unlikely role of *Granada Reports*' resident daredevil. It was his basic unsuitability for the role that made it appealing to viewers. The 'Kamikaze Kid' the papers called him. The posh-talking, butterscotch-haired reporter could be seen tickling lions, feeding alligators and being dropped into the sea then rescued by helicopter. One hang-gliding stunt – where Tony was required to launch himself from the top of a hill with virtually no training – left him unable to walk for several days. This wheeze would later provide the basis for an early comic scene in the film *24 Hour Party People*. It would prove to be of the few sections of the movie that were truly reflective of real-life events.

'He went out and did daring things,' confirms Gordon Burns. 'He abseiled and he jumped out of aeroplanes. Within the office the strand [series] was known as *Let's Kill Tony Wilson*. Phenomenal courage but great films.'

Tony loved being on the telly. Many onscreen reporters feign a slight distaste for the attention that being on television can generate. Tony revelled in it. What's more, he reasoned, if he presented the teatime programme rather than merely reported for it, he'd be on the telly even more.

'Tony was desperate to be a presenter,' says Burns. 'He liked the limelight and the fame. He was always pitching to be the presenter of *Granada Reports*. He was a better film-maker than a presenter in my view.'

As soon as he arrived back in the North West, Wilson sought out the company of musicians. 'I first met him when he first came back to Manchester in 1973,' says Durutti Column drummer Bruce Mitchell. 'I was a working musician and Granada was a platform for musicians. He was a bit too sophisticated for the TV audience at the time. He said comical things that were pretentious and bizarre. Tony just wanted to spend a lot of time with musicians. I've often thought the musicians haven't really been worthy of him. He'd say to them: "Look, you need to listen to me, because I've never made a mistake." When I challenged him on this, he admitted he'd once made a mistake about Neil Young. It was the only revisionist thing I ever heard him say. Looking back he *was* always right.'

Chris Lee of comedy art rockers Alberto y Lost Trios Paranoias was another musician Tony found on Manchester's pre-punk scene. 'He introduced himself backstage at a gig at a venue called The Squat in 1974,' says Lee. 'He came across as a hippy or a freak... a *head*. It was very obvious that he smoked dope and took acid. And when I met him in the flesh I discovered that he did. He was obsessed with music. His enthusiasm for music was reflected in what he did for music.'

Bruce Mitchell: 'He was everywhere. He'd go to opening of an envelope. Wouldn't you? Musicians reacted to his enthusiasm. He was always interested in those bands who had only just learned how to unpack their instruments.'

Tony's enthusiasm may have gone down well within Manchester's music community, but among the wider public he prompted extreme responses. 'I would be with him in public and there'd be varying reactions to him in person,' remembers Chris Lee. 'From "Pleased to meet you" to an almost psychotic hatred. I was amazed at the levels of abuse he got from people – and that was before punk. He was well used to it by the time punk came along. I was intrigued and amazed by the degree of animosity.'

'Wanker' was the favoured insult to throw at Tony. Wanker Wilson. He'd particularly attract abuse at gigs. 'I remember going to a Rory Gallagher gig in 1975 at the Free Trade Hall,' Tony later told *Spike Magazine*. 'There were 2,000 people and 1,999 people fucking hated me. And I just thought, What the fuck have I done to these fuckin' people? What shits they are. So people shouting abuse has happened for a very long time and I find it kind of amusing and irrelevant.'

Tony made friends far more easily in the Granada newsroom. Gordon Burns even used him as a babysitter. 'He came round to our house and he arrived with one of those ping-pong ball machine guns. Instead of putting my son to bed they spent all night shooting umpteen ping-pong balls at each other all over the house. That was typical Tony. There was lovely side to him.'

Tony also got himself a bijou cottage in the village of Charlesworth, close to Marple but just over the border in Derbyshire. His London girlfriend Eithme moved with him for a while, though the relationship wasn't to last long. Friends and colleagues remember being invited to regular parties in the remote spot, often leaving them in no state to drive home. Doris didn't approve of Tony's lifestyle and would travel the four miles up the road from Marple to clean the terraced house for her hippy son. She often found drugs paraphernalia and would flush them down the toilet.

But Tony's personality got him noticed. By 1975, Granada's press office was claiming that the 'handsome six-footer' was receiving 200 fan letters a week. Promoted in the local press as a bachelor after he'd split with Eithme, Tony Wilson became – unlikely as it may seem now – quite the sex symbol and with that came certain benefits. 'Whichever woman he was with, they would always be the golden couple sweeping in,' recalls Chris Lee. 'He was at the top of the pecking order because of his profile. His girlfriends were always lookers. Granada was where the usual pick-up pool was. He had a "Cut me another little heifer out of the herd" mentality.'

Tony played the regional celebrity game, taking part in charity events and even giving a talk at his old school. He'd been invited by Peter McNamara, who was now a teacher at De La Salle. 'I invited Tony in as he was doing some political reporting,' says Peter. 'We got a good turnout. But you had to be careful what you said in front of kids. Tony arrived. He had a fur coat on and a manbag. It was a handbag, but you'd call it a manbag today. And long hair. And he swore all the way through the talk, effing and jeffing. The kids loved it. The next day, the head teacher said, "I'm sorry I couldn't come to Tony Wilson's talk." I was bloody glad he didn't.'

Even at this relatively early stage in his career, it's believed that Tony received an offer from the BBC's *Nationwide* programme, essentially a networked version of a regional magazine show with news and fluffy filler sharing air time. Its current equivalent would be BBC1's *The One Show*. It's been claimed that he got as far as resigning, clearing his desk and driving to London to take up the reporter's post, before changing his mind and asking if he could have his Granada job back. If that's the case, then Granada's personnel department must have been extremely fond of the young presenter, because his record of employment with them remains unbroken from 1973 to 2003, with seemingly no mention of this resignation.

Tony's localised fame would prove immensely useful as his career progressed. It would help him get things done. With only three channels to choose from, his profile was inordinately high. Frank Cottrell Boyce, who would go on to write *24 Hour Party People*, vividly remembers Wilson's small-screen personality filling the North West at teatime. 'I grew up in Liverpool. Tony was our newsreader, although we were more of a BBC family than an ITV family. I felt very much that you lived in Granadaland. It was kind of great that it wasn't named after where you lived. Border was named after the border region, Thames was named after the Thames. We lived in this dreamy, other-worldly place. The North West is the footprint of a transmitter. And he was the face of that footprint.'

Martin Moscrop of Factory band A Certain Ratio: 'I was very aware of Tony on the telly. I was an apprentice at 16 and lived in a boarding house in Offerton. I shared a room with five smelly blokes. We used to get home from work and watch telly while we ate our tea. We watched *Granada Reports*. I loved the bits with Tony on. This was before he was doing anything musical. All I knew him as was as a TV presenter. He always had an interesting slant. He had a good way with people. He was young – a lot younger than the other presenters. Him having long hair was an added bonus.'

Andy McCluskey of Orchestral Manoeuvres in the Dark: 'Initially I took him to be just a local journalist on the telly on a regional news programme. Then I realised this guy always seems to do the musical bits. And he actually seems quite knowledgeable and has some interesting stuff, not like your average local TV presenter who knows bugger all about the "groovy" music that we're into. So in that respect it soon dawned on you that this guy was very different from your average suit-and-tie local TV news reporter. He was somebody who was allowing a window into our world.'

Don Jones, later Granada TV's head of sport: 'I always thought he was different and quite glamorous. Definitely a smart arse. In my pre-Granada days, I was a provincial newspaper reporter. I wasn't terribly impressed by his news persona. I never disliked him, I always thought he was an impressive character. I had long hair, that was me. He did too. I suppose he was a pretty right-on kind of fella but I couldn't quite square that with him doing the news show. I used to think that regional news on the TV was just nip in and nip out and not really cover the story properly. I always thought he was different and he was moving it on a bit. He was sitting alongside some very conventional people who were the kind of people you'd expect to see on regional news.'

Happy Mondays' Paul Ryder: 'I knew him as "The bloke on the telly." Then when he got his music programmes he was the first bloke off the telly that we saw without his "telly" clothes on. He was on *Granada Reports* with his shirt and tie on, then at 10.30 at night it was like, there's that bloke but he's got *normal* clothes on. I'd never seen that before. That made him more human to me. Granada was way ahead of its time; it was the best independent TV company.'

Tony had achieved an extraordinary amount in a very short amount of time. No one should have been prouder than his mum Doris but in 1975 she suffered a fatal heart attack. Tony Wilson, then just 25, was stopped in his tracks. The call went out to the Knupfers to come to *Oberlinden* but it was too late. Tony was hitchhiking in America and it proved difficult to get the news to him. When he did hear, he was distraught.

Geoff Knupfer recalls events several days later at Doris's funeral: 'I remember the funeral cortège, sitting in the car with Tony and he was detached. Whether he was detached because of the shock or whether he was detached because he was detached I don't know, but I remember being quite surprised by his manner. No visible signs of distress. I remember seeing him looking out of the window. I was sitting next to him. He was looking out of the window as if this wasn't something he was involved in. I wondered if this was his way of dealing with it or whether he really was detached from it.'

There's no doubting Doris's strength of personality and the impact she had on Tony's life. Whatever the reasons for Tony's apparent detachment that day, her presence would be felt for many years to come. Nearly 30 years after her death, Tony Wilson was asked a disarmingly simple question by the *Manchester Evening News* in one of those questionnaires that people like Tony Wilson are asked to fill in on a fairly regular basis. The question was, who do you love? He replied: 'Kids and partner, Manchester United, all my bands, Proust, Shakespeare and the rest. My mum.'

Tony said a prayer for Doris at Manchester's St Mary's church, tucked into a back street a short walk from Granada. Known as The Hidden Gem, the church was frequented by Granada's Catholics who would discreetly nod to each other from the pews at lunchtime mass. Actor Brian Moseley (Alf Roberts in *Coronation Street*) was a regular. Later in life, Tony would mainly go to mass when he was abroad, as his appearance in a church in the UK – and especially in Manchester – would cause a scene. He would make an exception on the anniversary of Doris's death.

Sydney was also distraught when Doris died. 'He absolutely adored her,' says Pat Dilibero. 'When she died his world fell apart. She was his total life.' When he later moved in quietly with a young male photographer in Manchester, it was never really discussed in the family. Two years after Doris's death, Pat Dilibero and her husband went to visit him and his friend to get some pictures taken. While they were there, Sydney dug out some photos he'd been meaning to show her for some time. When he showed them one of his 'wife' from his days in India, it was a picture of a good-looking young man.

*   *   *   *

When it came to interviewing pop stars passing through the North West, Tony was the obvious choice, but with varying degrees of success. After David Cassidy announced his retirement from live performing after the death of a 14-year-old fan at a gig in London, his final performance as a teen idol was to be in Manchester. He turned up for the interview wearing a sumptuous fur coat. Not to be outdone, Tony wore his own, slightly ratty version.

Paul and Linda McCartney ran rings around Tony as he tried to interview them about their new band Wings. The McCartneys had clearly noticed Tony's nerves and gave the reporter a stream of nonsense in place of answers. It must have been galling for Tony to be mocked by his Beatle hero, as McCartney and his wife told him how they wanted to be fairies when they grew up and that Paul was going to join the merchant navy. When Tony tried to ask them about the audience's expectations that they would play Beatles songs on a Wings tour? 'State of you and the price of tripe,' McCartney huffs, first at Wilson, then at the camera.

'He [Tony] would make outrageous remarks,' says Bob Greaves. 'I remember sitting in the canteen and someone mentioned drugs and he went on for about an hour about how there was no danger to any human being putting anything in their bodies. We all went, "Tony, come on." He gave us reasons why there was no proof that anyone was in any danger. We said, "But Tony, people *die*." '"They're going to die anyway, man," he'd reply. He was just great fun. And we took a lot of it with a pinch – a large *sack* – of salt.'

There was, however, at least one occasion in the Granada canteen when Tony was effortlessly outsmarted. Holding court and sporting that same coat, he was approached by Russell Harty. The effete presenter glanced disdainfully at the younger man and his ratty fur. 'Tony,' he sighed, 'you look like a cunt in a bucket...'

'Wilson was an extraordinary presence around Granada in that period,' recalls former Granada researcher David Liddiment, who eventually became director of programmes. 'He was on air a lot. He played a full part. He got into arguments about what programmes should be on the telly. He was a broadcaster. He'd gone into it as a career because he knew he had a feel for it. And he got better at it, more confident – not that he ever suffered from a lack of confidence – but his style was very particular to him and one of the strengths of *Granada Reports* at that time was that he was fronting it. It was because he loved the camera, he loved broadcasting, he was very fulfilled as a broadcaster. It was in his *being*.'

Tony made friends easily around Granada and one key relationship was with would-be band manager Alan Erasmus, whose acting career is often given little recognition. Yet he had a small but impressive list of credits, having acted alongside Ben Kinglsey and Alison Steadman in a Mike Leigh-directed Play For Today called *Hard Labour*, as well as working with writers like Jack Rosenthal and directors like Michael Apted. He had appeared in *Coronation Street* and was also adept at comedy, with appearances in *The Liver Birds* and the Diana Dors vehicle *Queenie's Castle*. He was also a regular face around the same haunts in the upmarket suburb of Didsbury that Wilson frequented. With its mix of money and grubby bohemia Didsbury fancied itself as south Manchester's Chelsea, and Tony did his socialising there despite living out in Charlesworth, nearly an hour away by car. Wilson and Erasmus had Granada, music and partying in common. More than enough to forge a friendship.

As well as presenting one edition of *Granada Reports* per week, Tony had taken over the arts and entertainment slot *What's On*, a ten-minute strand at the end of the Friday show. It was here that Wilson's music credentials – in television terms – began to be forged. Granada had always been a music-friendly environment, as Bob Greaves recalls. 'When *Scene at 6.30* [*Granada Reports* forerunner] was in its heyday, every evening there'd be music. Johnny Dankworth and Cleo Laine used to come in regular as clockwork. So there was a history of music on the evening programme. Then Tony developed that into separate programmes like *What's On* and then *So It Goes*, so it was a natural progression.'

Many of Granada's presenters branched off into their own shows. Bob Greaves had *Bob's Beat* and Gordon Burns did the popular science programmes that eventually led to *The Krypton Factor*. 'I used to do a half-hour audience participation, pop psychology thing where we did experiments. I even ate human shit in one of them.'

Tony had his eye on a politics programme rather than music. He'd already done some Westminster reporting and fancied more, enjoying the buzz of parliament and the company of MPs. On one occasion, Tony was sent out to interview Labour minister Tony Benn. Benn was being guarded that day by Tony's cousin Geoff Knupfer, who had become a Special Branch officer. Geoff stood behind Benn, just off camera, as Wilson interviewed the Energy Secretary. The cousins did not acknowledge each other. 'Our worlds were very much apart,' says Geoff today. 'I'd joined the cops. We were following different routes. He jumped ship from the family to a large extent.'

But unpredictability, unreliability and a penchant for recreational herbs had effectively marked Tony's card as being unsuitable as the main presenter of a political programme. Gordon Burns: 'He wanted to do the politics show. He was desperate to do it but they gave it to me. He sort of resented that. The bottom line was that Granada executives couldn't trust him on air. He was a loose cannon. He also had his little pouch with substances in it that he probably shouldn't have had. Granada were worried sick about him and wouldn't let him do the politics. In fact Tony didn't speak to me for over a year because I was doing what he wanted to do. Then along came *So It Goes*.'

The show was Tony's compensation for losing out on the politics. It was a half-hour music and entertainment programme, produced along similar lines to the regional output, but other regional television companies had the option to run it as well. In early production meetings it was decided to broaden the show to take on board comedy and social comment. 'We were turning it into a comedy show because there was, in our opinion, no music worth covering,' Wilson told me in 2001. 'It's hard to describe how bloody awful music was, how desperately bad it was, how our 1960s heroes had become boring and useless. Not only were they bad, they were badly *dressed*.'

As Tony and the team began preparations for *So It Goes,* new faces were brought in to front *What's On*. 'I was asked to go in and audition,' remembers classical musician Dick Witts, later of The Passage. 'I had to stand in the corner and talk to the wall as if I was speaking to a camera. I said, "I can't do this." Later they rang and offered me the job.' Also taken on were actress Margi Clarke (then styling herself as Margox), plus radio DJs Ray Teret and Mike Riddick. 'I think it said a lot about Tony that he had to be replaced by four people,' says Witts. 'Tony wanted to move on. He had ideas for programmes... starring him.'

As *What's On* quadrupled its presenters' bill, *So It Goes* – operating out of the same studio – was coming together. Australian television critic Clive James, another Cambridge man, was brought in to provide cultural comment in a slot entitled Brain Damage, along with another Cambridge graduate, the acerbic comic Peter Cook. Although delicate through drink, Cook was about to get a dubious career boost thanks to the potty-mouthed *Derek and Clive* recordings he'd made with Dudley Moore. The first transmission was scheduled for the first week of July 1976. Tom Waits, The Chieftains and The Jeff Raven Band were lined up for the show. All sorted. Unfortunately, as the *So It Goes* team moved into pre-production mode, the musical sands shifted right underneath Tony's platform-soled feet. He would need to negotiate some swift repositioning – maybe even a touch of revisionism – if he was to stay in touch and on trend.

THREE
GOOD COP, BAD COP

Punk, far from being a peasants' revolt, was just another English
spectacle; like the Royal Wedding
– JULIE BURCHILL

As the first series of *So It Goes* was coming together, two items arrived on Tony Wilson's desk. One was postmarked Stretford, the other Salford. From his home on Kings Road, Stretford, Steven Patrick Morrissey had sent Tony the sleeve of the New York Dolls' self-titled 1973 debut album. No disc inside, just the sleeve. It was accompanied by a letter advising Tony to get more music like that on air. Meanwhile, from a flat on Lower Broughton Road, Salford, student Howard Trafford sent Tony a tape and a covering letter, also offering Wilson advice. 'He said there's a new band from London,' Wilson later recalled. 'They're coming to Manchester on 4 June, I think you'll like them.'

The new band from London was the Sex Pistols. They had been playing London art colleges where the band's mix of 1960s garage and mod cover versions, plus half-a-dozen of their own songs, had been met with confusion and hostility, some of it generated by the group's own entourage. The Pistols had made the pages of the *New Musical Express* in February, claiming they were into chaos not music.

Howard Trafford and his friend Pete McNeish [now better known as Pete Shelley] had seen the Pistols twice in the space of one weekend, after turning up in London on spec and charmingly asking staff at the *New Musical Express* where they could find them. It's a measure of how far away this period in music really is when you consider that at one of the gigs, the Pistols were the support act for shock rocker turned politician Screamin' Lord Sutch.

Howard Trafford: 'Everything about the Sex Pistols impressed. Most importantly the music and the lyrics. The aggro of it was interesting. At the first gig John [Johnny Rotten] got into a bit of a tussle with somebody in the audience but kept singing under a small pile of people. Pete and I immediately had a model.'

After the show they cornered Malcolm McLaren, offering to lay on a show for them in or around Manchester. Their own band – now called Buzzcocks, eschewing the traditional The – had managed to play one gig at their college, the Bolton Institute. More accurately, they'd played four songs before the plug was pulled by college officials. Perhaps based on their one brush with Howard and Pete's taste in music, the Institute put a veto on the Pistols. Undeterred, the students opted for the Lesser Free Trade Hall in Manchester city centre instead, a theatre-style venue above the main Free Trade Hall.

Howard and Pete had a venue but not much by way of an act. Concerned they'd make fools of themselves in front of the Pistols, Trafford – now styling himself Howard Devoto – panicked and got the closest thing to a 'pro' band he could find to act as support to the Pistols – a progressive rock collective from Bolton called Solstice.

Howard personally issued the tickets at his flat, banging on the keys of a typewriter with a single finger to make each one individually. Many came out wrongly. Some of the 28 people who bought the 50p tickets found themselves promised entrance for a show on 4 June 1076. Among those who bought them were Morrissey (The Smiths), Paul Morley (*New Musical Express*), Manchester punk legend Jon the Postman (real name John Ormerod, real occupation postman), Steve Diggle (Buzzcocks) and Bernard Sumner and Peter Hook (Joy Division). 'It was absolutely bizarre,' Hook later recalled. 'It was the most shocking thing I've ever seen in my life, it was unbelievable. We just looked at each other and said, "*Oh my God.*" They looked like they were having such a fantastic time. You just thought, God, we could do that.'

Events that night at the Lesser Free Trade Hall, Manchester, would be claimed as a cultural ground zero for the city and for Tony Wilson. The mythology has it that the gig was the spark that ignited the Manchester music scene: all the city's key players-to-be mystically called together by the siren call of punk rock and sent on their way to start their own pop culture revolutions, armed with a blueprint drawn up by the Sex Pistols and handed out in the stalls of the Lesser Free Trade Hall.

No one was keener to push this brand of mythology than Tony Wilson. He would trumpet it to the rooftops at every opportunity. The gig formed key early scenes of both *24 Hour Party People* and the Ian Curtis movie *Control*. Tony would expound at length on the importance of the gig in terms of music, culture and Manchester. 'Something about the energy imparted that night set up a train of events,' he later told me. 'Factory Records would not have existed and my life would not have been what it was without Joy Division. And Joy Division got up on stage because they saw these buggers [Sex Pistols] on stage. If they can do it, we can do it. That was the message.'

More than 30 years after the event, mention of the gig can still start a fist-fight among men of a certain age in Manchester pubs. The issue that gets jackets tossed aside and dukes raised is this: who was really there that night? There's one name that causes more trouble than most. Co-organiser Pete McNeish took the tickets on the door: 'I knew of him [Wilson] because I used to watch him on TV every night. I've no strong recollection of him being at the first one. I don't actually remember him coming up to the box office and saying "I'm on the guest list."'

'I never saw Wilson either,' says Steve Diggle, who joined the band that very night.

'I'm sure Tony Wilson wasn't there,' says Jon the Postman.

Fanzine writer Paul Welsh was there to cover the gig for *Penetration*: 'I was at that first Pistols' show with nine other people, none of whom went on to form bands. As far as I know Mr Wilson wasn't there, although he said he was. I didn't see him and we knew each other by sight.'

Four weeks after the Pistols' gig the first episode of *So It Goes* was aired across several regions of ITV. The punk groundswell was becoming ever more convincing and the show now looked out of step. On 20 July, the Pistols played the Lesser Free Trade Hall again. This time, Buzzcocks were ready to prop up the bottom of the bill; Wythenshawe rockers Slaughter and the Dogs were up next, then the main attraction. This time the hall was full.

Tony Wilson would later claim he was on holiday as a way of cementing his place at the first gig. Fanzine writer Paul Welsh returned to see the Pistols for a second time and remembers it very differently. 'I took photos at the first gig and featured the Pistols in my magazine, which I took along to the second show and presented it to Malcolm McLaren. I then saw Tony dressed in a long velvet coat with a chiffon scarf, pink shades and shoulder bag. He asked me, "Have you seen Malcolm, man?" I directed him in McLaren's direction and that was it.'

Tony's new Granada colleague Dick Witts: 'I went with Tony to see the Sex Pistols. It was the second one in July. He went with me and my girlfriend.' Appearing to see the potential in claiming to have been at a sparsely attended first gig as a way of starting his musical affiliations afresh, Tony seized the chance. The spiel goes like this: *Manchester, music and popular culture were all rubbish, until me and a handful of chosen ones saw the Sex Pistols on 4 June 1976 and were inspired to make everything better.*

Back at Granada, *So It Goes* was soldiering on. Tony must have been acutely aware how much the show now needed to change. In among acts like John Miles, Soft Machine, Kevin Ayers and Lulu, there were nods to the changing tastes of the outside world. Eddie and the Hot Rods somehow slipped past the guards, as did Graham Parker and the Rumour and Patti Smith. But there was one band that Tony Wilson had been banging on the table to get on the show. 'The Sex Pistols had been in Tony's mind right from the word go,' says *So It Goes* director Peter Walker. 'Every pre-production meeting we'd have about who was going to be on the show, Tony would say, "When are we going to get the Sex Pistols on?" The show for Tony at that stage was a very different proposition. He wanted to have a lot of exposure. He was very much an egocentric sort of presenter.'

The penultimate show of the series featured Kiss at the Free Trade Hall. Described by Wilson as 'The biggest stage act since Nuremberg', Kiss were filmed backstage with him. Tony sported a scarf and a manbag as he camped it up with the make-up-plastered giants in a surprisingly positive piece. 'Don't knock 'em,' he advised in the studio outro.

The final episode of the series was a special edition featuring bands without a record deal. 'We were what you'd call a progressive band,' says Howard Kingston, the former lead singer of one of three unsigned acts featured on the show, Gentlemen. (The other two were Manhattan Transfer-style vocal group the Bowles Brothers and the Sex Pistols.) 'We were into Yes, Genesis, that kind of thing,' says Kingston. 'I was 23. We had to hire a hall near Manchester University to sort of audition for Wilson as we had no gigs coming up. He got us on the show, so he was OK by us. There was a feeling that he was an OK person, but also that he was out for himself. But I liked the way he managed to play the straight news guy for *Granada Reports*, then the music guy on *So It Goes*. He was good cop and bad cop.'

Tony had to play to both roles in dealing with the Sex Pistols and their entourage during rehearsals for the show. Punk queen Jordan came up with the band and upset everyone with her death-camp, Myra Hyndley look that included a swastika arm band. Johnny Rotten and Jordan called Clive James a 'Baldy old Sheila'. Sex Pistols' bassist Glen Matlock called Tony a cunt. The Pistols upset director Peter Walker and producer Chris Pye by trashing their stage set in studio two. All the while, Tony acted the peacemaker.

'Tony spoke to them because Tony was that kind of guy,' recalls Chris Pye. 'He'd talk to anyone. Tony thought the band were great. I've no idea what they made of him. I think that they thought he was some kind of ageing, naff person, because he was a TV presenter and had really quite nice hair.'

'We had to share a green room with the Pistols,' recalls Howard Kingston. 'They were obnoxious – drinking, making a mess, disrespecting musicians we had a lot of respect for: Joni Mitchell, Steely Dan... In retrospect, I get it. I see that although this was their shtick, music had got out of hand and needed to change, but I didn't like it. We nearly got into a fight with them – Clive James advised us not to. In a way I wish we had fought them – it would have been good publicity for us. They didn't like what we represented and we didn't like what they represented. There was an element that the show was all about the Pistols. They were the headliners after all.'

'I remember the Pistols were extremely badly-behaved all day,' Tony told me in 2001. 'I remember Clive James in the green room getting very upset with them. That was the day, the moment, that Clive James got old. Because Clive didn't get it.'

Gordon Burns: 'A lot of us were thinking, How can we let this go on air? All these horrible nasty groups spitting and swearing. Sex Pistols and that lot. At the time it was heavy stuff. A lot of people were saying that these guys shouldn't be allowed in the building and that it was disgraceful and "What's Tony doing?" But that was one of Granada's strengths. They backed him. Tony had the vision that we never had and it was another milestone in pop music.'

Gentlemen played first, with a new song from their set called 'My Ego's Killing Me'. 'There was an advert around at the time, "My girdle's killing me,"' explains Howard Kingston. 'The song was a play on that. Wilson messed it up – he said the song was called "My Ego's Hurting Me". That was sloppy. The song was

an attempt by us to do something more snappy and up-tempo.
We were changing.'

Next came the summery jazz of Bowles Brothers. After some
pop culture guff from Cook and James, the Pistols battered their
way through 'Anarchy in the UK'. It was blistering.

'As they hit the last chord,' remembered Tony, 'I'm sitting there
with a big grin on my face. The wonderful thing is, when the last
note hits there's complete silence. There's two hundred people in
the audience and there's nothing... complete silence.'

Wilson's first concern after the Pistols' performance was not
how it had gone down at Granada – really badly, as it happened
– but that someone else was going to pick up the punk ball and
run with it while *So It Goes* was off-air. 'I was shivering with
nightmares,' Wilson later told me, 'that someone at the BBC or
elsewhere would wake up and put all these bands on. Luckily, the
man at the BBC thought it was all about technique, so unless you
were technically proficient or American you couldn't get on *The
Old Grey Whistle Test*. What a dickhead. Wonderful for us.'

Wilson sat tight and when *So It Goes* returned the running
order was armed with a brace of live performances from a very
different set of bands. At a time when there was practically
nothing about the new wave of music on television apart from a
few news reports, Wilson and his team single-handedly filled the
archives for the benefit of every music documentary producer for
the next 30 years with film of Buzzcocks, Siouxsie and the
Banshees, The Clash, XTC, Elvis Costello, The Stranglers, The
Jam, X-Ray Spex, Magazine, Steel Pulse and Iggy Pop. As the *So
It Goes* film crews recorded the action, Wilson could be spied at
the back of the hall – not for him pogoing and gobbing – with
what onlookers assumed was the latest in his long line of
stunners. In fact it was his new wife, Lindsay Reade. 'She just
appeared,' recalls musician Chris Lee. 'She was very elegant in
that Biba-esque, hippie way. She wore all the right clothes.'

Tony and Lindsay's first date had been a visit to Portwood in
Stockport to see Slaughter and the Dogs. 'He was outwardly very

outgoing, very confident. He seemed very cocksure,' she later told researchers at Salford Museum for an audio-visual display about local music. 'He used to annoy people, but apart from little old ladies [watching him on *Granada Reports*] he wasn't that popular in those days. He could be pretty infuriating. What we were together was very exciting to me. He was just incredibly clever. He always had a literary reference to make. His mind was always working overtime. I always used to think it was all the drugs we took because he always seemed like he was somewhere else – I think it because his mind was always working.'

'They were very much in love,' recalls Chris Lee. 'There's no denying that. They were in love. Or in lust. One or the other.' Lee had been tasked with the job of organising Tony's stag night. 'Alan [Erasmus], myself and Tony went to see a band called Flashback – Alan's idea,' he says. 'We'd just dropped some acid and Alan said, "I'll do the driving." The great acid-fuelled stag party... Walking into a pub watching a load of hippies. I don't remember much about it, but the colours were great.'

Back at Granada, the powers-that-be had their patience stretched to the limit towards the end of the punked-up second series of *So It Goes*. Iggy Pop was filmed at Manchester's Apollo theatre, stripped to the waist, in leather pants and swearing. A lot.

'They'd had enough of me and I can't blame them,' Wilson later recalled in the pages of the *NME*. 'My boss said, "I don't need any more guys with horse's tails sticking out of their asses." When we filmed him – and a wonderful show it was too – Jimmy [Iggy's real name is James Osterberg] had this horse's tail sticking out of his ass. Plus, in the middle of "The Passenger" he yells out "fucking". So there's a week's debate over this one word, right? And I'm screaming "ART, ART, this is fucking ART!'

Horses' tails were one thing, swearing was quite another. The show was axed and Wilson was put back on regional news patrol. But he'd seized the moment and cut his first notch in pop culture's bedpost. Everything that was to come in Tony's musical life would be traced back to his achievements on *So It Goes* and the part the Sex Pistols played on his road to rock'n'roll Damascus. Time and time again he would come back to the Lesser Free Trade Hall as a way of explaining everything that was to come. It would become the undercoat for every music revolution for the next three decades. His presence at the first gig was key to this. 'I'm blessed,' he told me. 'I'm gig one.'

In fact, putting the Pistols on TV for the first time – three months before the band swore their way to infamy on Bill Grundy's *Today* show on Thames TV in London – was a much more important feat than seeing the band at the Lesser Free Trade Hall. Far more people were inspired to form a band by watching Johnny Rotten, Glen Matlock, Steve Jones and Paul Cook on *So It Goes* than by seeing the Pistols in the flesh. The show itself was also an influential television template for *The Tube*, *The Word* and Jools Holland's *Later*.

So Tony Wilson, the Sex Pistols and 4 June 1976 was now set in stone – certainly as far as Tony was concerned. The event even featured in the film ostensibly chronicling Tony's life – *24 Hour Party People* – more than 25 years later, so it *must* be true. Woe betide anyone who questioned Tony's version of events.

Thirty years on from the Lesser Free Trade Hall, Tony invited me on to his BBC Manchester radio programme *Talk of the Town*. The Saturday morning show was broadcast live from Cornerhouse, Manchester's art cinema/cafe/meeting place. Three characters from differing walks of life would come together to talk through the issues of the day with Tony as conversational ringmaster.

I was there to promote my new book, *I Swear I Was There*, an account of events surrounding that very gig. Also on the show were a nice lady from Salford Council and a bullish local businessman. Wilson was sporting open-toed sandals and black-painted toenails. I asked him, 'Why the new look?'

'It annoys people,' was his reply.

Tony allowed me free rein to talk about the book and that famous gig, which had recently been voted one of the most important concerts of all time, engaging the other guests in our conversation with his usual mix of deftness and tangential flurry.

During a break for headlines and travel news, Wilson leaned over to me. 'There was one thing I didn't like about the book,' he said in an off-air stage whisper, glasses teetering on the edge of his nose. 'Saying that I wasn't there – that was snide. You shouldn't have done that.' As I began to defend myself, saying I was just reporting what eyewitnesses had told me, he pushed up the fader and carried on with the show. He made no reference to the exchange and carried on in Tony Tigger mode. He never mentioned it again.

FOUR

THE BEST THING IN MANCHESTER FOR ABOUT SIX MONTHS

The quality of Mersey is not pure
– JOHN LENNON

Unceremoniously dumped back in the Granada newsroom, Tony's already less than serious on-screen personality became – if it were possible – more flippant than ever after the cancellation of *So It Goes*. 'Tony was quite posy on the telly,' states his newsroom colleague Gordon Burns, perhaps unnecessarily. 'He would sit in odd positions. He had this great trick where he would flick a pencil *as he was reading the news*. The viewing audience were split over Tony. Some didn't like him because of his posing and his self-confidence. Some people thought he was up himself. Others saw this great personality.'

David Liddiment was a researcher and budding director at Granada. 'It was fascinating in rehearsal. He would walk into the studio and plug in his earpiece, check the monitor to see that his hair was the way he wanted it to be, look into the camera and pout a little bit. He was quite vain, self confident, but just loved the thought that when we were live he was speaking to people in their living rooms and it made him a special broadcaster. He wasn't a renta-smoothie; he was a singular broadcaster.'

Whenever possible, Tony would accompany any on-air mention of Liverpool with a comment, an aside or a roll of the eyes to show his dislike of the city. 'There was a love-hate relationship,' confirms Bob Greaves. 'Some viewers thought he was the bees' knees. Everybody in Liverpool hated him. He used to slag the whole of Liverpool off deliberately. How he got away with it for so long before he was bollocked by the hierarchy I'll never know. He would demean Liverpool with every word... every gesture that he could.'

Gordon Burns: 'Tony was a typical Mancunian. In the same way Liverpool fans hate Manchester United fans and Manchester United hate Liverpool fans. Tony was a great United fan and he'd take every opportunity to knock Liverpool on air. I think he did it good-naturedly, but he did upset a lot of people. He wasn't liked at all in Liverpool for a long time.'

Bob Greaves: 'The favourite phrase I used to get whenever I went to Liverpool – as soon as I got off a train or out of a taxi or out of my own car – was, "Hey Bob, tell that Tony Wilson he's a wanker." That was the phrase. I must have had that delivered to me thousands of times. He alienated potentially half the audience.'

The on-screen pairing of Wilson and the infinitely more experienced Bob Greaves – on the face of it a terrible mismatch – produced real, mischief-laced chemistry. As the production assistant would begin the countdown to the end of the programme, the pair would stage a last-minute competition to see who could be the last one to say, 'Good night'.

'It was legendary that they were both wanting the last word,' remembers Gordon Burns.

'We were a team,' recalls Greaves, 'but he was ultra-competitive. He would slowly begin to get the last word in at the end of the programme. If the script said, "Bob says goodnight," he would chip in with a second goodnight. So I would do another good night. It became ridiculously competitive. The viewers loved it, but the bosses began to hate it and they gave us a severe rap across the knuckles. They threatened to separate us because they thought it was getting out of hand. But then eventually it would come back again. Very funny, very enjoyable times.'

Sitting in a south Manchester hotel recalling events of more than 30 years ago, Bob Greaves' reaction to Wilson's disruptive influence is one that would occur again and again through the years and Tony's many lives. No matter how annoying or irresponsible he could be, he would be forgiven for one simple reason: 'That's just Tony...'

'There was that love-hate relationship,' says Greaves. 'I used to think, You bugger... Just let me get on with it. But it was all good fodder, all grist to the mill. I never hated him. But there were moments when I wanted to. But he always amused me.'

Tony's playfulness could probably be attributed to a restlessness bordering on frustrated boredom. *So It Goes* had introduced him to the very world he had initially sought out when he returned to Manchester from ITN. The punk explosion set off by the Sex Pistols had sent entrepreneurial shrapnel across the city. Tony Wilson was the man who'd put the Pistols on television, yet others seemed to be taking the initiative. Buzzcocks and their manager Richard Boon had managed to put out a record – 'Spiral Scratch' – by January 1977, produced by Manchester University student and fledgling record producer Martin Hannett.

Hannett, along with musician Tosh Ryan, had also set up Rabid Records and released 'Cranked Up Really High' by Slaughter and the Dogs. Wilson was fascinated by Rabid and spent time in their office on Cotton Lane in Withington, south Manchester, ostensibly with a view to filming a piece about the label. Chris Sievey, a south Manchester musician with a flair for promotion, had become involved with the label from its early days. 'I went into Rabid and got chatting with them,' he says. 'Tosh was very interested in the fact I'd already put a record out ahead of everyone else. Tosh gave me a job doing publicity. Work for us, he said, we'll pay you. Tony Wilson was in and out of there all the time. Tosh hated Tony Wilson then, never mind later on.'

Tony's then wife, Lindsay Reade, confirms Wilson's interest in the label. 'Tony had been watching what other people had been doing, like Tosh Ryan with Rabid,' she would later say in the documentary *Shadowplayers*. 'Alan Erasmus was having a look too.' (Erasmus was managing the band that Tony had seen on his acid-fuelled stag night – the rather aptly-named Flashback.)

At the end of the working day, Tony's colleagues would usually head for the Granada bar – called The Stables – for a post-programme livener. Granada took the view that if staff were going to drink – and by God, they liked to drink – then it would be better if they did so on the premises rather than off it. In case of an emergency it would be easier to round up staff from their own bar than have to trawl around The White Lion, The Oxnoble and The Commercial looking for them. What was more, it meant that resident boozehounds were essentially handing back a hefty slice of their wages to the company. This resulted in the tale of a Granada film editor who was having his annual meeting with his accountant. 'You've had a good year,' said the financial advisor, 'but you've got to get rid of the horse.'

'I don't have a horse,' replied the editor.

'Then what about all these cheques to The Stables...'

Tony, by contrast, was rarely to be found in the bar. Once the red light went off, he disappeared. 'He was a workaholic,' states Bob Greaves, 'but it wasn't all for Granada. Most evenings he would simply leave the building and go to something else – and that would turn out to be the beginnings of Factory Records.'

Alan Erasmus's band Flashback were soon styling themselves with the punkier name Fast Breeder. When they split up Wilson took it upon himself to build a fresh band around the remaining members. Wythenshawe guitarist Vini Reilly was recruited from another Rabid act, Ed Banger and the Nosebleeds. Reilly would essentially take over the outfit under the name The Durutti Column. 'Alan introduced me to Tony,' Reilly told *Scream City* magazine. 'Tony came round to see me having never heard me play. Alan brought Tony round three times before I agreed to take part. Tony was really patient.'

Tony was casting his net wide for young bands. In April he'd been roundly abused by the lead singer of a group at a battle of the bands night at Rafters nightclub on Manchester's Oxford Street. Ian Curtis had faced up to Wilson, demanding to know why his group hadn't managed to secure a slot on the *What's On* slot.

Curtis, along with drummer Stephen Morris, bass player Peter Hook and guitarist Bernard Sumner, had changed their name four months earlier from Warsaw to the tastelessly eye-catching Joy Division. (Taken from the 1955 novel *The House of Dolls*, the name refers to sterilised sex slaves in a Nazi labour camp.) Their self-financed first EP, *A Design for Living*, was packaged in a fold-out poster that pictured a Hitler Youth drummer boy and a German soldier. Shocking, some might say; childish, others might counter. Guitarist Bernard Sumner: 'The climate was very different in those days. It was the time of punk and shock, sticking two fingers up to what we regarded as normal society – and that included some journalists. We knew the name was on dodgy ground and we did have reservations about it, but in the end it just felt like it was our name.'

Starting life in the back room of Bernard Sumner's grandmother's house in Lower Broughton in Salford, the band had moved from straightforward punk stylings to a slower, more mechanised sound. Their live performances were marked by Ian Curtis's onstage persona: a partly frightening, partly comic, jerking marionette. 'When we rehearsed as Joy Division, he would just sit in the corner and mumble into the microphone,' Stephen Morris would recall in the documentary *Factory*. 'Then when we started doing the first gigs with him he would do this dervish thing.'

Whether it was the strength of Joy Division's performance or the belligerence of their lead singer, they succeeded in getting Tony's attention. On 18 April, several days after the performance, Tony wrote to the band's manager Rob Gretton. On Granada headed notepaper, Wilson declared himself convinced of Joy Division's potential: 'I am totally in agreement, Joy Division are the best thing I have heard in Manchester for about six months.'

Wilson would use the same explanation for what he saw in Joy

Division time and time again over the years, a typical example of him quoting himself. 'Every band wants to be on stage, thinks they want to be pop stars,' he told me in 1998. 'The great bands have no choice but to be on stage. It's something forcing itself out of them, particularly Joy Division. It had to be expressed, it had to be said. It's as if they had no choice to be on stage. They had to be there.'

But stages were in short supply at this time. After the initial flurry of punk, Manchester's nightlife had shrunk, meaning that there was a serious shortage of places for Joy Division and like-minded souls to play. There was a real danger of the nascent scene falling apart. 'Tony tried his best to pull it together,' recalls Peter Hook. 'Tony was the first middle-class person I ever talked to. I mean Bernard and I were very working class, real working-class background. Bands like Buzzcocks were quite middle class so I don't think they could relate to us. We had a beer-boy attitude when they were quite a bit art school. It had become very difficult for us as a group because we weren't arty enough. It got very hard for us to get gigs for a while, we sort of fell out of the punk thing... It got a bit too arty, it wasn't punky enough for us.'

With his newfound, can-do spirit, Wilson figured that he would need to create his own space. The venue he and Alan Erasmus settled upon was the Russell Club on Royce Road in Hulme, a former club for drivers working for the bus company SELNEC. The club was close to The Crescents, a series of award-winning, deck-access accommodation developments that had fallen into frightening, crime-riddled disrepair. Initially taking four Fridays spread over two months, the pair dubbed the club night The Factory.

Peter Saville was a graphic design student at Manchester Polytechnic at the time. He painted a picture for me of the city's club scene before The Factory Club when I interviewed him in 2007. 'In the mid-1970s there were quite a few disco dance clubs, depending on one's taste I guess. I was a Roxy Music and David Bowie fan and I could be found four nights a week in Pips nightclub. There was a big northern soul contingent, there was a lot of classic dance clubs, some of which were great, and there was also a kind of fledging gay dance club scene happening. In fact, by the latter half of the 1970s there were some really great gay clubs in Manchester. When punk happened '76, '77, '78, there were a lot of quite astonishing venues, with the Electric Circus being probably the most memorable, but there were a lot of venues around Manchester for punk.

'Then, by 1978, disturbed by punk, the authorities found one reason or another to close down nearly all of those venues where punk bands had played, resulting in this situation that by early 1978, there was almost nowhere for the bands of the new wave – as it was becoming – to play. And that's how it came to pass that Tony and Alan founded The Factory night at the Russell Club. Friday night, every two weeks.'

Saville – who'd initially approached Wilson at a Patti Smith gig in Manchester to offer his services – designed a striking yellow-and-black poster to publicise the first night, Friday 19 May 1978. Manchester gig-goers were offered the temptation of The Durutti Column and Jilted John that night. Or they would have been, had the poster ready in time. Famously, it was finished too late to fulfil its purpose; Saville also managed to spell the name of the Russell Club wrong. The poster would later be dubbed FAC 1 – the first item in the Factory catalogue.

Late or not, the poster brought Saville into Wilson's coterie and what would become Factory Records. 'Nobody was involved in it commercially,' states Saville. 'Tony had his job at Granada. Alan was an occasionally working actor. I was a student at the art college in my final year of graphics. So I think when Tony and Alan instigated the nights at the Russell Club it wasn't the first step in a vision towards something else, it was a necessary opportunity. It was a facility. There had to be somewhere for the new wave bands to play. Manchester had been such a great city of venues and Tony thought it was important that these bands had somewhere to play. It wasn't part of the larger entertainment project. So he and Alan just got it going, I think really as a gesture of good faith more than anything else.'

Wilson, Erasmus and Saville were photographed outside the club: Saville sports big hair and a long dark coat; Erasmus is bearded with his afro covered by a flat cap; Wilson sports a skinny tie and a tweed jacket with the collar turned up rakishly. The picture was taken by Tony's fellow De La Salle alumnus Kevin Cummins. 'Because he had a proper job he dressed very straight,' Cummins told me. 'He didn't try to dress like a punk – he'd turn up in the suit he'd just presented *Granada Reports* in. So he was always a figure of fun to some people. His heart was in the right place. He wanted to promote music – it was his passion.'

Musician Chris Sievey of The Freshies remembers the atmosphere of the club. 'It was quite frightening. It was in the middle of Hulme, which at the time was like going to the Bronx. We had drum kits nicked straight out of the van and they went straight into the flats. Tony would always be there. It was a working men's club, all maroon seating with a cabaret stage for having a turn on each week. They didn't put anything in – it was the same for Factory nights. It was those punk days – this'll do, let's put it on here.'

A steady tide of bands were enticed over to the Russell Club from around Manchester and beyond. Liverpool's Big In Japan, Cabaret Voltaire from Sheffield, Wilson favourites Joy Division and local lads A Certain Ratio, whose Martin Moscrop remembers the speed at which Wilson was operating. 'I used to go to Factory night at the Russell Club and see bands like Pere Ubu. Tony seemed to have his finger in everything. It was Rob Gretton who saw ACR at Band on the Wall supporting Warsaw and got Wilson to come and watch us and book us at the Russell club. That's when he asked if he could manage us. He was that man on the telly. That's how we thought of him. You're a little bit star struck when you see people off the telly when you're at a young age. In those days it was unique to know someone on the telly.'

Tony used his position as someone on the telly to get Joy Division the slot on *Granada Reports* that singer Ian Curtis had so abusively requested at Rafters. Local bands were pre-recorded for the programme, so the tapes could be used as standby items in case a news story fell out. Joy Divison were introduced on 20 September 1978 by Bob Greaves and Tony. Bob commented to camera that he thought Joy Division had a nicer ring to it than their old name. 'We hope that we're launching them on a real joy ride as we have before with many others, haven't we, Tony?'

It looked like it was live, but Bob was handing over to a pre-recorded Tony Wilson. 'Seeing as how this is the programme which previously brought you first television appearances from everything from The Beatles to the Buzzcocks,' Wilson said, next to a pink-shirted Ian Curtis, 'we do like to keep our hand in and keep you informed of the most interesting new sounds in the North West. This, Joy Division, is the most interesting new sound we've come across in the last six months. They're a Manchester band, with the exception of the guitarist who comes from Salford, very important difference. They're called Joy Division and this number is "Shadowplay".'

Joy Division's tentative performance had a big impact on other young musicians. Across the region, nascent bands began to realise that Tony Wilson was the connection between their world and possibility of wider exposure through television. Orchestral Manoeuvres In The Dark were a duo from the terminally unfashionable Wirral peninsula on the wrong side of the River Mersey. OMD singer and bass player Andy McCluskey: 'In October 1978 we had dared ourselves to play at our local club Eric's [in Liverpool]. We played there previously in our art school rock band called The Id. Because of what we saw onstage at Eric's we dared ourselves to do onstage what we'd been writing since we were 16 – German/Brian Eno/disfunctional/electronic music. We dared to ask for a gig. We got a gig. The very first time we did a gig it was supporting Joy Division. We'd barely heard of them. We were told that Eric's had a reciprocal relationship with this place in Manchester. "That's why Joy Division are here. Do you want to go and play over there?"

'We only did it as a dare to do one gig. Then we got a second gig and the opportunity to go over to Manchester and play at The Factory night at the Russell Club in Hulme. We supported Cabaret Voltaire. And obviously we met Tony. Then the penny started to drop. The fella off the telly who's into the interesting bands has got his own club thing – and these Joy Division guys are associated with him. I see. He was very nice.'

With remarkable speed Tony Wilson had established a club night, started managing bands and become a magnet for aspiring musicians across Manchester and beyond. He was also doing his day job at Granada. Putting out a record was the next logical step. Alan Erasmus's flat on Palatine Road in West Didsbury was designated as the record company's offices. To tie in with the club night, Factory was chosen as the label's name.

Their first release, a double-disc EP, bore the legend *A Factory Sampler*. It featured an eccentric grab bag of acts within Wilson's immediate circle: Joy Division, Durutti Column, Cabaret Voltaire and comedian John Dowie, who'd previously appeared on *So It Goes*. Produced by Chris Lee of the Albertos, his tracks – 'Acne', 'Idiot' and 'Hitler's Liver' – seemed rum company for the other acts, but Dowie's inclusion was Tony's idea. 'Astonishingly and unprecedentedly, they – or rather, Tony Wilson – chose me,' Dowie told writer Ian McCartney in *Scream City* magazine. 'I lived near Manchester at the time and used to play gigs at the Russell Club. I think Tony Wilson had a side going spare as he only liked three bands.'

The label started as they meant to go on. In Wilson's words: 'The musicians own everything, the company owns nothing. All our bands have the freedom to fuck off.'

Two more posters would form the next numbers in Factory's strange catalogue system. The second record released was A Certain Ratio's 'All Night Party'. Tony was hands-on with ACR, even driving them to their early gigs in Liverpool, Sheffield and

London in his Peugeot. Most people in television swoon at the prospect of doing the job they are paid to do, let alone finish work and start afresh doing unpaid labour during the weekends and evenings. But Tony Wilson was engorged with enthusiasm for the possibilities that were opening up before him. Punk had been a short-lived shower of sparks, gone before it had really begun. Here was a chance to guide something from the start. If that meant multi-skilling then he was the man for the job.

'Tony had a full time job and he didn't want to take the piss out of Granada,' says ACR's Martin Moscrop. 'He had a full-time job but he still managed to run a record label and manage a band and do all that running around. I think that's pretty amazing. And he did it without getting stressed or knackered. He did think that musicians were whiners, but that's what you get with creative people. He did get stressed sometimes but for someone with so many jobs he remained relatively calm.'

Peter Saville: 'The Factory template was a platform for individuals to express themselves and do the work that they wanted to do. And that's what applied to the groups. No one told the groups what to do. No one obliged them to make singles or put singles on albums or to follow any of the commercial rules. Tony went about running a record company the way he felt like doing it.'

'Tony's genius was in spotting other's genius, not in making money,' Lindsay Reade would later tell filmmaker James Nice. 'He's never really had that hat on his shoulders.'

A Certain Ratio's Martin Moscrop: 'Tony managed ACR but he didn't tell us what to play. That's a good of example of how he didn't interfere with people's creativity, though he was a very creative person and a very creative manager. In music you get business managers who aren't creative but good at the business side of things. Tony was really crap at the business side of things but was very creative. Tony was really good at choosing the right people, which is a very good management skill to have. In business they choose the correct skill set and the correct people to make that business work. Tony did exactly the same thing with the Russell Club. He did exactly the same thing with Factory. He did the same thing with The Haçienda. He was really good at choosing the right people – Peter Saville, Martin Hannett – people who could help him create what he had in his head. I don't think he had preconceived ideas in his head, he worked off the cuff.'

Although there's little doubt that Tony was genuinely enthralled by the music of A Certain Ratio, Durutti Column and Joy Division, Factory's third record release would mark the start of a recurring theme in his relationship with music: getting behind something that he wasn't necessarily enthused about but others were.

OMD's Andy McCluskey: 'Within a couple of weeks of the Russell Club gig we saw Tony on Granada introducing The Human League. We thought, They're ahead of us but we've met him, we've played at his club in Manchester. Maybe we could be on the telly. Let's send him a tape. You don't get it if you don't ask. We had the "Electricity" demo that we'd recorded in our manager's garage, so we cheekily sent a cassette to Tony at Granada. A week or two passed and then he called up – Tony Wilson off the telly! – and said he couldn't get us on the telly. He rang our manager and said, "I can't get you on Granada but we're starting a record label. Would you like to make a record instead?" We were like, "OK... if you insist." A classic example of how doors opened for us. Extreme jamminess.

'Apparently he wasn't that knocked out by us but he'd left our cassette in his car and I later found out it was his wife Lindsay who'd heard it and said, "What's this sort of Kraftwerky, electro-punk thing?" Then Peter Saville said to Tony and to Alan, "Two hippy guys from the Wirral peninsula? But into Kraftwerk? You should sign that." Tony was surrounded by people saying, "You're wrong. That's cool. You should have that." Getting his ear bent had obviously changed his mind.'

How Tony managed to miss the yearningly pure pop appeal of 'Electricity' is a mystery, but having been convinced that the song was worthy of release, he made an offer to the pair. It was as breathtakingly simple as it was commercially suicidal.

Andy McCluskey: 'He told us that Factory was just a small label. "You guys should be on *Top of the Pops*. I can't get you there because Factory isn't big enough. We can't sell enough records to get you into the charts. So what we'll do is we'll just release one record as a demo for you. We will help you get onto *Top of the Pops* by getting you to a major label who have the money to get you there."

'Tony Wilson was the first person to say to us, "What you're doing is actually pop music. In fact, it's the future of pop music." If you said that to most people today they'd take it as a big compliment. We were like, "Don't you call it fucking pop music! It's bloody German-influenced experimental fucking music, thank you very much, Mr-fucking-Tony-Wilson. How dare you call us pop?" He saw something that we were unconsciously formulating. We wrote "Electricity" when we were 16. He saw in that the proto-electro-pop thing that two years later was going to sweep across the world as 1980s electro-pop. He saw that in 1978. He was the first person to say, "There's nothing wrong with being pop music." The idea that someone would make a record purely for the band's benefit – it's essentially carrying your own cross. There was no business sense to it. The only reason he seemed to do it because he believed in the music. Talk about philanthropic lunacy.'

Tony believed that such madness was largely the point of the fledging indie movement – to act as a feeder school for the majors. 'Factory was a very wonderful record label but there was a very arty, very clever record label a year before us out of Edinburgh called Fast Records,' he told documentary film-maker Dom Shaw in 2005. 'They had Gang of Four and Human League. What did they do? They sent the Gang of Four to EMI, Human League to Virgin. People forget that – that's what you *did*. When we started Factory it was to get my band Durutti Column signed, Rob's band Joy Division signed and Orchestral Manoeuvres signed. The first record that gets everyone excited is Orchestral Manoeuvres.'

The single was produced by Martin Hannett. The fact that he had crossed over from Rabid Records to their 'rival' Factory caused some ill feeling. Musician and Rabid employee Chris Sievey: 'Tosh Ryan was running Rabid, Tony was running Factory, but Tony was in a position to use his power. That always narked Tosh. Then Martin Hannett started producing stuff for Tony – it was like he'd lost one of his mates to Tony Wilson's side.'

Though they didn't care for Hannett's production of their song, Andy McCluskey and Paul Humphreys made the journey over to Manchester. There they got stuck into what was becoming a Factory tradition: get the band to pack their records in the sleeves in the dope-fugged surroundings of Factory's headquarters – otherwise known as Alan's flat. As McCluskey recalls, 'It certainly wasn't a record company office. When "Electricity" was manufactured we went to the front room of 86 Palatine Road. There were all these boxes. Five thousand seven-inch vinyl "Electricity"s in white-paper sleeves and each one had to be taken out and put into a black thermograph Peter Saville sleeve [a distinctive design featuring special shiny black ink on black paper].'

Radio 1 DJ John Peel – just entering his post-punk pomp as the nation's musical tastemaker – began playing OMD's single and within a week it had sold out. Tony took the trouble to drop off a copy off at the offices of DinDisc, a new Virgin subsidiary. Andy and Paul were offered a seven-album deal on the spot. Andy McCluskey: 'In hindsight people, might look at us and Joy Division and A Certain Ratio being on Factory and think that, Oh, that's cool and that isn't, and OMD turned into some crappy electro-pop band. But at the time we were all in the same boat: it was our art and very few people were interested in it. That's why Factory was the breeding ground for so many interesting things and why The Haçienda never made any fucking money and went bankrupt. They were run by people who liked music who just wanted to do something about helping other people who needed assistance. Rubbish businessmen, but praise the Lord for their determination to get involved in something they just loved the bones off.'

McCluskey and Humphreys were at the start of a run of peerless pop hits. Such was the speed of the duo's success that Andy didn't get the chance to properly thank Tony for what he, Lindsay and Factory had done for them. McCluskey vowed that one day he would make sure he thanked Tony personally.

'Electricity', although never a hit, created a wave of goodwill towards Factory. They could do post-punk. They could do comedy. They could do pure pop. They could also do weird, as the growing list of oddities that would be given a FAC number showed. Stationery (FAC 7), a prototype menstrual egg-timer by singer/artist Linder Sterling (FAC 8) and a film exhibition (FAC 9). Far from the austere image the label would later be saddled with, the early incarnation of Factory had a playful, whimsical feel, bordering on the hippyish.

FAC 10 was Joy Division's debut album, *Unknown Pleasures*, produced by Martin Hannett. The music press pounced on the record, holding it up to lead the way out of the perceived disappointments of punk. 'One of the best white English debut LPs of the year,' said *Melody Maker*.

'A haunting hypnotic experience ... morbid genius,' said *Sounds*.

Unknown Pleasures kept a foot in the punk camp with its low-mixed, distorted guitar, but there were enough bass pulses, peow-peow drums and background sound washes to firmly identify the band as the pathfinders for post-punk. 'Messing with those strange boxes and synthesisers,' Wilson would later say, 'Martin found in Joy Division a group as entertained as he was by technology.'

Feted by the music press, Tony Wilson was now a national pop culture figure, talking a great fight on behalf of his acts and often proving himself to be more entertaining than the musicians themselves. ACR's Martin Moscrop: 'He was interested in the social/political aspects of it. He was into Situationism. He was interested in how to create interest in something. He was in the media obviously being a journalist himself. He really knew how to get music journalists on his side, how to feed them what they wanted. Being a journalist really helped in his marketing and promotion. But it was the music he was into first and foremost.'

Tony's newfound fame made him the talk of Granada Television. Questions were being asked. Was it appropriate for an onscreen reporter to be mixing in the druggy swirl of the music scene? Many who asked were blissfully unaware of his long-standing taste for dope and psychedelics. Bob Greaves: 'Everybody in Manchester – by which I mean anyone who moved around Manchester and had any wit about them – had a view on what Tony was up to at night in connection with the music scene. Many of these views were based on a bit of personal experience by some, a bit of tittle-tattle by many, and a bit of listening to Tony himself by *very* many. We all put two and two together and reached at least four. Then there were the conversations in the canteen: "Hey, man, you can't do any harm to your body by experimenting with anything," which was such an outrageous thing to say. He sounded as though he meant it.'

More bands signed up – or more accurately didn't sign anything – for the Factory experience. The plaintive power-pop of The Distractions, the aching drones of Crawling Chaos and the European throb of Blackpool's Section 25. Singer Larry Cassidy: 'Our initial contact with Factory was through Rob [Gretton] and Joy Division. They were enthusiastic about the band. Tony was in the background. He was still a talking head on the telly. We did our first recording with Rob and Ian Curtis and the vehicle Rob wanted to use was Factory. Tony didn't like the demo. It came out anyway. I think he respected Rob's taste. It was a partnership. We became a Factory band, despite Tony. The hierarchy at Factory at that time was Joy Division, A Certain Ratio and Durutti Column. They were the core bands. They were like six-formers and we were the fifth-formers. We had to warm the toilet seat for them.'

Section 25's debut was 'Girls Don't Count' – FAC 18. 'Rob said, "Tony doesn't like it but we're putting it out anyway,"' recalls drummer Vince Cassidy. 'We didn't really think that Tony was that into music anyway. He was into what music *did*. It wasn't a requirement for Tony to like something for it to come out on Factory. It wasn't about his personal taste. It was right for Factory even though he didn't like it. I think that shows good judgement.'

Meanwhile, problems were piling up at Ian Curtis' door. By the end of 1978 he'd been experiencing seizures positively identified as epileptic fits. As well as taking debilitating drugs to temper the fits, he became gripped by the fear of where and when attacks would strike again. In April 1979 his daughter Natalie was born. Given that stress, flashing lights, alcohol and travel were all bad for his condition, Curtis was badly placed to avoid any of them. The fierce work ethic of the group saw the band gig relentlessly – it was their chief form of income. They played everywhere from youth clubs in south Manchester to art clubs in Brussels. At a gig at the Plan K club in Brussels – situated on the Rue de Manchester no less – Ian met up with Belgium Embassy worker and music journalist Annik Honoré. They'd met before when Honoré had interviewed the band in London. Curtis – married since he was in his teens – began a relationship with her that the other members of the band helped to hide from his wife Deborah.

Factory would continue to release records that at least one of their number were enthused by. Success was not sought; in some cases it was purposefully swerved. Despite this, real success – both financial and professional – would come Tony Wilson's way within a matter of months. The cost, however, would be too much for some to bear.

FIVE
I WAS PISSED OFF WITH HIM...

There is no refuge from confession but suicide... and suicide is confession
– DANIEL WEBSTER

World in Action was Granada's factual output flagship. It was what they quoted in response to accusations that the company was being too populist with its sitcoms, soaps and quiz shows. It had a visual motif of Leonardo Da Vinci's *Vitruvian Man* and prog-rock theme music that sounded like it could have been 'Nantucket Sleighride' by Mountain (but was in fact 'Jam for *World in Action*'). Within Granada's Quay Street building it was the programme you had to have high aspirations to work on. If a journalist or producer thought they were up to the task, they would set out their stall and hope to be noticed by the programme's editorial team. Between 1963 and 1998 its offices on the fifth floor were occupied at one time or another by Michael Parkinson, John Birt and Michael Apted (*The World Is Not Enough*).

Editor Ray Fitzwalter, now a visiting professor At Salford University, was always looking for ways to update the programme. 'Tony? He was just someone you saw in the building or on television,' he says. 'You were aware of a very frothy personality – a person who was developing very much in relation to music or *What's On* programmes or things in that kind of sphere. However, I did get to know him a bit better later and we became aware he was very interesting – quite sharp character with a very good Cambridge education, very bright man.'

World in Action prided itself in its boat-rocking and cage-rattling abilities and had run-ins with the security services, the military, the police and successive governments throughout its lifetime. Campaigning? Always. Courageous? Often. Leftist? Proudly so. But it was also perceived in some quarters as dry and earnest. Ray Fitzwalter: 'We were occasionally prodded by some of our colleagues that we had got set in our ways and we should be a bit more experimental. We were wondering whether or not we shouldn't experiment with Tony, who was still primarily a regional person, or was perceived as such.

'People thought *World in Action* was an investigative news series, but some of the things we did were not taken on board. For example we did occasional programmes on British culture and popular music. But we would only do so if there was significance to society in doing it. We did *Stones in the Park* [the 1969 Rolling Stones concert in Hyde Park] a long time ago, we did one with UB40 [the band on unemployment]. There had to be a reason or a depth otherwise there was no argument for it to be current affairs. We couldn't be seen just to be lapsing into, "Here's some new music."'

Just as Tony's night job was demanding more time and attention as the grim reality of Ian Curtis' condition became more pressing, he was set the biggest journalistic challenge of his career. He was called up to the *WIA* offices at the end of 1979 and offered a shot at the big-time: network current affairs.

From the start there were doubts about his suitability for the programme. Tony assumed that *World in Action* would afford him the opportunity to be seen by more people than on a regional magazine show, but star reporters were not *WIA*'s style. Ray Fitzwalter: 'There was a difficulty in that he wanted to be onscreen and we largely made programmes without reporters. It was only when I worked with him that I found out one of his weaknesses – and this was a real worry for us – he had almost no real research ability. He was a person who would throw out thoughts and ideas that were very insubstantial. Actually doing research and procuring a proper body of material, a proper story that could form the basis of a programme – most of our people could do that. The difficulty is that the person who can't do this tends to sit around and wait until someone comes up with something that he can then deliver. He could do that well. We realised he needed watching in other ways. He was not just an irrepressible character and very bouncy and bright, but he could also be a person who didn't listen and that could be a bit dangerous.'

Tony briefly shone when he was embroiled in one of the most contentious programmes in *World in Action*'s history. State-owned British Steel was going nose-to-nose with its unions over its decision to concentrate on key plants around the country while sacrificing non-essential sites. It was a story for which no research was required.

'We did an unbelievably controversial programme,' says Fitzwalter of the *The Steel Papers*, which went out on 4 February 1980. 'There was a strike and suddenly we got given to us, anonymously, a vast cache of British Steel documents that told us they were not telling the truth about what was going on. Tony came into his own here – at the last minute, literally the day of transmission – when we got the chairman of British Steel to agree to do an interview. Tony did it at short notice. It was a hell of a thing to take on. So he was useful there.

'Another occasion came up quite quickly and we used him,' says Fitzwalter. 'This is a good example of where it went wrong and brought out Tony's weaknesses. This was a programme relating to (then Conservative minister) Sir Keith Joseph [*Decline and Fall*, 17 May 1980]. I was concerned about Tony's volatility. I said to him, "Joseph won't be a easy interviewee, he's very skilful minister. You're on a hiding to nothing trying to get something really useful out of him."

'I had the chat with him the day before, the interview was scheduled for 10-11am the following morning and the crew and producer were already in London. I said, "Tony, you need to go to London tonight, have a good night's sleep, up early, having thought the thing through properly and try to imagine what all his frontline answers are going to be." Tony didn't do that. He had heard what I said, he knew what I said and he thought he knew best.'

A version of what happened next has entered into Tony Wilson folklore and features in *24 Hour Party People*. In Frank Cottrell Boyce's script, a spliffed-up Wilson drives through the night to get to London before insulting Sir Keith Joseph by calling him The Mad Monk. 'We had a very cavalier attitude to getting things right,' Cottrell Boyce concedes. 'Tony's attitude was print the legend. I've no interest in the anorak thing. It's a completely trivial film in a way – it's a comedy film. As a screenwriter, if you write a script it's probably not going to get made. So there's an air of irresponsibility about it that I wouldn't feel if I was writing a book or making a documentary.'

Here's what actually happened, courtesy of Ray Fitzwalter: 'He had this desire, always wanting to push things to the limit, push *himself* to the limit. He didn't go down the night before, he went down in the morning, driving himself in his car. Very bad weather, snow, got held up. Sir Keith Joseph is standing there waiting – producer, camera etc – no interviewer. Tony comes in puffing, blowing and is in a state. He isn't prepared. Another of his great features is that he thinks he can handle it, busk it. He can deal with the world, he's done lots of these people before. He made a cock-up of it, lost his temper – which was disgraceful, accused Sir Keith Joseph of calling other people liars in a loud voice and basically the minister had him for breakfast. We salvaged what we could. The minister had given an interview and we were obligated to use some of it. Tony was breaking the rules. For him to defy what I said was breathtaking and it brings out some of the kind of things we were thinking – can we keep him on this programme?'

Perhaps Tony had other things on his mind. Ian Curtis seemed increasingly unable to confront his own situation. Joy Division were also in London, recording a second album at Britannia Row Studios with Martin Hannett, and Curtis and Annik Honoré were sharing a flat.

Honoré gave the 'beer boys' of Joy Division as good as she got. 'She was very outspoken, dominant and very bolshie,' Peter Hook later told the *Sunday Times*. 'Ian became more dominant and outspoken himself as a result. As soon as she found out she could bully us, she just went for it and the only one that would tell her to fuck off was Rob Gretton. There was one time we were in Amsterdam for a gig, and the place where we staying was essentially a brothel. Annik thought it was disgusting and refused to stay there, until someone in the band made the point that she was knocking off a married bloke. She went apeshit!'

Curtis seemed to be doing his utmost to stay away from Macclesfield, his wife Deborah and one-year-old Natalie. A rare return trip in the first week of April saw him take an overdose of barbiturates, leaving Deborah a suicide note. He was rushed to hospital to have his stomach pumped. Tony took Deborah to visit him in hospital before driving the singer to an ill-fated Joy Division gig at the Derby Hall in Bury. A selection of Factory singers had been coerced into being on standby in case Curtis wasn't up to the performance. Given that it was taking place 36 hours after he'd apparently tried to kill himself, it's not surprising that he wasn't. Larry Cassidy (Section 25) Simon Topping (A Certain Ratio) and Alan Hempsall (Crispy Ambulance) took turns at playing with the remaining members of Joy Division.

Curtis looked on before somehow rousing himself to sing two songs before returning to the wings. 'He said he was standing by the side of the stage watching the band play without him and he just had this feeling that he was looking down and they were carrying on without him,' Lindsay Reade told documentary-maker Grant Gee in 2007. 'And that they were going to carry on without him. Which was kind of eerie.'

The return of the Factory 'all stars' to the stage proved too much for the crowd and a wave of bottle-throwing and fighting ensued. 'As we walked off some wag had picked up a bottle and lobbed it at this enormous chandelier suspended over the stage, sending shards of glass showering as we were walking off,' recalls Crispy Ambulance singer Alan Hempsall. 'Tony Wilson was by the door and I can hear all these bottles breaking against the dressing room door. Hooky's concerned because two of the roadies were out there and they're fighting to save the equipment. Hooky then has Tony hanging on to him around the waist shouting, "Get back in!"'

Lindsay Reade: 'We suggested that he come and stay at our house. Ian drove back with us that night from the gig.' The distraught Curtis would stay with them for the next fortnight before spending a week with Bernard Sumner, who tried everything he could to connect with Curtis. The pair walked through a graveyard and Sumner pointed out that if Curtis had been successful in his suicide attempt, a graveyard would be where he'd be right then. Sumner even attempted regressive hypnotism, recording the session on a cassette. The results were included in the 2007 documentary *Joy Division*: hearing Curtis talk dreamily of a mysterious 'book of laws' he was studying – the contents of which were known only to him – is an unsettling experience.

Curtis returned to Macclesfield towards the end of April and visited a local epilepsy clinic as well as managing to play gigs in Manchester, Derby and Birmingham as the band prepared for their first trip to America. He even filmed a video for the band's forthcoming single, 'Love Will Tear Us Apart'.

Meanwhile, Tony was back on *World in Action* patrol. He – and to an even greater extent his wife Lindsay – had taken Curtis under their roof to try and help ease the troubled singer's worries. Now he was called away again to his day job. The programme he was to present, *Britain over a Barrel,* couldn't have come at a worse time but, at the start of May, Tony started work on what would be his last *World in Action*. The programme was an investigation into how the government were planning to spend the proceeds from North Sea Oil. Tony was the reporter and one of his tasks was to grill trade secretary John Nott about the issue. 'It was where his ability to stand and deliver came well into its own and that was quite encouraging,' remembers editor Ray Fitzwalter. 'It was a fairly complex subject but he needed research back-up.'

The programme was set for transmission on 19 May in the regular 8.30pm Monday slot, which the production team would work through the weekend to hit. But even as Tony and his team pulled together the film – current affairs people always refer to even the shortest of pieces as 'films' – things had fallen apart 15 miles away in Macclesfield. In the early hours of 18 May, Ian Curtis took his own life. He hanged himself from a kitchen clothes dryer.

'I'd been warned two weeks earlier by Annik,' Wilson later recalled on BBC4's *Factory* documentary. 'I said, "What do you think of the new album?" and she goes, "I'm terrified."

'I say, "What are you terrified of?"

'"Don't you understand he means it?"

'I go, "No, he doesn't mean it, it's art." Guess what? He fucking meant it.'

Honoré had been travelling to England when Curtis killed himself. Fearful of what might happen at the funeral, she visited his body at the chapel of rest and then went to stay with Tony and Lindsay. 'Lindsay's and my job was to look after Annik,' Tony later recalled. 'I didn't go to the funeral because it was my job to make sure that Annik got on the plane back to Brussels and there was no scene at the funeral.' Annik spent five days at Charlesworth, listening continually to *Unknown Pleasures* and the imminent new album *Closer*. Tony bought her a plane ticket back to Brussels. When she got to the check-in desk, Annik noticed it had been booked in the name of A Curtis. Tony had never had time to discover her real surname.

The inquest into Ian Curtis's death was held the following month. If anyone had been in doubt as to the extent of his distress, then they couldn't avoid it after the findings put before

Macclesfield coroner Mr Timothy Dennis. He was told of a 23-year-old man in the grip of stress and depression over marital problems and epilepsy. It heard of his hospitalisation after taking the barbiturate overdose in April. It heard of his missed psychiatric appointments and of his self-harming with a knife. Deborah Curtis said that Ian had often talked of dying young and spoke frequently about killing himself. The inquest was shown a note left by the clothes rack where he hung himself. It read: *At this very moment I wish I was dead. I just can't cope any more.*

'He'd always planned to commit suicide,' Deborah Curtis told *Granada Reports* in 1995. 'He'd decided to do it before he met me, before he was in a band, before he became epileptic. I think having a band and building up his status was all part of the intention.'

Nearly 30 years on, the question remains of how much of Tony Wilson's attention was focussed on *World in Action* when it could have been aimed at Ian Curtis. This much I can offer. I have been involved in television the majority of my working life. For most people in the industry, it is their *lives*. A programme such as *World in Action* is all-consuming; it eats up time, lives and relationships and spits them out. It is frankly breathtaking that Tony Wilson was able to work on the programme – and be the face of other shows – and try to deal in any meaningful way with Ian Curtis's issues at the same time. When I discovered how close the transmission dates were to the final moments of Curtis's life I was astonished. This was multi-tasking on a grand – you could say foolhardy – scale.

Tony Wilson would spend the next 27 years trying to make sense of what Curtis had done, usually at the prompting of journalists like me. A question that would be asked again and again was: 'How did you feel about Ian's suicide?'

'If a friend of yours tops himself and leaves,' he told me in 1998, 'you're annoyed. In a friendly, loving way, you're annoyed. I was pissed off with him. He shouldn't have left, he shouldn't have left at all. But... his choice.'

Tony was on borrowed time and fading goodwill at *World in Action*. He'd somehow got away with the Keith Joseph incident, which should have been enough to see him shunted towards the fifth-floor lifts and back to the newsroom. But Curtis's death had made waves across the country – particularly in the music press – and there was inevitable sympathy towards Tony after the death of his young friend.

An upcoming *World in Action* investigation into the hyping of singles into the music charts had Tony Wilson written all over it. It even had a working title: *The Chart Busters*. All he needed to do was keep his head down and behave himself. Ray Fitzwalter: 'The thing that finished him off? He was in a taxi or a car, and he flicked the butt of a joint out of the window. He was seen. There was a police car if I remember it correctly. I don't know if they were watching him or whether it was accidental or whatever, but they got hold of him. It wasn't as if I hadn't tried to bring these things home to him.

'I said, "You're not playing in regional programmes here, it's network programmes. We've got a high profile, we are a target. Every time we make a mistake the press go for us. Usually it will be highly motivated and very unfair and they will try and do us a lot of damage. It will go to the regulator, the IBA. You've got to recognise that if you are going to be involved in our programmes, you are going to be playing ball in a completely different arena." All this had been said and to find that he's puffing joints at all and he's a known celebrity, it just made our position impossible and he was sacked. And that was sad. There was enormous talent there.'

Tony would make network shows again, but he was never truly rehabilitated on television. A reputation for being an unsafe pair of hands stayed with him.

Ray Fitzwalter: 'There were things in the mix of Tony's remarkable talents that ought to have carried him to network programming and a wider audience. He had the intellectual ability, he certainly had the fluency on screen. He was a remarkable talent. What he needed when he was with us was, I suppose, an astute minder. We were not in the business of providing minders. We were not a training ground. It's for real. You're talking about millions of people. It's a bit of a tragedy because it didn't make the most of him.'

SIX
A BIG DIRTY HALL

How inimitably graceful children are in general before they learn to dance
– SAMUEL TAYLOR COLERIDGE

A collective shudder went through Factory as they realised that Joy Division's final album *Closer* had a photograph of a tomb on it. It may well have been a tasteful Bernard Pierre Wolff picture taken in the Staglieno cemetery in Genoa, but in light of Ian Curtis's suicide there was considerable room for misinterpretation.

Tony Wilson would always remain acutely aware of the sensitivities in discussing the death. One of the few times that his laidback demeanour was ever truly rattled was when *The Face* magazine attributed to him: 'Ian Curtis dying on me was the greatest thing that's happened to my life. Death sells.' It has a particularly Wilson-esque bouquet to it, but Tony took every opportunity he could to rebut the quote. But in the immediate aftermath of Curtis's death, the uncomfortable truth was that interest in the band and the label soared. 'Love Will Tear Us Apart' went to No 13 in the singles chart; *Closer* went to No 6 in the albums. And the next chapter of Wilson's life would not have occurred without this swell of sales.

Factory designer Peter Saville: 'The bridge from the Friday nights at the Russell Club to The Haçienda is Ian Curtis. Ian's death prompted this astonishing investment of equity into Factory. As a result of Ian's death, the sales of Joy Division records – particularly *Closer*, the album released just after he died – were just phenomenal and unprecedented.'

Nine weeks after the death and without a band name, the remaining members of Joy Division took to the stage of The Beach Club in Manchester to play seven songs. Stephen Morris, Peter Hook and Bernard Sumner, assisted by a TEAC tape machine, sang two songs each and tackled an instrumental. In part they wanted to see who might be best placed to take over as singer, but they also wanted to do *something* to break the deadlock. 'The Beach Club gig was right for us,' says Sumner. 'I never considered doing anything other than Joy Division or New Order.'

Tony accompanied the band on a trip to America to continue the internal try-outs for lead singer and to fulfil Joy Division dates. 'The first gig was at Maxwell's Hoboken [New Jersey],' he later told me. 'A pub/club in the village across the Hudson from Midtown. People in Hoboken still talk about it. Joy Divison/New Order could always be shit and could be wonderful. New Order in particular can be *really* shit. It was utterly stunning. The whole point was Rob Gretton was trying out all three of them. Hooky would sing three of the songs, Bernard would sing three of the songs and Steven would sing three of the songs. Very bizarre. The gig after that was Hurrah's [in New York], the club we were originally supposed to play, as Joy Division, near the Lincoln Center. Bernard was obviously so nervous about having to be the lead singer. He'd usually drink half a bottle of Pernod before the gig and half after. He drank the whole bottle before the gig and was so out of it. So the nerves must have been enormous. Incredibly so. Brave of him to do that...'

Rob Gretton pushed for Bernard Sumner to become lead singer and he suggested the name New Order for the 'new' band. After the group had endured two years of criticism for the Nazi connotations in Joy Division, Gretton saddled them with a line from *Mein Kampf* – 'The New Order of the Third Reich'. He hadn't done it deliberately. 'It came from an article Rob was reading in *The Observer* about Prince Sihanouk of Cambodia,' says Bernard Sumner. 'We didn't know it had Nazi connotations.'

Change was also taking place back in the world of television. Film was being phased out and replaced by video, which didn't need to be sent off to a lab for developing. It was cheaper and supposed to save time, but for Tony it meant he could push deadlines even closer to the wire than he normally did. He could also indulge in his favoured professional pastime: making it up as he went along. If he screwed up he could just rewind and do it again. With the new format came new colleagues. Tony was no longer the bright young thing; he was an experienced hand, someone to be looked up to.

'I went in to Granada in 1980,' says Don Jones, who would later become Wilson's boss. 'I knew nothing about television – I'd done six years on newspapers. I arrived in January as a sports researcher. At the end of the football season – I'd had a very torrid time – I was cut loose into news for the summer. I'd never been out unaccompanied with a film crew. Now I was being told to go out, set it up and wait for the presenter to arrive. One of the first pieces I did was with Wilson. It was a complete revelation to me.'

They met at a local version of the boat race, with Manchester versus Salford on the River Irwell. 'He thought this was very funny as a Salford lad who'd gone to Cambridge. Wilson turned up and was completely taken with the whole idea. Of course he hadn't given it any thought. He turned up, stood on the bank and said, "Right...." He thought for about three minutes, then he said, "This is what we'll do. We'll do this shot, then that shot, then I'll get in that boat and row down the river, then I'll do the PTC [piece to camera] and interview that guy and that guy and it'll all be fantastic." We did what he said, and he threw himself into it.

'Then he got a bit of paper and scribbled down an order of how this piece would go together and gave me the paper with the tape and said, "Give this to the tape editor. I think you'll find it'll be fine." I was absolutely crapping myself because I'd never put anything like this together before.

'I took it back and told the editor, "Tony said, 'Put it together like this and it'll work.'"' And it did. It came as an absolute revelation to me. He'd worked it out in three minutes. He was a very clever guy and it was a witty, visually sound piece. He could take an idea and visualise it as a TV piece in lightning-quick time. In that one afternoon I learnt so much.'

Over at Palatine Road, Factory were also having to learn how to deal with a new concept: commercial success. Peter Saville: 'Factory were not a company, in the same way that the nights at the Russell Club were not an entertainment business. They were just a night in the same way that today a group of people might put on a night. Nobody was *employed* by Factory. There were no offices, there were no premises. There were no overheads. There were no contracts. So when thousands of copies of "Love Will Tear Us Apart" and *Closer* were selling as a result of the tragedy of Ian Curtis, Rob [Gretton], Alan [Erasmus], Tony, Martin [Hannett] and I, who were the fledgling partners in Factory, no one knew what to do with the money. There was no plan because the money was unexpected. So that's what built The Haçienda.'

Factory decided to become more organised. They formed a board to run the company with Alan, Tony, Rob, Peter and Martin all equal shareholders. More bands were signed to the label. South Manchester four-piece Crispy Ambulance had already released their own single 'From the Cradle to the Grave' in April 1980. It got them noticed. 'I remember being told in July 1980 that Rob had managed to get us on the label,' says singer Alan Hempsall. 'Up until that point Factory had been Tony and Alan Erasmus. But Tony was the main man. Just before Ian died the first Durutti Column album had been a bit more of a success than had been anticipated. Rob said he wanted Crispy Ambulance on Factory. The impression I got was that Tony grudgingly had us on the label.'

Rob Gretton's endorsement of Crispy Ambulance saddled them

with a tag that they were somehow the new Joy Division. The fact that they sounded nothing like Joy Division was neither here nor there. Tony took against the band from the word go. 'He didn't like bands without managers,' says Hempsall. 'He was right about that. We should have had a manager. We were Rob's band. There was a lot of the managerial side to Rob that people never saw. I don't think he was that bothered, he just got on with it. I think it probably suited him to let people think, I'm just a Wythenshawe thug. Let them think it. I think that was deliberate to a degree. I don't think he suffered fools. I don't think he tolerated costly errors and mistakes. He was very thorough.'

Rob had another idea what to do with the money being generated by record sales. Peter Saville: 'Tony and Rob had this bee in their bonnet about a club. Rob was a long-standing fan of dance music and liked the idea of a club and Tony liked the idea of giving the money back to the youth culture of Manchester that had supported Factory at those Friday nights. So The Haçienda was a gift back to Manchester.'

Maintaining a total press silence, New Order became a four-piece with the addition of Stephen Morris's girlfriend Gillian Gilbert, a Joy Division fan who'd once stood in for Bernard Sumner at a gig in Liverpool after Rob Gretton had hit the guitarist with a bottle. After a tentative first gig in their full format at Manchester's dingiest venue The Squat, New Order released a minor flurry of singles, starting with the Joy Division left-over 'Ceremony'. Tony managed to get time off from Granada to accompany them on further trips to America, with gigs in New York providing fresh ideas from nightclub visits to bring back to Manchester. 'We started going to [clubs like] Danceteria, Hurrah's and The Peppermint Lounge,' Sumner later told Q magazine. 'I literally saw the light when I was in New York with New Order. All of a sudden, this electronic music made sense. It was like being blind and someone came along and put glasses on you that made you see.'

At Granada, it didn't go unnoticed that Tony was spending

more and more time swanning around with his groups. Bob Greaves: 'Most people's working lives are their job but Tony would disappear for three days "by arrangement with the bosses". He'd come in on a Monday – we hadn't seen him since Wednesday – with a big bag on his shoulder, looking unkempt and it would turn out he'd been, "Hey, man" to New York.

'"New York, Tony? Why?"

'"Seeing people." He was forever on the move. He had more fingers in more pies than Mr Kipling's bakery.'

Lindsay was also heavily involved with the Factory organisation. 'She was doing international licensing,' remembers Durutti Column drummer Bruce Mitchell. 'I came to Factory once and she was there on the steps in tears. 'I said, "Tony, Lindsay's in tears."

'He said: "I know – I've just fired her." It wasn't always fun for Lindsay.'

Mitchell recalls an incident which sums up the couple's fiery, passionate relationship: 'Tony had bought these black Habitat tables to put his Christmas tree and the presents on at Charlesworth. Lindsay comes in and goes absolutely crackers. She's grabbing everything black and throwing them out of the door and onto the pavement and she's shouting, "Black, black... *Factory black*!" Tony was watching this, saying, "I knew then I probably couldn't live with Lindsay any more..."'

Lindsay is adamant this event did not take place – she claims they didn't even *own* any black furniture – and that it was she, not Wilson, who ended the relationship. Musician and friend Chris Lee: 'I think the break-up was caused by little Tony leading big Tony. I thought it was a shame.' Lee believes the culture of Factory at that time was very much stuck in the sexist 1970s. 'The attitude to women was very much, "Why don't you just sit back, roll a joint and give blow jobs?"' says Lee. 'Lindsay tried to be involved in the projects. She tried to be an active participant rather than a hanger-on. In that culture, that might have made her look a bit batty.'

Tony decided to leave rural Charlesworth to be closer to Manchester and moved to Withington, south Manchester. He found a rambling Victorian house on Old Broadway, a private road backing onto a park. The marriage did not survive the move, which bothered Tony greatly. 'Because I'm a Catholic, I felt very peculiar about the divorce,' he later told Manchester journalist Keith MacDonald. 'It's a very confusing area for me.'

Lindsay would – in a sense – have the last word, in the shape of FAC 64. She had recorded a Hoagy Carmichael song with The Durutti Column, and a year after their split it was released as a single. The song? 'I Get Along Without You Very Well'. *Touché*. But as Reade herself pointed out in correspondence for this book, a closer examination of the lyrics reveals the singer may well believe the opposite of the title, thanks to Carmichael's clever song construction.

With a site for The Haçienda agreed, work began on an incongruously placed former yacht showroom on Whitworth Street in central Manchester, close to the Gaythorn gas works. Peter Saville: 'It was quite impressive. It was a former industrial commercial space so it had a real aesthetic to it. Rob and Tony invited me to this empty warehouse and said, "We're going to take this place and make a club. You're the designer – will you do it?" I was flattered that they had the notion that I could do it, but I had the common sense to say, "Thanks but no thanks, but I know a man who could and who should." It was natural that Ben Kelly would pursue the same kind of idealism in doing the club that I was doing with the graphics.'

Saville's friend sized up the job: a massive, rented corner plot, as tall as a three-storey house but with little or no interior to allow headroom for the yacht masts. Tony Wilson and friends thought it would need little more than a swift tart up. They were quite wrong. 'For every job that most designers do there either exists a brief or you formulate a brief,' Kelly told me when I interviewed him for a Haçienda audio guide in Manchester's Urbis exhibition centre. 'Of course with this there was no brief.

There were a number of *conversations*. The organic thing was happening. It grew. It was at that point I had to take control to a degree to make it work from a practical point of view.

'It was a big, open space that had a rickety, old balcony and staircase and nothing else at all I don't think. Nothing. There was a basement. Physically it *was* what it *became* other than putting a new balcony and some bits and pieces. It was a big dirty hall. It wasn't like, there's a Factory template and I've got to roll that out. Peter doing sleeves for Factory bands was a logical thing. The records needed sleeves to go into and Peter was doing that – in a sense for himself, but for others as well. That's a two-dimensional product that contains sonic qualities. For me I have to wait for someone to come along and say we've got this building, this space and we need somebody to make into this, whatever that might be. So for me I was desperate for the opportunity to express myself three-dimensionally in the way Peter expressed himself two-dimensionally.'

Not everyone agreed with the club plans. Martin Hannett believed decisions were taken behind his back. Peter Saville: 'Martin Hannett believed the money should be put into Factory's core business which was by then making records. And Martin was probably right.' He would have preferred to put the investment into new music technology – specifically a Fairlight synthesiser/sampler – that he felt would push Factory to the forefront of 1980s music.

'Were it not for the utter stupidity of Alan Erasmus, Rob Gretton and Tony Wilson, he would have created the next generation of music because he was desperate to get a Fairlight,' Wilson later told *Spike* magazine. 'We had no idea what one was. What we knew was that it cost thirty-fuckin'-grand and we were running The Haçienda and you could fuck off. He never got a Fairlight, Trevor Horn got a Fairlight and the rest is Frankie Goes to Hollywood – and the rest is history.'

Hannett's subsequent legal action over how Factory money was spent would be given its own FAC number. The matter was finally settled – it's claimed that one tactic used by Tony during the dispute was to go to his house and offer Hannett compensation in cash; it's an offer few people with drug addictions could have refused.

Showing a disregard for finances that would become his calling card, Tony Wilson followed the Situationist tract that provided the club with its name – *The Haçienda Must Be Built* – regardless of the cost. 'It's youth culture expressing itself through Joy Division and New Order that's creating the money,' he told Channel 4 shortly after the club opened. 'So it's quite right that the money should go back in to that community, into the youth culture of Manchester. We are real suckers for our homeland.'

Luckily for Tony, just as The Haçienda was taking over his nights, his workload at Granada during the day was about to be reduced with the arrival of some new faces. 'I joined in 1982 from Radio City in Liverpool,' says former Granada journalist Rob McLoughlin. 'Tony was already a big name and a big star. The first thing we did together was the Labour Party conference. I remember he did an interview with Neil Kinnock before he became leader of the Labour Party. Kinnock was greatly impressed by his agility and his brain and the way he asked questions. He said to me: "Your boy is good. Your boy is very good." Tony was very well known on television. He was incredibly generous. There was no "star" about him.'

Tony co-presented *Granada Reports* with Judy Finnigan from Newton Heath in Manchester. She had recently returned to Granada after a stint at Anglia, where she'd been the company's first female on-screen reporter. 'Then Richard Madeley joined,' continues McLoughlin, 'so that was the presenting line-up: Tony, Judy and Richard.'

Richard Madeley had done stints at Border TV and Yorkshire TV before joining the Granada family. He and Finnigan were both married to other people when they met in Granada's newsroom on Madeley's first day.

'Tony Wilson was the epitome of laid-back, slightly arrogant cool,' Madeley recalled in the two-handed autobiography *Richard and Judy,* published in 2002. 'Judy Finnigan really stood out. She had an open, accessible style of presentation. She never flaunted her brightness – Tony did that (and he won't mind me saying so). I found Judy intriguing and I fancied her too.' Madeley and Finnigan became a pairing on screen and off. In 1986 they would become neighbours with Tony on Old Broadway. But to begin with, the two men's relationship wasn't quite so cosy.

'As far as Richard was concerned, there was a great deal of rivalry between him and Tony,' says Rob McLoughlin. 'Shortly after that period Tony was taken off the show. I remember Tony complaining sometimes about Richard coming in early and writing the promos.' These headline reads were designed to trail the programme in ad breaks and were always done in a set of three. In a show featuring two presenters, the person who said the first headline got to say the last line as well. Result? You're on air twice as much as your co-presenter. 'This meant Richard was at the top of the promo and at the end of the promo, ensuring that Richard said, "Good evening."'

Fellow presenter Bob Greaves also noticed a degree of gamesmanship going on in the newsroom. 'Tony was a one-off – there was no malice. As opposed to others – no names, no pack drill – a "famous presenter" would pop in the newsroom in the late afternoon when I was in the canteen and turn the start of the programme from "Bob to camera" into "X to camera". That wouldn't be Tony.'

Rob McLoughlin: 'I said to Tony, "Why don't you come in early and you write it?" Which he never did of course because he was too busy doing other things.'

One of the other things that Tony was too busy with opened its doors on 21 May 1982. The Haçienda's packed debut allowed invite-only guests to see the interior for the first time. It was big. It was greyish blue and yellow. It had a downstairs cocktail bar. And it was really cold. Future Haçienda DJ Graeme Park: 'I lived in Nottingham. I used to get the train up to see bands, more often than not in a place that was half-empty. You'd never take your coat off. They used to say, "Oh, Manchester, they love wearing those long macs and coats." After I went to The Haçienda few times I realised why. It wasn't a fashion statement – it was because it was so bloody cold in there.'

There was another reason why you didn't take your coat off in The Haçienda – there was no cloakroom.

In its initial incarnation – it would have many over the next 15 years – The Haçienda was a club only in the sense that you had to be a member. This allowed it to serve alcohol later than traditional pubs or venues, but its primary function was as to be a venue for live performances. Ben Kelly's industrial bollards and nobbly floors may have left design students salivating but he clearly hadn't spent much time watching rock bands playing live. You walked in to a right-hand bend, booths and tables to your left, bar straight ahead and chest-high stage to your right, with lots of pillars in the way to stop you getting a clear view of the acts.

There were also some major organisational differences that made The Haçienda different to venues such as your local Apollo or polytechnic. It had a playful, whimsical edge with its film shows, exhibitions and outré booking policy (from The Cramps to Dollar). Grub was on offer and you could even get a sandwich at lunchtime. The Haçienda felt like a heavily subsidised art space run by happy amateurs. Which is pretty much what it was.

Although the numbers bled away fairly swiftly, the early days of The Haçienda were a delight to those who stayed. And what a curious grab bag they were: left-over punks, Silvikrinned David Sylvian lookalikes, back-combed Billies and Brendas, rockabillies, psychobillies, goths, ghouls and suburban Siouxsie Siouxs, the long mac brigade and Princess Di puffball girls. The Haçienda was a post-industrial playground and a place of refuge.

'Being a student in Manchester in the early 1980s, the city centre was not a place where many people who liked music went,' remembers music writer Dave Haslam. 'I remember one night getting turned away from two clubs in Manchester – one for not being dressed up enough and the other for being too dressed up. So obviously I couldn't get it right. When The Haçienda opened I realised very quickly it was for people who didn't fit in or didn't want to go to the other clubs in Manchester. It opened as a gig venue.

'The story is that it was opened as a New York-style club with all the connotations of cutting-edge dance music – Studio 54, Paradise Garage – but it was really a gig venue. As far as the general public were concerned The Haçienda was somewhere that you went to see The Smiths, The Fall, The Birthday Party, New Order... As a venue it was poorly designed but the booking policy was great. I didn't look upon it as a doomed enterprise – I looked upon it as somewhere that put on the kind of bands I liked.'

Tony's energy for the club never seemed to flag, even with a full programme of news and regional programmes to deliver. Rob McLoughlin: 'In those days there was a huge amount of airtime. We had to broadcast seven-and-a-half hours of regional programmes a week so there was a lot to do. Tony was also still doing bits of network stuff. So actually there was more than just the news to focus on. Tony was always keen to go back to Granada because he regarded it as his home.'

Granada researcher Don Jones: 'There was a show called *Weekend* that went out on a Friday teatime. It was presented by Paul Jones, the blues guy, and cartoonist Bill Tidy. It was a kind of what's on/music/comedy show. Comedian Ted Robbins was on it and Tony was on it and Alexei Sayle was on it. We had The Boomtown Rats on. He did some wacky things on this programme. He did one film before Christmas where he suggested at 6.30pm that Father Christmas was all to do with Laplanders drinking reindeer piss. The reindeers had been eating magic mushrooms so the Laplanders were stoned and they imagined the whole thing – wacky stuff at teatime. All shot in Dunham Park with Wilson being very serious, talking about magic mushrooms and stoned Laplanders. Very weird but he got away with it.'

Bob Greaves: 'Tony was never safe. He was dangerous. I've seen him get away with murder. But they indulged him because they knew he was worth nurturing. He was a maverick. Everybody loved him. Apart from people in Liverpool, who probably had a grudging respect for him.'

Tony's ongoing, niggling war with the population of Liverpool reached its illogical conclusion around the same time. When Liverpool Football Club's manager Bob Paisley stepped down in 1983 after 44 years of service to the club, Tony was sent out to vox-pop people on the city's streets to get their reaction. As it was Tony Wilson, who had goaded them on-screen for the best part of a decade, no one believed him.

Then the people of Merseyside took the fight to Wilson's doorstep. And won. The day has has entered into Tony Wilson folklore. There are many and various versions of this tale from 1983 – let's go to the horse's mouth. Bob Greaves: 'Tony didn't have a car when I first knew him. After about four years of Factory Records – they never took money out of it – the accountants said to them, "You really should take some money." They had to be pressured to have a car each. Tony's was a Jaguar. He showed us from the first-floor window of the newsroom – "That's my car." A week or two later I was in the newsroom and the phone rang.

'[Best Scouse accent] "Sergeant Carruthers here from the Bridewell in Liverpool. Can you tell Mr Wilson that his car is in Eccersley Avenue in Liverpool 8?"

'Tony last saw his car outside Granada. Tony came in – I said, "I've had the police on, your car's in Liverpool."

'"Oh, wow, man, better haul ass." So he got the train over to Liverpool. Found his car. Three hours later his car was back outside Granada. Later that afternoon, I get another call.

'"Sergeant Carruthers here again. Can you tell Mr Wilson that his car is still here in Eccersley Avenue?"

'I said, "Tony, your car's back in Liverpool!" The scallies had watched him pick it up, followed him back, stolen it again and parked it in exactly the same place. Immediately returned it to Liverpool. Never damaged it. They played the game. They inconvenienced him. He'd obviously slagged Liverpool off one too many times. They followed him, they took it back and he had to go and get it twice in one day. He gave them grudging respect. "Gotta say, man. Good scam, man. Had to move ass, man. Fucking shit, man." Only in Liverpool.'

SEVEN

YOU CAN'T PUT A PRICE ON IRONY

The great secret of succeeding in conversation is to admire little, to hear much; always to distrust our own reason and sometimes that of our friends; never to pretend to wit but to make that of others appear as much as possibly we can; to hearken to what is said and to answer to the purpose
— BENJAMIN FRANKLIN

Tony's presence at the second-ever gig by The Smiths in January 1983 at Manchester's Manhattan club unsurprisingly made the band a fair bet to be Factory's next signing. When they played The Haçienda the following month, observers assumed it to be a foregone conclusion. Tony had kept an uncle-like eye on Morrissey's progress since he had written to him about the Sex Pistols in 1976. 'I always thought Steven [Morrissey] was going to be our novelist, our Dostoyevsky,' Tony later confided to Q. 'In fact, I lost a one-act play he wrote about eating toast in Hulme. But I got a phone call one day asking me to come over because he had something to tell me. I went to his mum's house and he took me into his bedroom – with a poster of James Dean on the wall – and he told me that he was going to be a pop star. I had to stifle my laughter because I thought this was the last person in the world about to become a pop star. Four months later I went to their second gig at the Manhattan club. It was stunning.'

'I remember Morrissey going over to meet with Tony Wilson,' Smiths' guitarist Johnny Marr told journalist Andrew Male in 2001. 'I don't quite know what went on at that meeting but when he came back he was fairly galvanised to go and sign to Rough

Trade.' Tony wasn't interested in doing anything with the band himself because he didn't think they would sell well, his decision influenced by a run of poorly-performing singles by bands such as James and Stockholm Monsters, provoking something of a crisis of confidence. Ron Gretton felt that the demo tape wasn't up to scratch. More precisely, he felt it was 'shit'.

The Smiths in turn felt themselves to be the polar opposite of what Factory – and by default Tony Wilson – represented. For example, Morrissey used flowers as part of his onstage show. 'We introduced them as an antidote to The Haçienda when we played there,' Morrissey later told *Sounds*. 'It was so sterile and inhuman. Manchester is semi-paralysed, the paralysis just zips through Factory.'

In March, Factory released FAC 73 – a single by New Order called 'Blue Monday'. The song, seven-and-a-half minutes of octave-stabbing bass, stop/start kick drum and light as a feather vocals from Bernard Sumner, grew out of a track called '586' on their *Power, Corruption and Lies* album. New Order had taken control of their sound from producer Martin Hannett, who was still in conflict with Factory over money and direction, not to mention with himself with a spiralling drug problem. Tony Wilson: 'New Order go on their own and what do they do without Martin? They create "Blue Monday". A changing moment in history. They had sucked everything out of Martin that they needed.'

Unlike some previous New Order forays into dance – 'Confusion' and 'Everything's Gone Green' – that still had an austere, Factory-esque tinge, 'Blue Monday' was a rock-solid invitation to the mainstream crowd to dance around their handbags – not just in The Haçienda (where it sounded great, ricocheting around the club through its terrible sound system) but in discos up and down the land. It started to sell in large doses. 'Blue Monday' showed that Factory still had what it took – Wilson got his hit and it lifted the self-imposed depression he'd gotten himself into. He also got to spin a yarn around the record that would take on a life of its own.

The Peter Saville designed sleeve of 'Blue Monday' was apparently so snazzy and cutting edge with its floppy-disc stylings, triple-cut-out versions and oblique, four-colour design that Factory lost money on each copy that was sold. As the song became omnipresent throughout the summer of 1983, the more it sold, the more money was lost. Apparently. It's easy to accuse Tony Wilson of being daft, but he wasn't stupid. To constantly reprint a sleeve that lost between 2 and 15 pence per item – depending on the version of the story being spun – would be commercial suicide. If, for some reason, one member of the organisation stuck to this insane game plan for the sheer glory of art, then 'Blue Monday' could have been simply deleted. Did the first run cost more than it was making after subtracting the 50/50 profit split with New Order and the per-copy publishing rights due to the band? Quite possibly. Would this be allowed to continue as 'Blue Monday' became the biggest-selling 12-inch single in UK history? Don't be daft. When I put this to New Order's Bernard Sumner even he couldn't back the tale up: 'Only Tony knows the truth behind this legend.'

Factory didn't spend money on marketing but a finely honed Tony Wilson flight of fancy came for free. Given a choice between the truth and the legend, it appears most people have gone with the legend. 'You can't put a price on irony,' as he himself commented.

'Blue Monday' would eventually achieve Top 5 status in America too, but the royalties from the single that should have come to Factory were employed in wedging opening the doors of The Haçienda. Within its first year, Tony estimated, The Haçienda lost a million pounds. 'We were very blasé about the way the club was run,' he told the *Manchester Evening News*, perhaps unnecessarily. 'We appointed enthusiastic friends and just messed about in a totally idealistic way. It went very silly. It was like having a conveyor belt running out of the club and we'd be pouring money onto it.'

The band, still in council housing and, in Peter Hook's case, helping out backstage at the club for a tenner a night, hit the road to provide themselves with an income. 'I think this was why we were pushed out on tours of the States so much. It was the only way for us to receive some money,' says Sumner today. 'Our royalties were being wasted on The Haçienda.'

In January 1984, the club pulled off a publicity coup by getting segments of Channel Four's teatime music show *The Tube* broadcast from the site. Wilson was on hand, in a dreadful baggy jumper, to talk to fanzine writer turned not-very-good presenter Tony Fletcher about the club and its place in Manchester music. Morrissey was also on the show, boasting about The Smiths' forthcoming album. 'I really do expect the highest of critical praise for it,' he told a flummoxed Fletcher. 'It's a very, very good album. I think it's a signal post in music.'

New American singer Madonna performed her single 'Holiday'. Madonna and her dancers Erika Bell and her brother Christopher Ciccone were shocked at how straight and – initially – unresponsive the audience is as they clump their way through the song. A few weeks before, the trio had been performing at the New York venues that The Haçienda was said to have been inspired by, but they find the Manchester club and the crowd not to their taste. The feeling is mutual. The audience decide to let their feelings about the singer and her pals known. 'Suddenly they started booing and throwing things at us,' Ciccone later recalled in his autobiography. 'I was hit with a crumpled up napkin, Madonna with a roll, Erika with something else. We're stunned. It's obvious this isn't about the music, it's about us. With cash in hand, we bolt.'

That *The Tube* and Madonna were paying The Haçienda a visit was a good indicator of how Factory were seen. With the success of New Order, Tony was in danger of becoming a genuine record company boss. Up to this point, he estimated he'd earned in the region of £7,000 from Factory, but it was now outgrowing cottage industry status. Martin Moscrop of A Certain Ratio: 'Tony stopped managing us in 84/85. As Factory got bigger he had more responsibilities, though he still managed to manage every band on Factory along with their actual manager. Rob managed Joy Division and New Order and did it really well but Tony would almost still be like a manger as well.'

Not long after *The Tube* broadcast, Tony visited a friend in Withington hospital, a mile from his new house on Old Broadway, and struck up a conversation with a young woman in a nearby bed. The woman – a gamine brunette five years his junior, who bore something of a resemblance to Lindsay Reade – introduced herself as Hilary Sherlock. She turned out to be the former girlfriend of Howard Kingston, lead singer of Gentlemen, the north Manchester prog-rockers Tony had booked on the 1976 *So It Goes* with Sex Pistols.

The pair started seeing each other and Tony would take Hilary out on the more far-flung shoots that Granada sent him on. He was filming a new strand called *Romantic Weekends*. Former Granada researcher Don Jones remembers: 'We shot one in Portmeirion, the Italian-style village in North Wales where *The Prisoner* was shot. Hilary came along.' Tony wanted to do scenes in a *Prisoner* style. 'He demanded that we get these massive weather balloons so they could chase him down the beach. It was blowing a gale and the first balloon blew away and Wilson was going berserk. Then the second one blew off as well. He went in after the second balloon, wading out to sea... the crew were pissing themselves. We never got the scene. We also went camping in Appleby in Cumbria. Comic Ted Robbins was there too. Tony wanted his girlfriend to cook a trout on camera – so I was knocking on doors in Appleby trying to find a trout.'

Tony and Hilary were soon married, Wilson-watchers noting that the relationship had developed even faster than the one he'd had with Lindsay. The ceremony took place in New York at the Supreme Court. Wilson acknowledged the haste in an interview he gave to the *Manchester Evening News*, which seemed to be geared towards promoting a more thoughtful, 'grown-up' Wilson. 'My first marriage was over, the divorce had come through. I wanted desperately to marry Hilary. I knew if I got married in this country it would have to be in a register office and I'd feel strange in a register office. So we decided to marry in New York.' The couple honeymooned on the Mexican island of Cozumel. On their return Hilary announced she was pregnant.

Tony took stock of Factory's output and The Haçienda's state of play. There was no questioning the commercial benefit of New Order – once the sleeve issue had been sorted out – but Factory were in danger of being seen as a one-act label when their other artists weren't selling anywhere near as much. They needed fresh blood and money coming in meant cash could be spent on new acts.

They found a band, from Little Hulton at the top end of Salford, whose very name mocked Factory's golden 'Blue Monday'. 'The first time I came across Tony was just after Factory said they were interested in us,' says co-founder and bass player with the Happy Mondays, Paul Ryder. 'Factory Records, the bloke off the telly, the one with the music programme... that's cool. Then I thought, Well, why do Factory like the Happy Mondays? We don't wear raincoats, we're not miserable. Which is the kind of impression people had of them. It kind of confused me for a while. We even had a name with the word "Happy" in it – why does he like us?'

There is an impression of the Happy Mondays as a raggle-taggle band of street urchins moulded by Wilson and Factory to be an E'd up Madchester super-group. The Mondays had started in 1980 as a covers band playing The Clash and Joy Division, and were being managed by Phil Saxe, a market trader at Manchester's Arndale Centre. They were centred around brothers Shaun and Paul Ryder, augmented by dancer Mark 'Bez' Berry, whose job it was to 'look after the grooves'.

'These were the days of Boy George. We used to get A&R men coming down and they'd see us in our trainers, trackies and Adidas gear and side partings and say you've got no image,' Shaun told writer John Warburton in 2000. 'They wanted Duran Duran type things. So Bez was brought on because he was a character and to do that image thing.'

Factory talent scout (and future leader of M People) Mike Pickering then got involved, but what Tony provided was a timely injection of confidence. 'I had 18 rejection letters from 18 major record companies from the first Happy Mondays tapes,' says Ryder today. 'Tony was the first one to say, "I want to do something with this band." Can you imagine having all those rejection letters and you start to doubt yourself? Then along comes the man from the telly who says, "You're really good. I believe in you." That's what he did. He had great faith in his bands.'

At the time, the Mondays were just another Factory act. Tony didn't take a great deal of notice. 'They were just another struggling local band who put out a record on Factory,' recalls music-writer-turned-DJ Dave Haslam. 'Tony didn't discover Happy Mondays, but if he hadn't got involved they would have fallen by the wayside. Maybe it's a question of semantics... maybe it's a question of rewriting history.'

Paul Ryder: 'For the first few months before the first record came out it was Mike Pickering who was courting us. He was a mate of Phil Saxe who was managing the Mondays. Mike was working for Factory. Tony kept his distance for a while – he didn't come down to rehearsals, he didn't phone anyone up out of the band. He let us grow a bit, which is what Tony was good at. He spotted the talent – I know it's gone down in history that the bands have the freedom to fuck off – he gave us freedom to grow, which takes a special man to do that because he must have had a lot of faith and trust.

'If he'd liked music as much as the bands he signed, he would have been in a band instead of being the 40-year-old compere. I think he liked the whole history of music... He liked the history and mystery of it. Maybe he didn't have the bollocks to go for it himself. I know from my point of view I must have had big balls to pack in a job with the Post Office with a pension to go on the dole to try to make it in the a band. Maybe he didn't have that inside, but maybe he had the insight to get a record label together and help musicians that way.'

Mike Pickering produced their first Factory release, the 12-inch 'Delightful'. New Order's Bernard Sumner then took a turn and oversaw their second, 'Freaky Dancin' – essentially recorded live at Stockport's Strawberry Studios. 'The Mondays were utterly, unbelievably lovely, lunatics,' Sumner said in 2007. 'I wanted to capture that rawness before they changed. They *didn't* change.' The vibrant block colour covers for both releases were done by Central Station Design, run by Karen Jackson and brothers Pat and Matt Carroll, cousins of the Ryders. Everything about the Mondays was a step away from the cool, arch style Factory was known for. The Mondays were the epitome of anti-Factory.

Photographer Kevin Cummins recalls the Mondays' first photo shoot. 'Tony introduced me to the Mondays – "They're from Salford," he said. Tony then introduced me to Shaun and said, "This is Kevin, he's from Salford too – he's photographed Joy Division and the Sex Pistols."

'Shaun looked at me and said, "They're all fookin' dead." What a good start.'

Cummins asked the band how they wanted to come across and they said they wanted to be photographed with Rambo. Wilson became greatly concerned on hearing this, but said he would do his best to contact Sylvester Stallone and see what could be done. Kevin Cummins: 'They said, "No, ya coont, there's a fookin' poster of him over the road..." Tony wasn't really a laddish bloke. He tried to be, but he was a lot better at his Didsbury dinner parties.'

Given the trouble that the Mondays would cause for Factory and for Tony, there's sometimes a suspicion that they were taking him for a ride. Streetwise lads from Little Hulton – actually a nice new estate when Paul and Shaun were growing up – running rings around posh Tony Wilson. Paul Ryder: 'There's no way we'd consider taking the piss out of Tony. It was just pure respect. He was daft sometimes and he said some daft things, but everybody does. No way were we running circles round him. We all had the utmost respect for Tony, simply because he stood up and said, "I want to do something with this band."'

By September, Tony and Hilary had a son – Oliver. Hilary Wilson would be frequently dogged by ill health during their relationship and spent more time in hospital during the early part of Oliver's life, which led to a strengthening of the bond between father and son.

Tony was, he declared, a changed man. 'I've married, I've settled down and had a son,' he told the *Manchester Evening News* just after he became a father. 'It makes me think that having my little Oliver has changed my perception of myself.'

*   *   *   *

In April 1985, Tony was preparing to travel to Japan with Durutti Column. He had high hopes that the band's ambient sound could do well there and had arranged for the gig to be filmed. On the 16th of that month Tony was due to do a live outside broadcast for Granada from Manchester's Royal College of Music. As he was getting ready for the show, he received a call from the police. Hilary had been attacked on the doorstep of their Old Broadway home and slashed across with the face with a carpet knife. Rushing to Withington hospital clutching a bouquet of flowers, Tony was collared by local journalist Margaret Henfield about the attack. Despite his shaken state, Wilson spoke with typical calm and clarity. 'One of Hilary's arteries had been cut and blood was pouring from it. She rushed through the door and onto the street. She managed to get to a vicar who was passing by and called for help. The woman stayed in the house... our baby was there too. When police arrived she opened the door and came out.'

After visiting Hilary, Tony went back to work and completed the live broadcast. 'It was a very complicated broadcast and no one else could have done it,' he said. If this seemed to show a certain detachment – similar perhaps to Geoff Knupfer's observation of Tony's behaviour at his mother's funeral – then that would be compounded by events that apparently followed. After again visiting Hilary in hospital, Wilson called in that evening at

The Haçienda. The attack had been all over the news and staff articulated their shock and concern over Hilary's welfare and Tony's well-being. It's claimed he responded with a shrug and the words: 'It was a rock'n'roll moment.' Soon after he boarded a plane to fulfil his commitment with Durutti Column in Japan.

The band – oblivious to what had happened – were waiting patiently for Tony to arrive. Durutti Column's Bruce Mitchell: 'We were doing a film in Tokyo. He was the director and the co-producer. We couldn't understand why he was late. Very unusual. His wife had been attacked – but he still flies out to do the gig. Don't know if I could do that. What he was concerned about was how to break this to Vini [Reilly, the band's key member].' The painfully thin guitarist had a history of ill health: 'Vini can be very fragile,' adds Mitchell.

Back in the UK, the details and background to the attack gradually began to unfold. The true nature of the incident turned from shocking to bizarre. Two days after Hilary was injured, a woman appeared in court charged with wounding with intent. She was named as 25-year-old Maryse Gabriel Gillman-Menage. She'd been living in the St Vincent Hostel for homeless women in the Victoria area of London just before Hilary was attacked. She had travelled up to Manchester two weeks earlier and called at the Wilson home, asking for Tony's autograph. Wilson was not around and it's believed the woman secretly spent the night in the couple's garage. She returned a fortnight later with flowers and cards. Again, Wilson was away. She later confronted Hilary and demanded the return of the cards. It was then that the knife attack took place. It's claimed Gillman-Menage shouted, 'What does he see in you? Why did he marry you?' as Hilary was slashed on the nose and cheek.

When the case came before a judge, prosecutor Mr Guy Gozem told that court that Gillman-Menage was not known to either Tony or Hilary, but that she had a jealous obsession for him. The case was widely reported in the press – WIFE'S KNIFE ORDEAL BY GIRL WITH 'FIXATION' FOR TONY was a typical headline. Gillman-

Menage was made the subject of an unlimited hospital order under the Mental Health Act and was sent to Broadmoor. The end of the court case brought a degree of closure, but the effects of the incident would be felt by the Wilsons for years. 'If you have a public life you're always aware that something like this could happen,' Tony told the *Manchester Evening News* in 1985, 'but you think about it in relation to yourself and not your wife. Hilary always said that she was scared in the house on her own. She always felt that because it is such a big house.'

The next time Tony flew out of Manchester, it would be to meet up with New Order on their US tour. In the process he inadvertently managed to get Bernard Sumner in major trouble. Sumner was waiting for his girlfriend Sarah Dalton to fly out to meet him but his wife Sue was, not surprisingly, unaware of this. Tony managed the impressive task of dropping Sumner in it with both women after agreeing to let *Smash Hits* cover the Santa Barbara leg of the tour without warning the band. Tony: 'One in the morning, I see this photographer and journalist from *Smash Hits*. I'd forgotten all about them. Two weeks later *Smash Hits* comes out and there's a photograph of these two girls, seven o'clock in the morning, running out with Bernard's underpants in their hands ... And because I forgot to warn him about *Smash Hits*, I get the blame. But then, I get the blame for everything.'

As if running a record company and a nightclub, being a television presenter and dropping the lead singer of your best-selling band in the mire were not enough to keep Tony busy, he then took on another responsibility. He became a trade union official. In journalistic terms, the father of the chapel – FOC – is the equivalent of a shop steward, an elected, unpaid union post giving the recipient the mandate to represent their colleagues in local negotiations over pay and conditions. He or she – a female journalist is the mother of the chapel – must be a steady pair of hands able to navigate choppy waters with tact and diplomacy. At this time at Granada Television, the person elected to the job was Tony Wilson.

Rob McLoughlin: 'I had the great misfortune of becoming his deputy. Tony was sometimes not the best note-keeper in the world. Sometimes we would go off and negotiate something on our behalf and afterwards you'd find out what he'd agreed to. One time he went off to America and we were in dispute with the management over a local election special, there would be extra work and we wanted paying for it. Management said, "But Tony has agreed to this." We said, "No, no one would agree to that." We nearly went out on strike. When he got back we said, "You'll never guess what management said while you were away! They said you'd agreed to this extra working – no one in their right mind would agree to that." He said, "Yeah man, I agreed to that." That's Tony...'

One example of Tony's ability to get into a less-than-serious ideological trade union tussle was The Great Powder Puff Battle of 1986. Granada was in the process of shifting some of its news operation to the refurbished Albert Dock in Liverpool. This was in some sense a political move as Merseyside was an important part of the Granada franchise and the area had long felt that the company was too Manchester-centric. There was even a feeling that Granada was anti-Liverpool, a sense not helped by Tony Wilson.

Granada presenters had been doing their own make-up since programmes started coming out of the Dock. Make-up artists objected to this and their union, BETA, protested they were being done out of jobs. It was decided that the best way to show solidarity was for Tony and his fellow journalists to down slap and appear without make-up during bulletins. 'We have been instructed by the National Union of Journalists at a national level not to do jobs which have been done by BETA members,' Wilson told the *Daily Mirror* in his official capacity as union rep. Typically, he couldn't resist adding a Wilson-esque flourish. 'It's unfortunate – I need the powder to hide the bags under my eyes.'

In August 1985, the recordings made by The Durutti Column in Japan were released. *Domo Arigato* was not available as vinyl or cassette, but on Wilson's new favourite format: compact disc.

'He put a pamphlet out saying, "CD is the new medium",' remembers Bruce Mitchell. '"Vinyl will be dead in two years." It was part of the first CD for Factory. The music press said, "What a pillock." He was right. He was right every time. Downloads? He predicted them too.'

Meanwhile, there was talk of the party finally ending at The Haçienda. Dave Haslam: 'Towards the end of 1985, beginning of 1986, Factory and New Order were aware that The Haçienda was losing a lot of money and a decision about whether to close the club had to be made. Before making that decision they somewhat belatedly decided to employ someone who was actually a club manager – they'd [previously] given jobs to friends. That was why the booking policy was great and the finances were shit. They asked Paul Mason to come up from Nottingham Rock City. He began working with [Haçienda promoter] Paul Cons. Mason and Cons along with [manager] Leroy Richardson really took the club by the scruff of the neck. Their first decision was to say, "You're booking all these bands but no one is coming to see them. A much more economic way would be to put DJs on. It'll only cost 40 quid."

'They started looking for DJs. Mike Pickering had been doing irregular Fridays. I was doing a night at The Venue, which was [also] on Whitworth Street. Mason and Cons set out on a mission to find DJs and went all of a hundred yards down the road. I remember being a bit hesitant. There was a moment where I thought I should stay. I had a good thing going and I didn't know anyone at The Haçienda and nobody went. Employing DJs was a last throw of the dice.'

The traditional Factory marketing model of not doing any marketing was re-thought. Manchester's massive student population – Europe's biggest – was actively targeted. Obvious really. Free buses were laid on shuttling students from the main halls of residence to Whitworth Street. Gay night on Monday. Funk night. For years The Haçienda had operated on a 'build it and they will come' policy; now they tried to *encourage* people to come.

In July, there was also the high profile Festival of the Tenth Summer, Factory's way of marking a decade passing since the Sex Pistols' gigs at the Lesser Free Trade Hall. There were film shows, exhibitions and a Peter Saville art exhibition, culminating in a massive gig at the G-Mex Centre featuring A Certain Ratio, The Smiths and New Order. Happy Mondays were relegated to a separate low-key gig at Rafters. The band weren't even considered worthy of complimentary tickets to attend the main event, much less play at it.

It *looked* like Factory was in a bullish mood. Tony went on holiday to China. Dave Haslam was by now a DJ at The Haçienda: 'I think he was soul searching – should the club close? I think he wanted to wash his hands of the whole problem by the summer of 1986. But in August – for the first time – Thursday night was full. Paul Cons phoned Tony in China and said, "We sold out last night." Tony later admitted that that was the moment he thought, Maybe there's a future for The Haçienda? The club never looked back.'

Tony's television career was not as healthy. He was essentially going through the motions. Granada researcher Don Jones: 'He was clever enough not to have to spend loads of time studying something before he did it. He could turn up and suss it very quickly. The trouble with that from a researcher's point of view is that he would turn up on the day and make outrageous demands. He'd arrive and have an idea: "To make this work we must have..." then ask for something outrageous. We went to the dry ski slope at Rossendale to make a mini outside broadcast with four cameras. Wilson obviously hadn't thought about this. As we pulled in to Rossendale he said to me, "What we need here, Don, is a St Bernard dog with a brandy barrel round its neck. I have this scene in mind..."

But in late 1986, a Channel 4 series was being proposed and Tony found himself in the hat as one of its presenters. The job description for *After Dark* might have better read 'facilitator' as the task was to guide a group of handpicked guests to talk about a chosen topic for as long as it was useful, interesting or pertinent to do so. 'I'd never heard of him until I was told he was *the* greatest live TV presenter,' recalls *After Dark* producer Sebastian Cody. 'We had a lot of trouble finding people who could take this show on. I didn't know about his work in music. What I wanted to test was whether he understood the idea we were working to. He instinctively understood it. I remember proposing him as one of our hosts and a sort of groan where they essentially said, "How can we have this idiot all over this wonderful show of ours?" My defence is very simple: someone who sells my show back to me better than I can sell it is someone who understands it. And that's what he did. We tested quite a few people; we ran quite a few pilots in one way or another. Then we did three real pilots and Tony Wilson was one of the three people we tried out. He must have convinced me because I gave him the first show of the series.'

Before he signed on the dotted line, Tony – ever the Granada boy – said he would only do the show if Quay Street agreed. Cody recalls, 'He was the only person to do that. Others said, "You'll have to talk to my agent about money" … "We'll have to think about dates" … "I'm not sure if can cope with a live show that goes on that long" … "Can I do it every week?" The only person who said – in a very corporate way – "I've got to check this with the bosses," was this man who in every other way didn't behave like a corporate man. And he said this every time. It didn't fit with the anarchic individual who wanted to poke a stick up everyone he met.'

With his hair freshly cut, his accent set to 'slightly posh' and captioned on the opening shot as Anthony Wilson, Tony introduced the first *After Dark* with a time-check of 'one minute past midnight,' to prove the show was live. He wore his watch on the inside of his wrist like a kid does. He promised us a new approach to a discussion programme. 'It's open-ended. All the people here can go on talking until such time as they choose to stop talking. This will result – perhaps not tonight, *perhaps* tonight – in a chemistry which will make it worth you staying up into the after-dark hours.'

The seven-strong squad of guests were arranged in a square formation and sipped juice and smoked as they discussed the topic of secrets. Wilson's guests on the first outing were a mix of pro- and semi-pro talkers (*Times* columnist TE Utley, civil servant-turned-writer Clive Ponting and prospective MP Peter Hain) and aggrieved individuals (campaigning farmer Isaac Evans and Margaret Moore, whose scientist husband had committed suicide two months earlier, one of a number of Marconi workers who'd died in strange circumstances). The initial hook was the Official Secrets Act but talk turned to personal secrets as the show progressed. The ad breaks came and went without any break in the flow of conversation.

'I don't want to overstate it but I never worked with a guy who could take two different sets of instructions from two different earpieces, one in the left ear one in the right,' says Sebastian Cody. 'That's a level of conjuring I've never been a part of. In terms of the technical relationship between the live presenter and the person talking to him, it was eerie. It felt like I was thinking things and they came out of Tony's mouth.'

Tony was one of a number of hosts who negotiated the late-night minefield over the course of four series. Broadcaster and lawyer Helena Kennedy (later a baroness), health and ethics academic Professor (later Sir) Ian Kennedy and the late psychiatrist Professor Anthony Clare were among those who also helmed the show. A lawyer was always on hand in the live gallery, though the only time the show came briefly off air was when tanked-up actor Oliver Reed rolled around on top of American feminist writer Kate Millett.

Wilson was, on occasion, 'sin-binned' for taking too much control of the show, or for just being too... Tony Wilson. Sebastian Cody: 'My only sanction was to say you can't come back. On one notorious occasion he overstepped the line by telling everyone that some comment he was making wasn't his idea – it was all the idea of this person whispering in his ear. Which was very much in the style of the thing – the transparency. Why shouldn't people know that presenters are being guided? But it got my goat. Because it looked like a piece of performance art, another bit of Tony – "Look at me". We were aware of this exhibitionist quality to him that didn't help the show. But it was still a mistake to ground him. We ended up working with people who were less good.'

Seven years after he had blown his ITV network chances with *World in Action*, Tony's application to the job in hand – and his good fortune in finding a format that suited his singular style – paid dividends and *After Dark* became one of Britain's most talked-about shows. *The Guardian* called it 'quite the best idea for a television programme since men sat around the camp fire talking while, in the darkness, watching eyes glowed red.' *The Independent* wrote that, 'the series has brought to television the rare acts of listening, thinking and thorough and subtle discussion.' Many reviewers singled out Wilson for praise.

'*After Dark* was important to Tony because it was national,' says Sebastian Cody. 'But I don't remember a political calculation of this being his step to the big time.'

The programme was, however, significant for another reason: it saw the national debut of a new Wilson identity. As the series progressed, Tony morphed from Anthony into Anthony H Wilson. Sebastian Cody: 'He was indeed Anthony H Wilson whenever he did *After Dark*. That was very, very firm. I remember Granada members of the team saying [best Manc accent] "Ay, Terrrny, since when 'ave yoo bin Anterrrny H, then?" And he said, "*After Dark* is an important programme and for *After Dark* I am Anthony H Wilson." As far as he was concerned, *After Dark* was his *Question Time*. It was prestigious, it was national, it was serious, it was a programme that *The Guardian* and *The Independent* and all the big papers paid attention to. He wasn't just Tony Wilson – he was Anthony H Wilson and we indulged him. We didn't argue. This was a man who was on top of what he was doing and that's what he wanted to be.'

'Tony is a more dismissive way of referring to oneself,' Wilson told Manchester diary journalist Guy Meyler at the time. 'I think most Tonys hate the name. Most Tonys find it rather undignified.' Wilson claimed he'd always been an Anthony but had inadvisably plumped for Tony while at Cambridge on receipt of his first byline for *Varsity* and had got stuck with it. This was patent nonsense as his school friends called him Tony, as did his family – with the notable exception of mum Doris. With this later name change, he was laying himself wide open to mockery, particularly from the Manchester media. The fact that Tony – please let's just stick with Tony for our purposes – actually got the Granada press office to send out a media release whenever he chose to be known by a slightly different handle didn't help matters.

The *Evening News* Diary page – one part gossip to two parts spleen in those days – would make a feature of 'accidentally' getting Wilson's new name wrong and then apologising in the following line. When you look back at each of his name changes, you see they coincide with the day of one of his new programmes – so he may have appeared foolish but he got publicity for each project.

In *After Dark* Tony had found a television format to fit his talents, but his reputation as a musical tastemaker was running low. If Joy Division/New Order were taken out of the equation, Factory's commercial profile was almost non-existent. Crispy Ambulance singer Alan Hempsall offers this by way of financial illumination: 'I was cycling past Palatine Road and Alan Erasmus pulled out of the drive and he chased me down the road flashing his headlights. He caught up with me and said, "I'm glad I've seen you. Your ten-inch single is finally in profit – I've got a cheque for you." It was for 80 quid. This was nearly ten years after it was released.'

As the label prepared to enter its tenth year some were wondering if Factory's best days were behind them. Something fresh was needed and no one was more acutely aware of this than Tony Wilson. 'I gave a speech to the Factory staff in the autumn of '87, saying, "There's another musical revolution around the corner,"' Wilson told author John Warburton for his Happy Mondays book *Hallelujah!* 'It might not happen in Manchester, but keep your eyes open. At the same time one member of the Happy Mondays, a group we'd signed 18 months earlier, was standing on his own in the middle of The Haçienda dancefloor waving his fucking arms in the air. Another two of them were selling these little tablets around the back. We were sitting on top of the explosion.'

The intimate euphoria brought on by the little tablets – 3,4-methylenedioxy-N-methylamphetamine or MDMA – meant that things that had previously been drawbacks at the club would suddenly became assets. One of the drug's original nicknames was 'empathy' and it certainly seemed to create an understanding between The Haçienda's boomy, industrial space and the clattering repetitive beats that were beginning to fill it. Suddenly, the place seemed to make *sense*. 'Everyone in the place was on E and it made us look better and sound better,' Happy Mondays' lead singer Shaun Ryder later told *Q* magazine. 'The whole Manchester thing was nothing to do with the actual bands. It was the E scene that started it off.'

Graeme Park was asked to cover for Mike Pickering in late 1987. He'd been a gig-goer at the club in the early, cold and empty years. 'I worked in a record shop so I was in a great position to get hold of imported records. I was playing what's now become known as house music, imports from Chicago. There's a whole other book in who played house music first, north or south. But I know that me and Mike Pickering were the first DJs in the UK to play house music. I was playing it in Nottingham at the The Garage, a small, sweaty, seedy club. Mike was doing exactly the same at The Haçienda in a cavernous club that could hold 1500 people. We were both aware of what we were doing. Mike was due to go on holiday. I went up to The

Haçienda a week before to check it out. I was like... *Oh my God.* He was playing the same music as me but the difference was the little white pill called Ecstasy. I've forgotten a lot of things over the years but I'll never forget those three weeks at The Haçienda. I stayed.'

*   *   *   *

Christmas 1987 was a dark time for the Wilsons. The problems Hilary Wilson had experienced since the doorstep attack 20 months earlier overwhelmed her and she was hospitalised at the Cheadle Royal in Stockport. When news leaked out, Tony for once refused to comment, but a Granada spokesman was quoted in *The Sun* as stating: 'The scar is still visible and is a constant reminder of what happened. This has led to a delayed breakdown.' To emphasise what the paper saw as the actions of a disturbed woman stalking the family of the man she was obsessed with, the article was accompanied by a photograph of Michael Douglas and Glenn Close in *Fatal Attraction*.

EIGHT
YVETTE

I am proud to wear the scorn of fools
– THOMAS DEKKER

The combination of a drug he'd never heard of, a style of music he didn't like and a band he was ambivalent about would provide Tony Wilson with a vital second wind that would seal his reputation. At the same time – again by total chance, there was no master plan here – Tony found himself with another new television outlet.

It's hard to recall now, but British television – with the exception of *After Dark* – tended to finish pretty early in the 1980s. ITV stations in London, the South and the Midlands had experimented with *Night Network* in 1987 – quizzes, comedy, music and re-runs of 1960s *Batman* shows running after midnight – before the concept went nationwide the following year. As in 1976, a stroke of good luck saw Tony find himself on the cusp of a musical revolution with access to airtime.

Another running theme in Tony's television career was the way that when junior staff – researchers in particular – achieved positions of authority, they would remember his kindness. Granada researcher David Liddiment had gone on to direct the news and *What's On*. By the late 1980s, he'd progressed even further. 'I was running entertainment,' says Liddiment. '*So It Goes* was long gone and Tony hadn't got quite the same place in the company. But he still had that hankering to capture popular culture.'

Granada weighed into *Night Network* with three main shows: *Quiz Night* with over-the-top sports pundit Stuart Hall, *The Hit Man and Her* – basically a couple of cameras in a nightclub with record producer Pete Waterman and kids' TV presenter Michaela Strachan – and Tony Wilson's *The Other Side of Midnight*.

'It was Wilson, a researcher and a producer/director called Julian Jarrold,' says Liddiment. 'Just three of them and they just blagged. They had incredible vision on no money. We got the studio. Tony wanted an all-white set, he wanted the *OSM* tablet [graphic logo] in the top right corner – now they are everywhere, then they weren't. He had a real sense of what the show should look like. They were like weekly essays from Wilson about what was out there, what struck him – and he delighted in that.'

Dave Haslam: 'In January 1988 I was walking through town with a bag of records and bumped into Tony. He said, "What have you been buying?"

'"A bit of acid house."

'"What's that?"

'A couple of weeks later he said, "I want you to come on *The Other Side of Midnight* and talk about acid house." Then a few weeks after that I was at an event and Tony was there, saying, "Let's face it, the future of music is acid house." That mindset where it sounds exciting, it's current, let's put it on the telly. Somehow it's taking ownership of it. He never really understood dance music. Tony was Leonard Cohen/Sex Pistols. Disco was the enemy.'

A Certain Ratio's Martin Moscrop: 'He could be a bit fuddy-duddy about new things like acid house. There were certain times when he just should have shut up. He had no experience or love of dance music at all. When he did start talking about it, it was like, "Oh shut up, Tony."'

David Liddiment: 'We used to have these big debates. I was really into dance music – he scorned dance music. He just thought

I was off the mark. He graciously conceded that I wasn't off the mark when dance permeated the alternative music scene that he'd been part of. We had wonderful arguments.'

The Other Side Of Midnight wasn't all about talk. As well as doing features on cinema and advertising, it hosted dance acts like Bomb the Bass and The Rhythm Sister, along with The Fall (in their glamorous period featuring Marcia Schofield and Brix) and Wilson-related acts. Peter Hook performed the New Order off-cut 'The Happy One' on his own and fast-rising Happy Mondays did 'Wrote for Luck'. Paul Ryder recalls going to the *OSM* studio to record the show. 'I used to deliver telegrams to Granada, so I knew where it was. There was always a big queue of autograph hunters outside waiting for the *Coronation Street* people. I thought, Wow I've made it. Maybe it was just a local TV programme but it was like going to the moon. You're no longer a Post Office delivery boy: you're in a band and you're on the telly.'

Any reservations Tony may have had about promoting Factory artists or other outside interests had clearly evaporated. 'Just about every other music is complete crap,' he told the *New Musical Express* when they came to visit the set. 'I'm very happy if people think, Oh, Wilson's putting his own stuff on. It makes me look like a nasty person and I find that an amusing image to have.'

Paul Ryder: 'He had already started dropping our name in the press. New Order had a record out and Tony and New Order were mentioning the Mondays. Then he got us on *The Other Side of Midnight*. That was one of the perks of being on Factory.' It wasn't just Factory acts, though. Tony introduced The Stones Roses performing 'Waterfall' on *OSM* by stating he'd seriously disliked their 'rock'n'roll stance' in the past – but was wrong. And he apologised.

'The Stone Roses I hated,' he later stated. 'I'd seen them in the early 1980s when they were a goth band and badly dressed. By the time they started spreading their names all over Manchester they were managed by my ex-wife, my ex-business partner Martin Hannett and two ex-protégés from The Haçienda were also working with them. So everyone who was an ex in my life was involved with the Roses, so I completely ignored them.'

'*OSM* was a thrilling thing to do because it gave Tony that voice again,' says David Liddiment. 'And it also had the challenge of having no money. The music thing took off in such a big way that it masked the other side of him, the TV side, which was just as much a key component of him. The two met in *So It Goes*, *What's On* and *The Other Side of Midnight*. All the other TV things he did were his day jobs.' He was initially billed as Anthony on *OSM* before including the H as well, as on *After Dark*. The additional consonant was met with universal local derision, but Tony lapped up the attention.

'When he came to Granada he was Tony, then he became Anthony,' remembers colleague Bob Greaves. 'It was difficult to remember what to call him. Then the H appeared. Then he interviewed one of his heroes, Anthony Burgess.'

The author of *A Clockwork Orange*'s full name was John Anthony Burgess Wilson, so he was entitled to an opinion on the subject of names. Bob Greaves: 'Burgess saw the end credits and said, "What's with this Anthony H? Get rid." And he did. Tony took the word of his idol. Then eventually, he virtually dropped the Anthony. No one ever said to me, "Tell that Anthony H Wilson he's a wanker." It was always, "Tell that Tony..."' Even so, the end result of this dalliance with name changes was that for the rest of Tony's life, no one ever knew quite what to call him.

As well as a return to music television, 1988 saw a typically full plate for Tony. He revealed plans to open the first of a series of drinking establishments, even announcing the kind of drink that people would be necking in it. It was his new discovery and he was very excited about it: Mexican beer with slices of lime shoved down the neck. The bar/restaurant venture – initially talked up in the press as being called 'Dri and Hungry' – would be the first of a series. Sites earmarked were Los Angeles, Paris and – rather charmingly – Leeds. Tony was adamant that there were no plans to open a London branch.

The name was eventually shortened to Dry. 'That was Bernard Sumner's idea,' Tony told me in 2006. 'Brilliant name for a bar... *Dry*.' Tony wanted Dry to be on the site of an old carpet shop on Oldham Street, the tatty end of Manchester city centre better known for porn and joke shops, feeling that the area was ripe for regeneration. Bernard disagreed. 'Bernard, stupid bastard, wanted us to put it on Oxford Road [centre for Manchester's enormous student population]. Imagine, putting a bar on Oxford Road where all these students would pass by and buy drinks. Absolutely disgusting. So I won the debate. Bernard was right and I was wrong.'

In fact Tony was right – just 15 years before his time. That tatty area around Oldham Street is now known as the Northern Quarter and bustles with cafes, shops and creative industries. Tony's vision cost Factory – by his reckoning – 'a few million quid'.

Haçienda designer Ben Kelly was brought in to do the honours for Dry, something he has mixed feelings about today. 'I feel personally responsible for that God-awful thing called designer bars. In a sense Dry was the first one. It set in motion a kind of more European sensibility of going out in the day and spending time in somewhere that wasn't corporate or wasn't steeped in tradition. I do think that's what Dry did. This horrible tag "designer bar" and lots of not-very-well-designed places did spring up, but it gave a lot freedom to a lot of people all over the country. That in turn eventually led to having cafes and bars almost everywhere and I think Dry played a part in that.'

There was also bullish talk of an 'international youth exploitation film' about Manchester car thieves with 'at least three high-speed car chases', to use Tony's description. He wanted £2.5m for the movie and had approached Warner Bros with little success. Perhaps it was the subject matter that was off-putting. 'It won't glamorise joyriding,' he insisted, 'but express youth.' Or maybe it was the title: *The Mad Fuckers!* (Their exclamation mark, not mine.) Tony told the *North West Times* in 1988 that he saw the title as a test to see if a studio executive 'got' the film. 'When someone in the movie world says: "That has a swear word on the front cover, I will read it when you change that front cover," that says everything you need to know about those people.'

If all this wasn't enough, he was voted Britain's Worst Dressed Man for 1988. According to the list, Tony Wilson was a 'crumpled mess' who 'tries to look trendy but it doesn't come off.' Tony professed himself delighted with the award – he even pulled a quote out of the bag for the occasion, dismissing the award as 'the scorn of fools'. Among those he beat to the title were all-round entertainer Bruce Forsyth, newsreader Sandy Gall and chat show host Russell Harty, the very man who'd told him he looked like a 'cunt in a bucket' all those years ago in the Granada canteen.

Bob Greaves has a typically succinct view on the Wilson style: 'He didn't care. None of us had heard about designer labels. They were just starting up in America. We didn't know anything about clothes having a name on them that was worth talking about. He came in one day wearing what I thought was an old sack from a farmer's field. It was grey and hung on him like a sack. He was obviously proud of this jacket. He told us the price, like $650 – I'm talking about many years ago. "But it's John Paul Gaultier, man."

'He had no style. You could often hear him coming down the corridor with the soles on his shoes where they were broken at the front and flapped. '"I wear 'em till they go, man. Shoe polish, man? What's that?" He simply wore a pair of shoes till they wore out. He would wait till they did that (slaps hands) on the studio floor till he got rid. He didn't care. He wasn't arsed and he always looked lop-sided. Even a smart jacket looked like a lump of shit on him.'

At this time Tony was to some extent a figure of fun at Granada. However high he soared there was always some quick-witted cameraman or grip with a one-liner to drag him back down to earth. One day a windsurf board appeared firmly attached to the roof of his Jaguar, with Tony declaring himself a convert to the cause of the fashionable sport. As he was being mocked mercilessly by a gang of film and sound editors, one of them secretly licked his finger and ran it down the side of the board, making a long groove in the dirt. Several weeks later, the gang saw the mark was still there and loudly pointed this out to Tony across the car park. He was forced to admit that the nearest the board had come to water since he bought it was the editor's spit-covered finger.

At The Haçienda, Tony watched in amazement as house and acid house took hold. DJ Graeme Park: 'Tony was down the club most weekends. What was his role? That's interesting. With hindsight he was interacting with people. He accused me and Mike Pickering of destroying The Haçienda because we totally committed the club to dance music, to house. He was like, "But Graeme, darling, it took over and it became exclusively about house music. Previously it had been everything and anything." He was right, we did. I don't think he got the dance music thing. But he could see what was going on. He couldn't argue with the queues around the corner. Tony might not have understood dance music but he totally got The Haçienda. One night Tony came into the DJ box with Seymour Stein [Sire Records boss]. He was like, "Oh my *God*, this is just like *Noo Yawk*." The man who signed Madonna is saying our Friday night is like a club in New York!'

Fellow DJ Dave Haslam: 'Having DJ'd at The Haçienda nearly 500 times between 1985 and the night it closed in 1997, I only had one conversation with Tony about music policy. That was in about 1989 when he came up to the DJ box and said, "I've been in London all day and someone at EMI gave me this record. It's reggae. Do we play reggae?"

'I said, "No."

'He said, "Well, have it anyway."

'I remember saying to him – quite laughingly – "I'm the mill hand and you're the mill owner." You can imagine back in

Victorian Manchester there'd be people working their butts off in the mill... in the factory. Then there was the mill owner. The mill would be named after him and he'd be riding with the hounds in Cheshire while you laboured and he'd turn up once a year at the annual party and philanthropically give you free drinks. That's kind of how I feel about Tony through some of that Haçienda period. He was like the mill owner. But everyone owed the mill owner everything.'

As sell-out nights began to become commonplace, Graeme Park paints a picture of how DJs were treated by The Haçienda management at this time. 'We always got paid properly. I'd submit my invoice at the start of night, at the end I'd be paid plus VAT. My hotel always got paid. There'd be dinner, room service, people would come back for a bit of a party. When I checked out I had never had to pay anything. The Haçienda always picked up any extras on my bill. Maybe that's why they went bust.

'I stayed at the V&A [Victoria & Albert] hotel and at the time it was owned by Granada. Every room was themed. There was a *Coronation Street* suite with flying ducks, a *Jewel in the Crown* suite which had an Indian theme – there was even a *Grumbleweeds* room. One night I was really tired, lay down on my bed and there's a huge picture of Tony Wilson looking down at me. It was the *Granada Reports* suite. I rang down to reception, "I want to change rooms..."'

Back at Granada, Tony was asked to do a favour for his colleague Mike Spencer, who was due to show to show a young, would-be journalist and presenter around the new Liverpool studios. Her name was Yvette Livesey.

'I was a journo in the GTV newsroom,' says Spencer. 'Yvette knew Mike West, a presenter I had worked with at Radio Lancashire, and he rang me to ask whether I would show Yvette round the newsroom. A time was agreed but on the day I was sent out on a story. Tony was upstairs, preparing for one of the daytime bulletins, and I asked him if he'd show her round instead. I remember Mike saying that she was a former Miss UK, information I'm sure I passed on to Tony and which would have helped the cause.'

'All my cultural growing up, I did with Tony,' says Yvette Livesey. 'It made me who I am. I was a spoilt rich girl. Tony and I just clicked, we were so alike – people didn't see it, but we were so alike. Our attitudes towards people were exactly the same. In a funny way, I found my home with Tony as soon as we met. We loved the same books, we loved travelling. All the things I love and I am, Tony was as well.'

After being born in the small Lancashire town of Oswaldtwistle and spending part of her childhood in South Africa, Yvette had grown up in the monied Lancashire village of Whalley. Her father's successful engineering business paid for private education, and modelling work from the age of 14 added to her sense of independence. 'Three days after my A levels I ran away as fast as possible. I was always supposed to inherit the business, but it was my worst possible idea of life and hell. So as soon as I'd done my exams I ran away to London.'

A modelling agent suggested she entered beauty contest to boost her confidence. 'She entered me into Miss Leeds, which lead on to Miss West Yorkshire, which led me into the Miss England competition. So I became Miss England in three steps, then went to the Miss Universe competition in Singapore. It was pretty wacky – travelling the world as Miss UK on my 19th birthday. I ended up in places like El Salvador during the civil war, meeting the president, staying in hotels with half the hotel missing. People say to me, "If you had a daughter, would you let her model?" I'd say, God, yeah. You get these experiences – so intense at that age – but you've got to grow up quite fast. You travel the world and earn a lot of money.'

After her Miss UK tenure, Livesey began knocking on the doors of regional radio stations and made some headway at Red Rose Radio in Lancashire and Manchester's Piccadilly Radio – the biggest station outside London. While at Piccadilly she began seeing one of the station's news reporters, Chris Roberts, now an anchorman on Sky News. It was the height of Gunchester and Manchester was at the top of the nation's news agenda. Add to that the attention being received by The Haçienda – a club Livesey had never been to – and you couldn't escape the feeling that something was happening in Manchester.

'It felt like the city was dramatically changing. At that time Manchester was dirty and grubby. You were careful what you wore and you certainly didn't walk down the streets alone by yourself at night. But Granada was this huge company and if you wanted to get into telly and get anywhere, that was where you wanted to be. That cool factor – Tony always said I had a "Whalley" look – prim, proper, pretty kind of look, the opposite to being cool. The sensibilities of being a Mancunian – of morality and attitudes to people – are who I am today. I feel that Manchester made me and shaped me. I know who I am and that's fine. I'm not a snob and Tony wasn't either. You'd think Tony was a snob but he wasn't – about people or things – he was a populist in a funny way.'

When she met Tony at Granada the pair embarked upon an elongated and secret courtship. It was also rather prim, which may surprise many. 'It took two years and I was very upright and proper about it,' says Yvette. 'I was like "Sorry, Tony, you're married." He explained the situation of his marriage, so we spent a lot of time going out for dinner and just being with each other and being quite obsessed with each other. We both knew it was life-changing. It wasn't just an affair. It was something more special than that. I would never have gone anywhere near Tony if I thought he had a happy marriage. At that age you have certain standards and morals. I was very prudish about it. We knew how we felt about it other but that didn't matter. I was brought up very well.'

While Tony expressed unhappiness with life on Old Broadway, his commitment to his son Oliver – plus a large dose of Catholic guilt – caused him great confusion. Matters would come to a head, but not before the news that Tony was about to become a dad for the second time. Yvette: 'Nine months before Tony left, Hilary had obviously got wind that there was something wrong. She got pregnant. I remember Tony ringing from the hospital saying Isabel had been born and I thought, Well, that's it then – he's got to stay. But he made the decision he couldn't stay. At that point we were still just friends, but I actively thought then that it was not to be between us.'

The relationship between Tony and Yvette would remain covert over a two-year period and although she would become a familiar face at The Haçienda and at Factory, the pair's status was not the subject of comment. As with Ian Curtis and Annik Honoré, Bernard Sumner and Sarah Dalton before them, Tony and Yvette's relationship was their business and it was not spoken about. At Granada, Tony's personal life was a closed book as always.

Bob Greaves: 'Did we talk about our love lives? No, not a great deal. When Tony finished at seven o'clock at Granada, he was not a man who would go in the Granada bar. He would disappear and pursue his other interests. He didn't have long, lingering "let's talk about our personal lives" conversations. It was work and then he'd dart off to do his other things.'

NINE
FURY OF TV WIFE

Like art and politics, gangsterism is a very important avenue
of assimilation into society
– E L DOCTOROW

As sold out nights at The Haçienda started to become the norm rather than something to ring Tony in China about, a certain logic about the club began to develop among some Manchester criminals. The music brought in the people; the music sounded better with the drugs – everyone said so; the more people who took drugs the better The Haçienda experience would be. Therefore people who had drugs to sell were surely to be welcomed with open arms at The Haçienda.

Given the pronouncements that had come out of the scene thus far, the criminals could be said to have had a point. After 16-year-old Claire Leighton died in the club in July 1989 after taking ecstasy – great effort was made to point out she hadn't bought or taken the drug inside the premises, as if that mattered – The Haçienda became a target for the police. To them, Tony and the rest of the lefties, rabble-rousers and bohemian anarchists involved in the club were the root of the problem. To Greater Manchester Police – under the stewardship of arch-conservative chief constable James Anderton – they might as well have been from another planet.

What's more, those running The Haçienda were initially reluctant to seek police help in tackling gang-related problems.

'Tony and Rob didn't know how to deal with the police,' says Dave Haslam. 'They were caught between these two gangs, the criminals and the police. Rob wasn't going to ask the police for help. When the police came in Tony would "address" them. The police don't take too kindly to being lectured by men off the telly. The police weren't helpful that's for sure. But they [Rob and Tony] weren't about to align themselves with the forces of law and order. Which is why the criminal element took over.'

Yvette Livesey: 'Tony did want help. The police said, "We don't put police on doors." He said, "You do for football. Why don't you help us?" They were desperate for help, but the police were convinced that they were part of the drugs and the gangs.'

Undercover officers from Greater Manchester Police made a hundred visits to the club. The most they saw was people rolling and smoking joints. They were missing the gangs behind the drugs. Great show was made by the criminal element of their snowballing confidence. Free drinks were demanded, queues were jumped and security staff were shown who was in charge. To add to the problems The Haçienda was in the middle of a geographical gangland triangle. To the north of the city was Cheetham Hill, where the gangs specialised in drilled, chillingly efficient armed robberies to provide their funds, which were then ploughed into drugs. To the south were the younger, leaner soldiers and dealers of Moss Side. To the west, in Salford, protection rackets were the order of the day with licensed premises the favoured target. All the gangs were within a handbrake turn of the centre of Manchester and all of them considered the city their territory.

Greater Manchester Police hit back with Operation Clubwatch, coming down hard on the gangs who were flashing guns to get free entry into clubs. On any given Friday or Saturday night, police estimated that there were a thousand people in the centre of Manchester who had the express intention of causing trouble. Venues like Konspiracy and The Gallery suffered alongside The Haçienda. Konspiracy co-owner Marino Morgan summed up the problem to local crime reporter Steve Panter: 'The gangs come in. Without Robocop on the door, they are difficult to stop.'

The Haçienda's solution was to in a sense to heed Morgan's advice. Money was spent on providing the club with their own Robocops – über-doormen capable of facing down the most intimidating of club-going gangsters. This came at a cost and Wilson estimated that at the height of The Haçienda's gang troubles, £375,000 was spent in the space of 12 months on maintaining the door, bringing the Cambridge graduate into contact with a whole new type of Mancunian.

Haçienda DJ Dave Haslam: 'By the end of 1989 the start of 1990, things had changed. Everyone connected with The Haçienda was on a magical mystery tour. Make it up as we go along, make it better than it was last week. You have this wonderful, naïve, organic, spontaneous upward curve of brilliant adventure, but when it starts to go wrong you're not prepared for it.

'It also got caught up in a change in the wider culture – the Happy Mondays thing really. Things were more gang-orientated, a bit rougher. That somehow became part of lad culture. Among some people – and I think Tony was guilty of this – there was a notion of getting a bit distracted by gangster chic. Tony suddenly meeting people who'd shot people – shot *two* people – and got away with it. Tony with his restless, challenging personality found them interesting people to deal with. He didn't see them as other people might see them, as destructive knobheads who needed putting away.'

Manchester's destructive knobheads were attracting attention across the country. 'Gunchester' was the tag given to the city as shootings became so commonplace that the local news media only reported the 'best' ones. DJ Graeme Park: 'My mum was picking up *The Daily Record* – a Scottish tabloid – and reading about what was going on at The Haçienda on the front page. People would say to me, "Oh, The Haçienda, people have guns there." I never saw it. The worst violence I ever saw in the club was when Mick Hucknall tried to punch me.'

On a more cerebral plane in the autumn, Tony trumpeted Factory Classical. 'One of the best things about Factory starting a classical label,' Wilson told the *NME* in October 1989, 'is that as a pop label we pioneered the classical look of record covers without pictures of the groups on them. Now, as a classical label, we can pioneer the pop look of records with pictures of the musicians on the front.' The Duke String Quartet, The Kreisler Quartet, oboist Robin Williams, pianist Rolf Hind and composer Steve Martland made up the first batch of releases. Underlining Wilson's point, Martland's release featured a cover picture of the composer shirtless with a rockabilly haircut. Wilson-watchers will note the concept of marketing younger classical musicians in the same way as pop stars would be a commonplace sight within a few years.

John Metcalfe – a member of both the Duke and the Kreisler quartets – was given the job of overseeing the first Factory Classical releases. 'I was a kid in a sweet shop,' he told Cerysmaticfactory website. 'I chose the artists and with them organised the recordings, editing etc. It was important for the music to be 20th century with at least one British piece on each CD – the point being that you didn't have to have a World Cup or a shit disco beat over the top or another bollocks version of Mozart's "Eine Kleine Nachtmusik" to make excuses for classical music to an already patronised and assumed dumbed-down audience. Beyond that the musicians could do what they liked.'

Speaking of which, the Happy Mondays were on a swift ascent. They spent the last two months of the 1980s on a UK tour – including a riotous night at the Free Trade Hall – and made their first appearance on *Top of the Pops* to promote their 'Madchester Rave On' EP. Stone Roses appeared on the same edition and the Mondays barely made it on time after Shaun Ryder was arrested on Jersey for cocaine possession. The tabloids were becoming very interested in the band and Wilson revelled in their notoriety. 'I'm sure he did do,' says the band's Paul Ryder today. 'All publicity is great publicity. But he wasn't doing it in a nasty way. Tony was probably just giggling thinking you can't *buy* publicity like this.'

In April 1990 – just as the Happy Mondays were playing two packed gigs at G-Mex, the very venue for which they couldn't even get tickets less than two years earlier – it was discovered that the police were planning an objection to The Haçienda's licence when it came up for renewal. The action was based on their undercover findings. Tony began to plan his defence. He'd kept the doors of the club open by fair means or foul for eight years and he wasn't about to give up without a fight.

At Manchester Magistrates Court, officers cited 'continued use of controlled substances' as their chief reason for revoking the licence. Tony went on the offensive and wrote an article defending the club for the *Manchester Evening News*. Wisely, he avoided attacking the police or the gangs, instead bigging up the club's value in terms of youth culture, international kudos and the local economy. 'The statistics are simple,' he wrote. 'In considering The Haçienda's value to the community, calculate the foreign money – the yens and the dollars and the pesos – that flow into our city and circulate in our confident new environment.' The fact that Manchester City Council supported the club as culturally valuable also helped. The services of celebrated QC George Carman were retained as the fight loomed.

Elsewhere, there was the matter of FAC 293, a number one single, to deal with. 'It fell to me to pull the whole thing together,' Wilson told me with customary modesty when I asked him how 'World in Motion' – the official England song for the 1990 World Cup – came about. With New Order effectively on hold after an ill-tempered American tour, Bernard Sumner had formed a partnership with The Smiths' Johnny Marr under the banner of Electronic. They'd already scored a hit with 'Getting Away With It' with the Pet Shop Boys, the first of a series of collaborators. Meanwhile, Stephen Morris and Gillian Gilbert had formed The

Other Two and were producing singles and soundtracks at a very reasonable rate. Musicologists might note that one of their pieces – the theme tune for the BBC's *DEF II* programme – bears a remarkable similarity to the finished England song.

The Football Association, tired of the pub singalongs that normally passed for football songs, had approached Factory with a view to New Order doing the honours. 'None of New Order were interested,' Wilson later recalled. 'I set about finding someone who could do lyrics about football. I spent a month and a half ringing up witty and literate people who I thought might be right.' New Order's Bernard Sumner eventually brought in comic actor and semi-professional rock sidekick Keith Allen to write the words and the song was credited to ENGLANDneworder. Wilson's contribution was the three-note 'EN-GER-LAND' chant, though Allen disputes this. Either way, the result was the least worst football song of all time. It was also New Order's last single for Factory.

Back at Granada, Tony began work on a new series. Several ITV regions had started experimenting with a new format of late-night, confrontational discussion programmes. As ever, Granada wanted their show to be different. ITV head of entertainment David Liddiment: 'The Granada one wasn't like the other ones. Because of Wilson I think, because of his personal style. That was him wanting to get stuck in with what was going on.'

The purpose of *Granada Up Front* was to generate studio argy-bargy, the forerunner of the kind of morning shows that are still made at Granada's studios. 'It was the Nicky Campbell show, it was the Matthew Wright show, it was the Jeremy Kyle show – it was the precursor to all of those programmes,' says Mark Alderton, one of a team of researchers who worked on the show. 'It was populist, it was serious, it was funny, it was contemporary, it was edgy, it was live, it was late-night, it was well-funded and it had two really good presenters in Lucy Meacock and Tony Wilson.'

Chester-born Meacock had joined Granada the previous year from *London Plus*. A presenter in the Judy Finnigan mould,

Meacock was spikier and less easy to get along with than Wilson. The show was split into two – with one of them tackling the week's serious subject, while the other took on a lighter topic. In the middle would be up-and-coming stand-up performers such as character comedienne Caroline Aherne and impressionist Steve Coogan.

'We would research subjects all week,' says former *Up Front* researcher Peter Berry. 'You noticed a difference in the briefing sessions. Tony's would be ten minutes around a computer, print off a copy, roll it into a scroll and say, "Right, I'm off to the rugby club. I'll see you later." He used to disappear until the programme was ready to go on air. With Lucy it was a much longer process. She wasn't as confident. She needed reassurance and plenty of briefing. With Tony it was all up here all in his head. He carried it round with him. It was hard to judge their relationship. In many ways Lucy looked up to Tony. He was obviously more experienced. There no question that Tony was more comfortable in the role than she was.'

Mark Alderton: 'They worked really well together. I imagine there was a competitive edge, but that's good. She respected Tony and he respected her. To use a footballing analogy it was a Keegan-Toshack thing. They played off each other's strengths.'

Peter Berry: 'Subject-wise we did things like the Germans taking over Rover – we had Stan Boardman on that. Then we'd have George Melly on what is art?'

In October 1990, the show got noticed when several participants – including Tony – got hurt. At the end of a debate on whether wrestling was a fix, a 'fight' broke out on the studio floor. Tony was floored by masked grappler Kendo Nagasaki, who then stormed off set after his mask was ripped off. Fellow wrestler Marty Jones was also hurt, while Granada make-up artist Lois Richardson was knocked flying and needed hospital treatment for an injured back. Nagasaki's manager branded the whole show 'a set-up'.

'This is the last thing we wanted or expected to happen,' *Up*

Front executive producer Charles Tremayne told the *Daily Mirror*. 'We're just glad no bones were broken.' Never ones to miss a chance to make Wilson look foolish, technicians took a screen grab of the presenter getting decked and printed it off as a photo. It graced the wall of the *Up Front* office for years to come as the show became a staple of Granada's schedule.

After the run of *Up Front* Tony decided to go abroad. He was continuing his protracted courtship of Yvette Livesey and invited her along. 'Tony said, "I'm going to Lake Como, Verona. Do you want to come?" And I said, "Yes." It was very funny. We got there and he'd booked a single room. I went absolutely bonkers and said, "I'm not sharing a room with you! I have principles." So he booked separate rooms. Tony and I were just friends, despite how we felt about each other.

'It took us the best part of the two years to accept that we had to be together and there was no point in denying it any more. We came home, then at Christmas we realised that this was getting serious. That spring I said, "We either do something or we don't." And that was it really.'

Steeling himself to deal with his personal life, Tony began the new year with at least one piece of good news. Magistrates had decided to give The Haçienda a six-month reprieve in light of 'a positive change in direction at the club'. The police admitted that there was better control; even Chief Constable James Anderton said he was willing to see the case adjourned until the summer.

But the fear of gang violence remained. Yvette Livesey: 'I remember walking out and a bouncer walked down the street with us. I said to Tony, "This isn't funny any more. I'm really worried you might get shot. It feels that bad." It felt like it had got that dangerous and that wrong.'

The menace meant that while the club's doors may well have been open, people were increasingly reluctant to walk through them. 'The DJs in their box 20 feet in the air were pretty much unaware what was going on,' remembers Graeme Park. 'We wouldn't know about any incidents till later on when we have having a drink and getting paid. In the three weeks before it closed all we saw were dwindling crowds. I thought, Shit, we've lost it. We saw the vibe wasn't the same and we thought it was about the music. It wasn't. It was because it had become not a nice place to be.'

The gangsters saw the club as theirs – Tony Wilson and friends were not really their concern, nor were the rules and restrictions that applied to 'civilian' clubbers. They demanded the right to enter without the constraints of queues and the hassle of handing over entry fees. They wanted service – pronto, regardless of who else was waiting and how long they'd been there. Then they wanted everything for free. If the club had men on the doors who were too intimidated – or too friendly – to do anything about the gangsters, then all the better.

It would be unfair to leave the impression that this was a problem confined to The Haçienda. The Gallery, formerly a music venue near the Lesser Free Trade Hall, had become a centre of activity for the city's black gangs. Konspiracy became a centre for the white Salford gangs and their distribution of E. In September 1990, 600 clubbers were locked inside Konspiracy by police to maintain a crime scene after a student was stabbed on the dancefloor.

After both The Gallery and Konspiracy closed, double the trouble headed towards The Haçienda. Konspiracy had a legendary hard man on the door: Dessie Noonan. Noonan was a gangland enforcer and a towering physical and psychological weapon to have at the front of any operation. His brother Damian would later be made head doorman at The Haçienda, a move that was seen by some – including the police – as a clear indication that the club had lost control of its entry system.

Former Haçienda manager Leroy Richardson – who started at the club as a glass collector and holds the distinction of being the Factory organisation's longest-serving employee – disagrees. 'People say Damian Noonan and Dessie muscled in and took the door. They didn't. I was the one who introduced them. It had its downside but it had its upside. Without them, the club would have closed years earlier. Everybody says they took it over and they ran it, that it was protection money. It wasn't. They got paid very well and I think whatever they got paid it wasn't enough. I wouldn't have done it. I did it a few times 'cos Rob [Gretton] asked me and I used to have to wear a [bulletproof] vest.'

Haçienda staff member Elliot Eastwick watched as serious money came in through the doors of The Haçienda – and promptly went back out again. 'There was always these stories that the band [New Order] were having to bail the club out and it was like, "What do you mean bail the club out? There's a queue at nine o'clock that snakes around the block, you can't get in after 11pm." Then you see the doormen with big bags of cash coming out through the reception... Aaah, right. *That's* what happens.'

Leroy Richardson pinpoints the moments when – from his perspective – the atmosphere began to change in The Haçienda. 'Two incidents,' he says. 'One guy got attacked in The Haçienda. It looked like half his nose and face were hanging off. The doormen didn't seem to be *doing* anything. I got between him and the guys. I bundled him into the cellar and he was a proper mess. It was then I thought the viciousness could be a big problem.

'Another incident: a part-time doorman got attacked. Because I knew them [the gangsters responsible] from earlier years they might not do anything to me. I never got touched. This is dangerous now and something really needs to be done about it.

'I would have gone down the lines of *doing 'em*. These people were causing so much trouble round the city centre. The police were powerless. The police view was if we didn't have the clubs we wouldn't have the trouble. So their policy was: get rid of the clubs. We tried to hire the police like they do at football matches – they wouldn't have it because they didn't want to set a precedent. We tried to hire off-duty officers. We went to talk to some very serious security companies. There were certain people who said we can solve the problem for you and that's the way I would have gone, to tell you the truth. But you never know, you

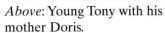

Above: Young Tony with his mother Doris.

Above: Tony at play.

Above: Herman Knufper, Tony's grandfather.

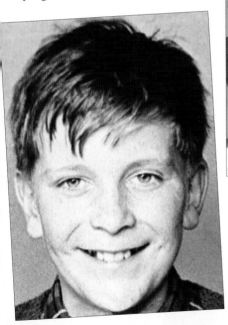

Above: Tony (rear right) backstage in the school theatre.

Left: Marple school boy, Tony Wilson.

Below left: Tony (left) and the De La Salle debating team.

Below: The boy who would be king: Tony in *The Lark*.

Right: *Granada Reports*, 1974.

Below: With David Cassidy on the set of *What's On*.

Below: Tony waits for his week's 250 fan letters.

Left: Tony's first wife, Lindsay Reade.

Above: Tony (foreground) with Factory band Section 25.

Left: 'Anthony H Wilson' presents *After Dark* on Channel 4.

Below left: Tony, Oliver and Sydney Wilson.

Below: Happy Mondays' Paul Ryder.

A mind map of the Manchester music scene… with Tony at its heart.

HACIENDA FAMILY TREE 2008.

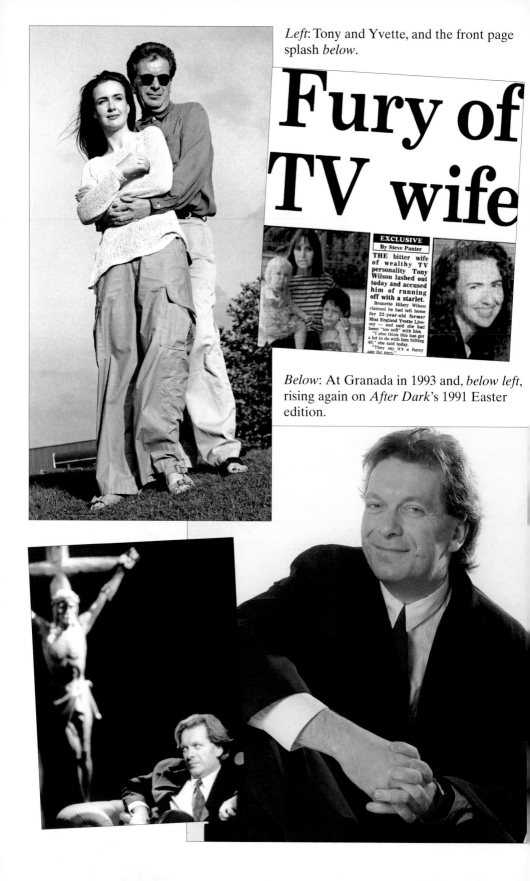

Left: Tony and Yvette, and the front page splash *below*.

Fury of TV wife

EXCLUSIVE
By Steve Panter

THE bitter wife of wealthy TV personality Tony Wilson lashed out today and accused him of running off with a starlet.

Brunette Hilary Wilson claimed he had left home for 22-year-old former Miss England Yvette Livesey — and said she had been "too soft" with him.

"I also think this has got a lot to do with him hitting 40," she said today.

"They say it's a funny age for men."

Below: At Granada in 1993 and, *below left*, rising again on *After Dark*'s 1991 Easter edition.

Above: with Yvette in 2005.

Right: with Jenny Winstone on *The New Friday*.

Below: Tony at Channel M in Manchester preparing for his last music TV show.

Above: Tony and Yvette at the Coachella Festival, Palm Springs.

Left: Looking to the future – Yvette Livesey today.

Below: Tony at the end of the *Politics Show* run in 2007.

Left: The Peter Saville-designed invitation to Tony Wilson's funeral.

might be causing more trouble for yourself with the people who are sorting it than the ones you had the trouble with.'

One key gangster on the up was to bring about the first of The Haçienda's closures. 'White' Tony Johnson was a young man in a hurry who knew the power of publicity. As a child he'd lived with his grandmother Winnie Johnson in Fallowfield, south Manchester. Winnie regularly took calls and visits from local and national journalists over her own son, Keith Bennett – 'White' Tony's uncle. He had been spirited away by Moors Murderers Ian Brady and Myra Hyndley in 1964 and his body has never been found. Winnie knew that by keeping Keith's story ticking over in the press, she increased the chances of his body being discovered on Saddleworth Moor, where it is believed to be buried.

'White' Tony was soon aware of the power and importance of the press. His message was that he was the new force to be reckoned with and the stage he chose to deliver it was the door of The Haçienda. The costume of choice was one that he would single-handedly popularise: the bulletproof vest. He was already an accomplished armed robber and had been adopted into the Cheetham Hill gang to the north of the city. He was under suspicion of the murder of one man and of being involved in the murder of two others.

'It was targeted trouble,' says Leroy Richardson. 'One group against another group – or one person who was dealing – rather than against the club or people who went there. But if you happened to be in the way...'

Sitting in the stale daytime atmosphere of the club he runs now – all nightclubs smell awful in the daylight – Richardson acts out a typical encounter with the vest-toting Johnson over entry to the club.

'White' Tony: 'You're not showing me any respect.'

Leroy Richardson: 'What respect are you showing me? You could buy and sell me ten times over and you're giving me shit on the door for three quid.'

WT: 'I *could* do something.'

LR: 'I'm always here, so you know where I am if you want to.'

WT: 'You're a cheeky bastard, you.'

LR: 'If you *ask* me, "Can I come in for nothing?" rather than telling me, that's different. I'm not going to argue over three quid, but you are.'

WT: 'So I'm all right for coming in then?'

LR: 'Yeah, three quid.'

WT: 'Cheeky bastard.'

LR: 'You pay to get in and I'll get you a drink.'

The initial emphasis with the gangsters on the door was on conversation not confrontation. 'That's how the relationship with him was,' says Richardson. 'There was always the point with him where he could quite easily flip.'

Johnson also spread the bad vibes to Dry bar as well, demonstrating his ability to start trouble anytime, anyplace, anywhere... with anyone. Leroy Richardson: 'At Dry bar the licensing police came round. Tony knew who they were – he was sat on the bonnet of the car. They turned round and they asked me to ask him to get off. I went out and said, "Look, I'm going to get some right shit. Would you please get off the car?"

'"Why aren't they coming out to tell me?" he said.

'"Because they know they can make me do it, Tony."

'He went, "All right, then."'

But by January 1991, it was decided enough was enough. Johnson threatened one of The Haçienda's door staff with a gun and it was decided to make a protest at the way the likes of he and other gang faces were using and abusing the club. Tony Wilson effectively went on strike.

Ever the showman, Tony held a press conference on the club's dancefloor. 'The Haçienda is closing its doors as of today,' he told reporters. 'It is with the greatest reluctance that for the moment we are turning the lights out on what is, for us, a most important place. We are forced into taking this drastic action in order to protect our employees, our members and all our clients. We are quite simply sick and tired of dealing with instances of personal violence. We hope – we must believe – we can reopen The Haçienda in a better climate. But until we are able to run the club in a safe manner and in a way that the owners believe will guarantee the role of The Haçienda at the heart of the city's youth community, it is with great sadness that we will shut our club.'

Yvette Livesey: 'He was making a big show because the police wouldn't help him. He was making a point. To say, "We can't handle this. We don't want the gangs here – we want your help." That was Tony all over. Everything had to be dramatic. Everything was over the top.'

DJ Graeme Park: 'When he did his press conference saying The Haçienda was going to close because he couldn't guarantee the safety of his employees, it was a really masterful PR stunt. Everyone was talking about The Haçienda even though it was closed. Then when it re-opened it was exactly like it had been.'

While The Haçienda's doors were shut, on 22 February 1991, 'White' Tony Johnson and an associate known as 'Black' Tony McKie were both shot and wounded in Cheetham Hill. As Johnson tried to crawl away from the scene, one of his assailants pushed a gun into his mouth and pulled the trigger. Shortly after that incident, The Haçienda reopened and four men were put on trial for Johnson's murder: Paul Flannery, Michael Sharples, Dessie Noonan and Dominic Noonan. They were tried twice for the murder. The first trial collapsed, at the second they were cleared. No one has ever been convicted of Johnson's murder.

* * * * *

Tony turned his attention to a new project, the flagship Factory headquarters on the corner of Charles Street and Princess Street, close to the BBC. Designed by the man who created The Hacienda, Ben Kelly, it cost three quarters of a million pounds and was a major statement with exposed brickwork, steel girders and a tear-shaped boardroom table suspended on wires from the ceiling. Wilson was in his element as he showed journalist Andy Spinoza around. 'I wanted to triangulate the town with Ben

Kelly,' he said, referring to Kelly's other designs for The Haçienda and Dry.

'I like to think we've moved forward,' added Kelly. 'The Factory building is a step forward from Dry. We don't remain static – we don't rely on mileage we've already got.'

In April – at the very time The Haçienda was preparing to reopen – news came through of the death of producer Martin Hannett. After decades of excess, the man who didn't want to spend Factory's money on a nightclub in the first place died of heart failure aged just 42. Tony would rarely, if ever, miss an opportunity to trumpet Hannett's place in the Factory story. 'I hope that I have a facility for spotting genius,' he later told documentary-maker James Nice. 'Although he was a genius – I knew that at the time – I think I've only just understood what a genius he was. It's a word that's used too often but there's no way that it's overused for Martin.'

The Haçienda's closure gave Tony Wilson something he rarely received: time to think. Several weeks after Hannett's death, Tony decided to leave Hilary to be with Yvette Livesey. The pair moved to Comberbach, near Northwich in Cheshire, living in a rented cottage. The news of Tony's split with Hilary lay dormant for two months. National newspapers had got wind of the story but couldn't get a confirmation, with Hilary refusing to speak.

Even so, journalists were gathering en masse on Old Broadway, the street where the Wilson family lived. But it had nothing to do with Tony and Yvette; it was Tony's near-neighbour Richard Madeley who was the cause of media interest. Madeley had opted for trial after being charged with shoplifting at a Tesco supermarket in East Didsbury. The hacks had been there to greet Madeley and Judy Finnigan morning and night and the drama had been incorporated into their vastly popular *This Morning* show, broadcast daily from Granada's studios at the Albert Dock in Liverpool. Madeley was acquitted and the press pack swelled even further.

It can't be a coincidence that at this precise moment, with her road swarming with reporters, Hilary Wilson decided to break her silence and go to the press with the news that Tony had left her. The paper she chose was the *Manchester Evening News* and reporter Steve Panter was despatched to interview her. 'I remember knocking on her door,' says Panter. 'She was very cooperative. I remember thinking how attractive she was, hence the words in my piece describing her as "a striking brunette". She obviously made an impression on me.'

Hilary – so reticent to talk to the press in the past – let fly at her errant husband. 'I've given seven years of my life to bringing up his children, while giving him the freedom to do what he wanted,' she told Panter. 'I think I have been too soft with him. This has got a lot to do with him hitting 40. They say it's a funny age for men.'

'She was very pleasant and down to earth but talking in a sort of bitter way,' recalls Panter. 'She retained her composure but was obviously willing to confirm what had happened. I suppose the fact that she had two young children in tow would have fuelled her anger.'

The story made front-page news in the early edition of the following day's *Manchester Evening News* under the splash headline 'FURY OF TV WIFE'. Hilary posed for pictures with Oliver and Isabel and the *Evening News* also ran a photo of Yvette Livesey, describing her as a 'starlet'. Panter's story was promptly picked up by the nationals. 'There was probably an element in there of the old "print versus broadcast" thing,' he said. 'Tony was a broadcast person and we were the poor print relation. I imagine somewhere – not with me, of course – there would be some print hacks who would have raised a glass to his discomfort. You either loved him or hated him, simple as that. He was the sort of person that journalists would talk about.'

Yvette Livesey: 'For Tony, it was the hardest decision he would ever have to make, but it was an inevitable one because you can't help who you fall in love with. It was a really tough decision, but it was a decision I left to Tony. Neither of us wanted to hurt anyone, but we also had the discussion that there was no point in Tony living in an unhappy marriage for the sake of the children. If he was a happier person, that would be better for everyone.'

Despite vehement denials that the pair were living together, Tony and Yvette spent six months in Comberbach before moving to a converted chip shop in Lymm and then to Barrow Bridge near Bolton. Not everyone approved. The relationship caused a schism between Wilson and some of his closest associates. Alan Erasmus in particular was affronted by Tony leaving his wife and children for a model many years his junior. It would prove to be the start of a falling-out between the two men that lasted 16 years, until another shattering event brought them back together.

TEN
YOU'LL NEVER MAKE MONEY UNLESS YOU FOCUS

Factory windows are always broken, someone's always throwing bricks
– VACHEL LINDSAY

Just two weeks after the newspapers had been plastered with pictures of Tony and Yvette Livesey, they were in the press again; this time for the announcement of a new music venture – In the City. As The Haçienda reopened, Yvette had been ensconced in an office at Manchester town hall working on an idea for an annual music conference. Funded by cash from Factory and Simply Red managers Elliot Rashman and Andy Dodd, the plan was to lay on a four-day event in Manchester in autumn of 1992 to rival similar US events. They had a year to pull it together.

There was a general assumption that In the City was Wilson's gig and that Livesey's presence was a combination of window dressing and a way of legitimising her. Yvette Livesey: 'It's very difficult if you are pretty and 23 and running a company to get people to take you seriously. I fought really hard. I was outraged. In the City was *mine*, I was the director. I learnt to live with it. Every partner Tony ever had had the same problem. Rob Gretton had the same problem. But in every interview he ever did, he made it clear In the City was mine. Tony had a lot of belief in me.'

The pair flew to New York in July 1991 to launch the event on Madison Avenue during the city's New Music Seminar showcasing conference. The trip also had the effect of getting them out of the UK and away from the attention news of their relationship had generated. On their return Wilson and Livesey posed for photos with Elliot Rashman to promote the new venture and spoke bullishly of their intentions for a 'glossy and stylish' seminar.

'It's ridiculous that Britain is the centre of the world's pop music and we have nothing like the New Music Seminar,' Wilson told reporters when the idea was launched. 'Manchester is the perfect place. In the City will make concrete the international gains that Britain has already made. Manchester chose itself. For decades now it has been club city, a concentration of superb venues within walking distance at the heart of the city.' Wilson talked the talk to such convincing effect on behalf of In the City, it was no surprise people assumed In the City was his; such was the strength of the Wilson ballyhoo, it sometimes felt like he'd invented *everything*.

But by the autumn of 1991, it was beginning to become apparent that there was trouble in Factory, with the announcement of a small number of redundancies – 'tightening of belts' was the reason given. In fact, a dizzying array of mishaps, poor decisions and bad luck were building up like a drift of misfortune while he was engaged with In the City.

'When the problems started with Factory, Tony spent more and more time in my office in the town hall and became more and more involved,' says Livesey.

One of Factory's problems was Tony himself. His bohemian swagger was so infectious that work just didn't get done when he was around. 'Everybody in Factory was trying to be Tony,' says Livesey. 'They brought a financial controller in and *he* started acting like Tony. Nobody wanted to sit down and do the sums. No one would turn round and say, "You can't do that."'

Martin Moscrop of A Certain Ratio: 'When New Order and Happy Mondays were doing quite well, that's when they weren't a small indie any more. It's when the beast gets too big – that's what happened. It wasn't this creative outlet any more – it becomes a big company. And Tony was a crap businessman – big companies don't work with crap businessmen, do they? They never had a really good businessman in that whole set. The one thing they needed was someone to say, "This isn't working properly, this isn't being run properly." But they never had that.'

Photographer Kevin Cummins: 'Everyone who worked for Factory knew they were surfing on some wave that could come crashing down any minute.'

The bold decision to shut The Haçienda was one of the key sums that weren't being done. Nightclubs with closed doors don't make money. Though the crowds did initially come back after the reopening, so did the trouble, particularly from Salford gangs. It was an expensive gamble that didn't have the desired effect.

Despite the accumulation of trouble, new members continued to join the Factory family. Former *NME* journalist Cath Carroll – previously with Factory band Miaow – came on board. Press kits for her debut album contained images of Carroll taken by photographer Robert Mapplethorpe. His work didn't come cheap. Carroll later moved to America. 'A couple of people have mentioned that they heard I came here after taking all of Factory's advance money and Tony Wilson's pension fund, which is somewhat amusing until people actually believe stuff like that,' she told *Proper* magazine in 2003. 'Of course, I did have my head up my butt during my days at Factory and for that must take some responsibility, but the money did not come with me. In reality, everyone at Factory knew very well where the money went. The album I recorded, *England Made Me*, was a very colourful and easily expressed symbol of the unravelling at Factory. However, take it out of the equation and the same thing would have happened.'

Fey indie-poppers The Adventure Babies were snapped up by Wilson after they staged a private performance for him. Tony signed them without consulting anyone else at Factory. The band would have the pleasure of being the label's last signing.

Perhaps a box-set CD history of the Factory story so far –
named *Palatine* after the road in Didsbury where the label began
– could bring things back on track? It brought together
recordings from 1979 to 1990, but didn't actually come out until
November 1991. Photographer Kevin Cummins: 'They had all
these grandiose plans. *Palatine* was going to save them. I did the
sleeves for them and obviously I never got paid. I hardly ever got
paid by Factory. I got paid for shooting the Mondays. All the Joy
Division stuff I shot myself.'

Then there was the lack of a contribution from the old Factory
cash cow: New Order. Relations within the band were low and
getting lower. The US tour to promote their 1989 *Technique*
album had been a particularly sour affair, not helped by the
feeling that the band were working hard to generate cash for
doomed enterprises. Bernard Sumner: 'There was no soul to what
we were doing. We were just fishermen with a large net, catching
money and then giving it away.' With New Order's plethora of
offshoots and side projects – Electronic, The Other Two (Stephen
Morris and Gillian Gilbert) plus Peter Hook's unloved and pricy
Revenge project – no one was in any rush to get back into the
studio. It would be 1993 before New Order's next album would
be released, by which time Factory had been and gone. The group
sat and watched the label's demise from the sidelines.

Then there was the small matter of Happy Mondays. What had
seemed laddishly charming and titillatingly dodgy four years
earlier now bordered on the squalid. Necking a few Es is one
thing – being a smackhead is quite another. The single 'Step On'
had made them a Top Five act and *lads du jour*. Schoolyards
across the country were rife with talk of melons being twisted as
the band went overground. Their 1990 album *Pills 'n' Thrills
And Bellyaches* had gone to No 1. But heroin had swamped the
Ryders, with singer Shaun singularly unapologetic about his
habit. 'It's a horrible thing to say,' he told *Q* magazine in 1999,
'but to me the gear was pipe and slippers. Comforting. I tried to
get off it a few times. I used to say that if we made it I would get

off the gear. By the time I was 30 I really wanted to get off it, 'cos who likes a 30-year-old sad, old junkie cunt?'

Meanwhile, the band had been 'appointed' guest editors of top-shelf magazine *Penthouse* in 1991. It was the kind of thing that wouldn't have played well with Tony Wilson's Didsbury pals. Neither would apparently homophobic comments made by sideman Bez. By now there was more than a whiff of sordid panto about them.

It was decided to ship the band off to Barbados at the start of 1992 to keep Shaun away from heroin, which was unavailable on the island. Unfortunately, crack cocaine was. Paul Ryder managed to score on the day they arrived. The trip went from chaos to anarchy. Two jeeps were written off in drunken smashes; Bez broke his arm in one crash, then managed to break it *again* in another. Producers Chris Frantz and Tina Weymouth of Talking Heads had issues getting paid by Factory. Tony stopped the band's daily subsistence payments for fear of what they'd be spent on, though he would later delight in telling the story of how Shaun Ryder was caught loading a studio sofa into a van to sell it for drug money. He did toy with the idea of going out to the island and taking control of matters, but baulked when he realised the distance involved and the commitments it would mean missing.

'I think one of Tony's regrets was not intervening when the Mondays were in Barbados,' says Paul Ryder. 'I'm sure Shaun would have listened to him if he'd flown over. We'll never know. He usually knew when to keep his distance and he knew when to say something wasn't right. That takes great skill, to know when to take a step back.'

When the Mondays' *Yes Please!* album was finally released it went Top 10 but didn't stay around for long. The band's 1992 singles fared badly. 'Stinkin Thinkin' stalled outside the Top 30 and the follow-up 'Sunshine and Love' only managed a placing of 62.

And across town from Factory's offices, there were problems at Tony's other 'home'. Granada chairman David Plowright – the man who gave Tony a job 20 years earlier – was ousted as a new regime took over, led by managers of the food and leisure group Compass. Their removal of Plowright prompted an infamous fax from his friend and *Monty Python* star John Cleese: 'Why don't you fuck off, you jumped-up caterers...' With Plowright gone, Granada changed almost immediately. The bohemian enclave that Tony had known since the early 1970s became part of a business group involved in motorway service stations and bowling alleys. It would never be the same and Tony's favoured status at Granada would never recover; his place and his standing there dwindled over the 1990s.

Tony's former researcher Don Jones was by now a producer. 'Suddenly there was a different set of priorities. We'd moved away from this golden age where people were allowed to experiment. If it didn't work it wasn't a disaster but if it did work it could be wonderful. That whole period where people were chancing their arms was brilliant for someone like Wilson. Suddenly everything had to be right on the day. The problem with Wilson was he wasn't everyone's cup of tea. There were only so many formats he could fit into in this new, boring world.'

In the shadow of these problems, the first In the City took place in July 1992. Bands showcased included Radiohead, Suede, Elastica and a band that Factory were keen to sign called Oasis. It never happened. Music writer and Haçienda DJ Dave Haslam: '1992 was a very interesting year in the life of Tony Wilson. He launches In the City as the same time as his own record label is sinking. That's a remarkable feat.'

The fatal last wringing of Factory's neck came with the collapse of UK property values in a three-year recession; their key assets were simply not worth what they had paid for them. 'They were unlucky,' says Yvette Livesey. 'People always say Tony was a really bad businessman. He wasn't – he was really good with money. But he didn't give a toss about money. He didn't care. They moved into the property market and got a ridiculous mortgage for The Haçienda from a German company. Having bought the new

Factory building for a ridiculous amount of money, they spent a ridiculous amount of money doing it up. But it wasn't about the money – it was all about what was fun and what was right and what was artistically correct rather than, "Can we afford it?"'

Kevin Cummins: 'There was a certain desperation towards the end. It was like having a close relative dying of cancer. They went bust owing me about 15 grand. But they gave me a great archive of work. It didn't worry me too much. The archive is mine forever. I was more concerned [about Factory staff] who lost their livelihoods. I could carry on. That's cruel, but businesses go bust all the time.'

As The Haçienda approached its tenth anniversary in May 1992, Tony was still talking a good fight, predicting great things for the upcoming New Order and Happy Mondays albums and fresh releases from Factory Classical. 'Every year we have a party but this year will be something special,' he told the *Manchester Evening News*. 'There will be books, albums, the whole bit.'

But behind the scenes, talks were underway with London Records (a subsidiary of Polygram) to buy part of Factory to provide much needed cash to tide them over. News that the label could be partly sold off caused ripples of disappointment. *NME* writer turned columnist Tony Parsons bemoaned the potential loss of independence for the 'Tamla Motown of Manchester' in his *Daily Telegraph* column. 'Tony Wilson has done more than anyone since The Beatles to decentralise England, to drag pop out of the boardroom and back to the council estates of pale provincial kids. That a chunk of Factory is being sold to a company called London is a bitter irony indeed.'

But Factory's accounts – hopelessly out of date – didn't make good reading for potential investors. Things were closing in on Tony Wilson. Even Morrissey, the man Wilson had once mentored, turned on him, witheringly describing him in an interview as 'the biggest pop star in Manchester, who lords it over the Manchester scene and tramples on anyone who disagrees with him.'

Money was departing from the Factory coffers by every means. In August a five-man gang armed with shotguns and machetes staged a robbery at Dry bar, stealing more than £10,000. On 24 November 1992, Factory Communications crashed with debts of more than £2 million. Unfortunately for the headline writers it was a Tuesday, thus denying them their 'BLUE MONDAY' splash. They had to settle with 'UNHAPPY TUESDAY' instead. Not quite the same, is it?

Receivers Leonard Curtis and Partners announced they were actively looking for a buyer, but were frankly pessimistic. 'Unless someone comes up with an awful lot of money,' stated joint receiver Dermot Power, 'I don't think there's any prospect of Factory trading in its current form.' The firm specifically cited reasons for the collapse as a decline in demand in the music industry, the effect of interest rates on property owned by Factory and the late arrival of 'specific records'.

Tony himself was in typically flowing form when asked to make a statement to the media gathered outside the Factory building. 'Factory tried to do too many things, from adventurous buildings to ambitious recording projects, at a time when signs of a negative economic climate ahead suggested restraint. Our principal sadness is for the people we have had to lay off. We regret the failure of our efforts to survive this crisis intact.'

London Records was the obvious choice to take on the business – until they realised there wasn't one. 'It was always presumed by London Records that we had no contracts with any of their artists,' Tony told journalist Paolo Sedazzari in 1994, 'but there was a contract drawn up in 1979 to say there was no contract, which I signed in blood. It was just a page-and-a-half and I'd forgotten it existed. It turned up in the tax investigations. We faxed it to the solicitor. He got very upset and said, "Don't you realise? If you don't have a contract you don't own the group's future, right?" Right.

'"But you do own the back catalogue which you paid for the production of. Unless – you have a piece of paper like this that specifically says that you don't."

'And we went, "Oh sorry...."'

The non-contract mantra that Factory was based on – *the musicians own everything, the company owns nothing. All our bands have the freedom to fuck off* – meant there was nothing to buy.

New Order went to London – discussions about going to the label had been taking place for some time. Yvette Livesey: 'If Rob hadn't signed New Order to London, they would have had a saleable asset. Rob sold New Order to London… there was no Factory.'

Durutti Column's Bruce Mitchell: 'Within a year we got music out again. Without contracts the music wasn't taken as an asset by the liquidators.'

There was contractual paperwork for some bands, including Happy Mondays, but in a final Wilson-esque move, Tony explained to the Mondays how to get out of the contract, freeing them to move on as well. Paul Ryder: 'If it hadn't been the way it was, then we wouldn't be talking about it now. You can't afford to have regrets. They were out for the ride. I always considered Tony an adult. Rob Gretton was an adult, Alan Erasmus was certainly an adult. But they were like adult *children*. And that's great.'

Yvette Livesey: 'Tony was too big a character – people didn't trust him. The whole music industry actively stood by while Tony got screwed over when Factory went. I know Tony had signed contracts in blood saying, "We don't own anything" – well done! But if they'd invested in *Tony* it wouldn't have happened. But he was too scary – too out there.'

A Certain Ratio's Martin Moscrop: 'All good things come to an end. I think it'd be really crap if Factory was still going now. I think it probably lasted just slightly too long than it should have done. Could have ended slightly earlier, same with The Haçienda.'

As Tony left the Factory offices on the day of the collapse, he was spotted from the pub across the road, the Lass O' Gowrie, by two men having a quiet pint. One was former Freshies singer Chris Sievey, the other was Tosh Ryan, former head of Rabid Records and a robust critic of Wilson throughout the Factory years. The pair were in the habit of filming anything and everything that caught their eye at this time – and Tony Wilson coming out of the Factory offices on the day it went bust definitely caught their eye.

'Tosh went to the Factory offices,' says Sievey. 'He hadn't particularly gone to film Tony Wilson. We were in the pub when it happened. Tosh just wanted it for his own personal amusement. I always remember Tosh dancing around when Tony went bankrupt.'

The pair ran out of the pub and Ryan began filming Tony. He had a simple question: 'Who won, Tony? Who *won*?'

'Apparently,' Wilson later recalled in *The Times*, 'I said, "The music won," which is slightly more intelligent than what I would have expected to say at that point in time.' There's a punchline to this story and to the apparent history of needle between Ryan and Wilson. It can be found in the cast of characters section at the rear of this book. In fact, there's another punchline. The day the news broke about Factory, Tony was at work at Granada recording one of his favourite shows, one whose message he could have done well to heed.

Flying Start was a studio-based teatime programme that was a forerunner of the kind of business-related TV shows that are common currency today. It was a competition to find successful North West businesses. Tony always lobbied for *Flying Start* to be recommissioned every time a series came to an end. 'He got the value of the entrepreneur to our society way before it became fashionable,' says David Liddiment. 'That's a little bit of Granada and an awful lot of him.'

Tony's Granada colleague Rob McLoughlin: 'Just look at a show like *Flying Start*. Trying to make business sexy and connect with people. He was totally committed to it. Before *The Appentice* and *Dragon's Den,* when did you ever hear anyone talking about cash flow and business plan? Mind you, he should have taken some of his own advice...'

In every episode, *Flying Start* would have a guest from the business community to judge the entrants and their companies. One week the guest was Virgin entrepreneur Richard Branson. After the recording, Branson – who was aware of Tony's work – took him to one side and gave him some advice. 'You know Tony, you'll never make money unless you focus....'

ELEVEN
LONDON RESISTED HIM

The man who is tired of London is tired of looking for a parking space
– PAUL THEROUX

After the collapse of Factory, Tony was obviously open to ridicule as the presenter of an entrepreneurial showcase like *Flying Start* – and oh, how the studio crew had fun at his expense. When he checked his diary he couldn't help but notice another unfortunate booking: 15 December 1992, give talk to 50 aspiring music industry entrepreneurs on how to succeed in business. The event was at the British Council's swanky Manchester headquarters, just across the road from The Haçienda. The invite from the Prince's Youth Business Trust in Manchester had been in place for some time and they assumed that Tony would be a no-show after the events of the previous month. Not the greatest timing, but Tony went ahead and gave the talk. 'It just goes to show,' organiser Eric Newman told guests, 'that no matter how hard you work and what you do, you don't always succeed in business.'

Flying Start, though it was very much David Plowright's baby, continued as one of Tony's regional shows, as did *Up Front*, but in typical Wilson fashion he'd landed jammy side up with a new network TV show – Channel 4's *Remote Control*. The show, a UK version of an American show on MTV, was to feature former Rabid Records' publicist Chris Sievey in his incarnation as the Timperley-based, papier-mâché-headed innocent, Frank Sidebottom.

Chris Sievey: 'Tony phoned me up and he said have you seen this programme *Remote Control*? It was my favourite programme. MTV 11am *Remote Control*. It was a great slant. The game show with the irreverent sidekick.

'He said, "We're looking at getting the rights. Are you interested?" Definitely. I ended up doing all 33 episodes.'

The programme, which also featured comic and impressionist Phil Cornwell, was a jokey, slacker quiz show aimed at a student crowd. Chris Sievey: 'I loved doing it. Everyone always says Tony Wilson's a cunt. He wasn't – he was a really nice bloke and dead professional. A lot of people on that show were surprised how cool he was and how focused he was on making it work. It doesn't always across like that on-screen – he comes across as a smarmy bastard. That's the image a lot of people have of him and that's a shame.'

The show went on air just as the altogether more cerebral *After Dark* was ending. Tony's image on *Remote Control* – roomy, designer suit with slicked-back hair – didn't play well with everyone. 'I saw him on this awful programme, looking like a junkie, trying hard to look 20 years younger,' says *After Dark* producer Sebastian Cody. 'What was he doing to himself and why does he feel obliged to do it?'

Meanwhile, post-Factory, the label's premier acts had fortunes that could at best be described as mixed. Happy Mondays just about made it into 1993 before collapsing. The tarted-up Barbados sessions – *Yes Please!* – had been Factory's last album, arriving just weeks before the collapse. Heroin had re-entered the band's itinerary and Shaun Ryder had become disenfranchised from the rest of the Mondays in internal wrangling over who was the group's true leader. It became the stuff of legend that Shaun walked out of high-end talks with EMI for a KFC and never returned, KFC being band slang for heroin. In fact, both versions were true: he did go to a Kentucky

Fried Chicken outlet close to EMI's Manchester Square offices and had some heroin with his meal.

'Shaun's main crime was that he was the leader of the gang and he kept letting his gang down,' Tony told writer John Warburton in 2000. 'The final letdown – even though I think he was probably right to do it – was going for a Kentucky when EMI were going to give them nigh on a million pounds.'

New Order's *Republic* album finally came out on CentreDate/London Records shortly after the Mondays' implosion. A shiny, cosmopolitan affair, it contained at least one slam bang hit in the shape of 'Regret', signalling their account was in a healthy state. But the grim reality of being in each other's company through the year to tour the album proved too much for the band. Sumner took to wearing a cardboard sign around his neck saying 'Fuck off, don't talk to me,' during the American leg of the campaign. They would last till the end of the summer before bowing out at the Reading Festival and wouldn't play together again until the end of the decade.

Meanwhile, Tony and Yvette began to spend more time in America. 'It became our lifestyle,' she says. 'We would end up going to America five, six times a year. Tony couldn't go out in Manchester because he would get harassed. There was an ease about America. We'd have a three-week stint at a time. New York and LA. It became an easier place to be.'

Tony had been obsessed by New York for years. 'I always say it reminds me of Manchester,' he told the *Manchester Evening News*. 'I find them similar places in terms of the people. In New York, people at a bus stop will talk to you. They won't in London, but they will in Manchester. I feel more at ease going from Manchester to New York than to London.'

There was something else that fascinated Tony about New York: people living in the city centre in converted loft spaces. Manchester was awash with old and empty warehousing, but at the time of the last census, only about 250 people actually lived in Manchester city centre. The pair began searching for suitable spaces.

As the headlines about their relationship had faded, Tony and Yvette could have been forgiven for 'settling' and opting for a quieter life. 'Tony never settled,' says Yvette. 'He once said something to me about relationships along the lines of, "Treat 'em mean to keep 'em keen." The kind of thing a 12-year-old might say. He would wind me up. He had an inability to *grow* into a relationship. We kept trying to get rid of each other. Eventually he said, "You know we're really special, we are..." 'I went, "*Duh*, I've been trying to tell you this for years."

'Things never calmed down. Because we were totally and completely and utterly in love, and if you're in love the both of you are completely jealous and totally obsessed. We were both as bad as each other. He was explosive – like a rhino coming through a thicket – then it would blow over and be done with. From the outside looking in, people would say, "Tony completely adores you..." Well, why doesn't he fucking show it then? He did sometimes. He was very romantic.'

Meanwhile Tony dipped his toe in a few new puddles, but without the abandon of the past. He filmed a pilot for a late-night music and arts show with pop producer Pete Waterman, with the pair touted as a rock'n'roll Saint and Greavsie. He also tried his hand as a columnist with the very paper who had splashed his relationship with Yvette on its front pages, the *Manchester Evening News*. He wrote about football, sustainable development, *Sonic the Hedgehog* and CD-ROMs. Reading his columns was a little like having Wilson bend your ear in a wine bar, but as we know from his stint on the *Post & Echo* all those years ago, he was no newspaper man. He was still a figure of fun, however. Comedian and actor John Thomson started doing a new comic character at this time – a pretentious, self-obsessed darts player called Jocky H Wilson. In all, it was a perfectly reasonable media portfolio, but positively low-key by Wilson standards.

In the summer of 1994, Tony managed to grab the headlines with the announcement of a new record label, Factory Too. Though not exactly humble, this was a slightly different Wilson, fronting a very different proposition. There would be no place for back-of-a-napkin deals signed in blood here. Factory Too was owned by London Records, part of Polygram. 'I always said that Factory was an experiment,' he told the website Zani, 'so here's another experiment – can you be an intelligent record company when you're owned by a major? The first release will come in October – an album by Durutti Column. I thought it would be a lovely way to start. Vini Reilly of Durutti Column has been loyal and stayed with me. After that we want to sign two or three young bands. London trust our judgement totally, they've given us full artistic control. That's why we're working with them.'

Factory's playfulness was soon in evidence again – one of the earliest Factory Too 'releases' was a woolly hat. It all seemed reassuringly familiar, but there is a telling first picture of Wilson at the Factory Too offices. He looks the same as ever – crumpled shirt, granny shades, mouth in full flow – but there isn't a stick of furniture in the room apart from the chair he's sat on and he is all alone. But Wilson was still keen to show he was on his game, gently chiding London Records for being too dance-orientated and needing his help to find rock acts. He made some play of one of the first acts he was chasing – Shriek – and that things at the new label would be more businesslike – in an experimental sort of way.

Behind his usual bluster, those closest to Tony believe that Factory Too and the other Factory incarnations that would follow weren't just Wilson playing at being a label boss. Yvette Livesey: 'They were genuine attempts to remain in the music industry and put stuff out, things that he believed in. It *was* serious to him but the bands weren't right.'

The Durutti Column had come along as a matter of course. The first act to be scouted and signed were London/Oxford band Hopper, led by the owlishly-fetching Rachel Morris. Wilson's criteria for choosing the band – who had already released material on the Damaged Goods label – was that no one else seemed interested in them. 'There were only half-a-dozen people when I saw them in London,' Tony told the *Manchester Evening News* when the band's signing was announced. 'It was the same with Joy Division and Happy Mondays. I always think it's a sign that one is right.'

Hopper – described at the time by music weekly *Melody Maker* as 'foot-chewingly tedious' – didn't quite live up to the Wilson ballyhoo. Yvette Livesey offers mitigating circumstances: 'He was totally tone deaf – couldn't sing a note – but had the best pair of ears in the business. Hopper were good but they realised that the person who wrote the songs wasn't in the band by the time they were signed.'

Tony was never happier than when he had a buzzword to fling around. Around this time he found himself a new one: *download*. Here's a crazy idea – rather than have the inconvenience of going to an old-fashioned record shop and buying music over the counter, why not access it via the internet and siphon it straight onto your computer? The name of the download website was Musis33.com. For 1995, this was revolutionary stuff. Yvette Livesey: 'The idea was both of ours. The site was the first fully functioning legal music download site, charging 33p per track, but we couldn't get any credit card company to take micropayments. We were in talks with one big bank, but couldn't make it happen. This was between the majors trying to set up a site together and their talks fell through. Then iTunes came along and the rest is history.'

While looking to the future, Tony was also looking to the past for Factory Too's inspiration. The label released *A Factory Sample Too*, aping the original 1979 Factory release, this time with tracks by East West Coast, The Orch, Italian Love Party and K-Track, but the next big thing always seemed tantalisingly out of Wilson's reach.

Factory Too's next signing were the Space Monkeys – the band's dance-rock single seemed to sum the problem up: 'Acid House Killed Rock And Roll'. There was something out of kilter about Tony's choices. The Space Monkeys' sub-Jesus Jones grooves were never likely to find a home and he used the same shaky 'nobody else likes them' criteria when deciding if he should sign them.

'Our first gig was at The Haçienda,' Space Monkeys' singer Richard McNevin-Duff recalled on www.isnakebitecom. 'Tony came down and missed us, but everyone in the club was fucking raving about us, saying, "Oh, you should have seen the Space Monkeys, they fucking blew the joint up." Next thing we know he's come to see us at a party we were throwing the week after. Tony came down to one of them and said, "Where's the dressing room?"'

'So we pointed to the car park and said, "It's out there."'

'He was like, "Oh, cool." So we were all standing in the car park while all these fucking 14-year-old kids were getting off with each other, smashing bottles and stuff and he said, "How do you fancy signing to Factory?"'

'We were like, "Why not? No one else has offered us a deal."'

Yvette Livesey: 'The Space Monkeys were good but they weren't changing the world. At one stage he was after [dance-rock act] The Music and wanted to sign them. He played them to me and they were stunning. He took a major label to see them in Yorkshire – and they went behind his back and signed them.'

The Space Monkeys' *The Daddy Of Them All* would inadvertently bring about the end of Factory Too. Tony had managed to keep things on an even keel until the start of 1997, when London Records delayed the release of the Monkeys' rather ordinary collection of dance-rockers. Wilson was 'flabbergasted and horrified' and the relationship came to an end. Tony put out a typically cocky statement to explain the demise of Factory Too. 'We loved London's money, but we hated being controlled by them. Being fired by a multinational means we are in this strange and wonderful position of owning ourselves.' Tony set up a new identity – Factory Limited – to release the Space Monkeys' remaining material, which London had kindly handed over.

There was one other noteworthy addition to the Factory Too/Factory Limited family: Natalie Curtis, the daughter of Ian

Curtis. After she had expressed an interest in a media career, Tony had taken the teenager out filming with him for Granada, then quietly gave her an office job at Factory Too. 'It remains a family,' Tony told me in 1998, 'in the same way as with Manchester music – there's a broad family. Don't always get on with each other like most families don't, but there's a family thing about it. So yes the fact that Natalie works in the office gives me a warm glow, if I'm honest.'

Despite the reduced circumstances of his record label, Tony still played the man about town, involving himself in a dizzying array of projects, plans and argy-bargies. He paved the way for wider web access as Dry became Manchester's first cyber-café, linked to what was described at the time by the *Manchester Evening News* as 'the internet – the vast worldwide network of databases' – allowing punters to log on during a night out. He hosted a TV debate with Pete Wylie of The Mighty Wah! about the history of enmity between Liverpool and Manchester. He got involved with the Marketing Manchester campaign because he didn't think it was being done properly. He hosted the Young Jazz Musician of the Year awards, and he helped launch an awareness campaign for tackling depression in men.

By this time Tony and Yvette had totally bought into their long-term project of a loft lifestyle. For £80,000 they found the top floor of a three-storey printer's building at the Knott Mill end of Deansgate, the main drag that connects the edge of Manchester city centre to the unloved Arndale Centre. On 15 June 1996 the nauseous yellow-fronted shopping centre, along with a million square feet of Manchester city centre, was partially wrecked by the biggest bomb ever planted on mainland Britain. There would be many people – Tony Wilson prominent among their number – who could lay claim to being instrumental in the architectural, economic and cultural rebirth of Manchester in the late 1990s. The truth is that the faceless IRA men who parked their bomb just outside the Arndale branch of Marks and Spencer did more to clear the way – literally – for the city's upgrade than anyone.

Although no politician was willing to go on record and say the bombing was 'good' for the city, behind closed doors the planners cracked their knuckles in secret delight at having a tilt at the most extensive city refurbishment since World War II. This was their chance to buff Manchester up into the European cafe society city that many – especially Tony Wilson – had always wanted it to be, but had been stymied by a lack of funds and political will, as well as an inability to get round town hall red tape.

By way of contrast, just a thousand yards from the bomb site, the pioneer of the design-led, Euro-Manc lifestyle was on its last legs. The bills had been bumped up still further at The Haçienda by a management team keen to demonstrate they were serious about keeping trouble out. They implemented such measures as cameras, an imposing metal detector at the entrance and door operators who had reputations as intimidating as some of the men they were paid to keep out. A sense of control had been established but in the end it wouldn't be the guns and the gangs that brought about the end of The Haçienda.

The venue had by then outlived its usefulness as the nocturnal culture it championed and inspired took root and sprouted in little pockets across Manchester and beyond. Bars sprung up around Dry as the Northern Quarter began to attract revellers and creative businesses. Neon signs were turned on along the length of the city centre's run of canals. The gay village pioneered a path of regeneration around Canal Street and the red light district of Sackville Street. Ancoats throbbed with Sankey's Soap club nights.

Even the Knott Mill end of Deansgate where Tony's new gaff was situated was taking off. Tony himself got embroiled in a planning row over a lap-dancing club being opened near the loft, taking the moral high ground as the city centre was – in part thanks to him – on its way to becoming a place where people actually lived and that his children stayed with him several nights a week. 'There would be a problem having a sexually-related club going on 'til two or three in the morning in what is very much a residential area,' was his argument. 'I think ladies around here would be uncomfortable with it. It should be rejected.'

With newer, shinier, *groovier* places to go, the gangs also stopped coagulating in The Haçienda. The problems didn't disappear, they just spread out over a larger area . So did the civilian crowd and they took their money with them. At 15 years of age, The Haçienda was becoming a little *gamey* and for some the end was overdue. Yvette Livesey: 'It probably went on too long. Some people may have thought it was Tony taking his eye off the ball but it wasn't. The time was right.'

'The Haçienda was all-consuming,' says DJ Graeme Park. 'I never imagined it would end. I did notice towards the end, though, it was going a bit weird. People started going to Cream in Liverpool. There were coaches outside The Haçienda taking people to Cream. Then you get Gatecrasher in Sheffield and the Ministry of Sound opened in London. You started to see Manchester clubbers in these places. Not a good sign.'

Park describes Wilson's influence on the club over the years. 'What Tony did was to get everyone to feed off everyone else. My introductions to Happy Mondays or New Order or all the bands were all via Tony. His talent was winding people up behind the scenes, saying outrageous things and getting people to do stuff together. He would pour the paraffin, flick the match in, stand back and watch what would happen. He never interfered. He might make a cutting remark but then he made cutting remarks about everything.

'Without Tony, The Haçienda would just be another club. Peter Hook would come down The Haçienda and be a grumpy bastard, wondering how much money it was making, how much it was going to cost him. Tony would come down and be... *louche*.'

The Haçienda would bow out with such a whimper that many on the staff didn't actually know it had ended. By June 1997 it was enjoying something of a late flush, with full nights at the weekend not entirely out of the question. Though Tony and senior managers knew that the end had arrived, they took the decision not to tell frontline employees. The final DJs on the night were Elliot Eastwick and Dave Haslam. 'The end was very, very messy and totally unplanned,' says Haslam today. 'Probably could have been avoided. Me and Elliot were the DJs on the last night. The Saturday night was doing really well, but it wasn't doing particularly well on the other nights of the week. The culture had changed. A lot of people wanted a more intimate clubbing thing rather than the big warehouse experience. Plus there was what some people might call a protection racket being run by the people on the door which bled the club.'

There was no grand exit. No Tony Wilson speeches to the clubbing throng. No instruction to the crowd to take what they wanted. That image of Tony on the last night of The Haçienda is a fabrication, courtesy of *24 Hour Party People* scriptwriter Frank Cottrell Boyce.

'Wilson was nowhere near the club on the last night,' Elliot Eastwick told me. 'He *knew* it was going to end. None of them were there: Gretton, Hooky, Bernard. It was a big Saturday night.'

Dave Haslam: 'I've never understood why the closure of The Haçienda becomes something controlled by Tony. The whole *24 Hour Party People* thing gets people confused – it conflates the end of Factory Records and the end of The Haçienda – it looks like they happen at the same time. As we know, it struggled on for another five years.'

As Tony tucked into a takeaway half-a-mile away at his loft apartment, Elliot Eastwick played the last ever record to boom across The Haçienda – 'Post-Modern Sleaze' by Sneaker Pimps – and went home happy. Eastwick had started in his teens as a glass collector and rose to Saturday night DJ. He'd made it. The next day no one would return his phone calls. On Monday he saw a *Manchester Evening News* headline. It read: 'HAÇIENDA CLOSES FOR GOOD'. 'Imagine finding out you've been sacked by reading a billboard outside a shop,' he says. 'I remember looking down at it thinking, *You fucking cunts*.'

Dave Haslam: 'There were a couple of days of people running

around hoping to do a deal – close one company and open another and start afresh. I was told, "Don't worry." I even went on BBC local news. I was told to say, as far as I know The Haçienda will be open on Saturday. It never did.'

Tony Wilson would quickly wipe his hands of The Haçienda and consign it to history, refusing all attempts at any form of nostalgic revival. A year after the closure, the Manchester Civic Society would try to save the club from the developers' bulldozers, arguing that the building was as important as The Cavern in Liverpool and the Wigan Casino, both of which had been knocked down to later regret. The chief opponent of the scheme to save The Haçienda was a Mr AH Wilson of Knott Mill, Deansgate. 'I received a circular from the Civic Society recently,' Tony told *Mr Manchester's Diary* (the gossip column of the *Manchester Evening News)*. 'It went straight in the bin. The Haçienda's memory will be preserved forever, but it shouldn't be turned into a museum. The Civic Society is holding Manchester back.'

Yvette Livesey: 'He brushed stuff off. If he passed Factory or The Haçienda building, it would be, "It was good fun at the time, but you can't regret anything and always look forward, never look back."' The venue was knocked down to make way for a block of lookalike flats also called The Haçienda. In 2002, Peter Hook did the honours and started the demolition live on *Granada Reports*. That was that. Or at least until the club was rebuilt for a film shortly afterwards.

If there was one constant in Tony's musical life it was Vini Reilly's Durutti Column. Of all the bands he'd been involved with, they were the bedrock – he was and always had been their manager. Until 1998 that is, when he was sacked. 'It was a real shock and very, very difficult because first and foremost Tony Wilson was a very close friend,' Vini Reilly later told *The Independent*. 'We disagreed profoundly over some of the things that were happening. I felt that Factory had lost its identity and that was the problem, so I left. I was very, very sad to leave and

Tony was very upset and felt personally rejected. It was just a very difficult thing to do and a very sad time really.'

With no Haçienda, one band on his record label and work from Granada dwindling, Tony was talked into getting an agent to take a serious stab at his TV career. London-based agent Vivienne Clore began to look after Tony's television profile and he got an ITV network gig – a music and arts show called *Content*. It might have helped that the person in charge was former Granada researcher David Liddiment: 'ITV used to put it out at the latest available slot in the south. It became his signature in a way – North/South antagonism. He rather liked the idea that London didn't get him. It became part of his identity. London resisted him to the end.'

Yvette Livesey: 'I remember watching him in a studio in London and thinking, You're just not being yourself. Maybe because he was out of his comfort zone – in Manchester he could be himself. It wasn't him. It was him playing at being a serious TV presenter. He preferred to be infamous than famous. He liked being under the radar.'

Although *Content* would continue into 2000, it wasn't recommissioned and its conclusion would signal the end of Tony's wider TV ambitions. Though he would still tell anyone who would listen that his dream was to present the BBC's political discussion programme *Question Time*, the fire seemed to have left his belly. Even Granada stopped calling, in slightly humiliating circumstances. Tony was on a retainer of £13,000 per annum to be 'available' to Granada. That could mean popping up as a talking head for pundit shows or doing some presenting, but the reality was that he was rarely called. If this was the way his association with Granada would end, it didn't seem fitting on either side.

The end of the decade would see a return to the public stage for some of Tony's former charges. New Order – who had steadfastly refused to admit they'd ever actually split up – reformed without Gillian Gilbert. They walked onto the stage of Manchester's Apollo theatre in July 1998 and pretended they'd never been away. The first song they played was 'Regret'. New Order would continue and produce two new, but largely unloved albums, *Get Ready* and *Waiting for the Sirens Call*. Hardcore fans went out and bought them on the day of release but critics were largely unimpressed.

Tony would be politely dismissive of the band. 'It's very difficult when you get older in a young man's business,' he told me in 2006. 'New Order's way of keeping going is they keep thinking they're writing new songs – or keep thinking they're doing something useful.' New Order would continue thinking they were doing something useful until Peter Hook's long, messy, public exit from the band in 2006-7. That's how long and messy it was – it stretched from one year into another.

1999 saw the return of Happy Mondays. Paul Ryder says it was for the music. Brother Shaun said it was for the cash. 'I have no problem with the Mondays reforming to make some money,' Tony told *Mojo* magazine. 'They deserve it. Frank Sinatra managed to have quite a long career and Shaun Ryder is no less talented.'

On Saturday 15 May 1999, Rob Gretton was found dead at his home in Chorlton. His death at the age of 46 was attributed to heart and thyroid problems. He was buried in nearby Southern Cemetery – the sprawling burial ground that inspired The Smiths' song 'Cemetery Gates' – in the middle of a hefty Mancunian downpour.

'I think Tony's relationship with Gretton was really interesting,' says Dave Haslam. 'A lot of the things Tony is renowned for doing, Rob Gretton had a really big part in. The Haçienda was an example. I don't think The Haçienda would have happened without Rob. It's what he wanted. I always felt Tony's, "We opened The Haçienda because my colleague Mr Gretton wanted somewhere to ogle women" – that's quite funny. But give the guy a bit more credibility. Gretton actually knew what he was doing.'

Rob Gretton's widow Lesley later published his notebooks to give an insight into his working methods. Called *1 Top Class*

Manager, they showed the incredible extent of thought and detail he put into his dealings with Joy Division, from detailing costs and expenses down to the last penny, to his thoughts on how the band should present themselves to the media.

1999 would see another huge loss for Tony. Nearly a quarter of a century after the death of his mother Doris, his father Sydney died. Tony sometimes liked to drop a reference to his father into relatively random conversations: 'Oh, my dad's boyfriend knows that hotel...' as if to gauge the other person's reaction to the information. Those closest to Tony believe that he never really dealt with his father's sexuality.

Yvette Livesey: 'It dawned on him. The conversation was never had with his mum. He realised after his mum died. But he and his dad never talked about it either. I don't know if he ever came to terms with it. He was closer to his uncles. His dad never did any "dad" stuff with him. Sydney wasn't particularly great with Oliver and Isabel. He wasn't great with kids.'

Tony kept a photo of Sydney in the loft apartment that he shared with Yvette. He would sometimes point to the photo when guests were there. 'Look,' he would say sadly. 'That's a picture of my dead gay dad.'

TWELVE
TWAT

This is the West, sir. When the legend becomes fact, print the legend
– MAXWELL STOTT IN THE MAN WHO SHOT LIBERTY VALANCE

Many people's concept of Tony Wilson, what he was like and what happened during his lives and times has been coloured, filtered and maybe even tainted by *24 Hour Party People*. Writer Frank Cottrell Boyce and director Michael Winterbottom had first met Tony at Granada, working on *Coronation Street* and *Cracker*. They approached Tony with the idea of him investing in a film they were interested in doing – Tony turned the tables by trying to interest them in the script for *The Mad Fuckers!* Again, not my exclamation mark.

'We went to Tony thinking he had money,' says Frank Cottrell Boyce. 'He probably has less money than anyone in Europe but he had a *suit*. He was generous with his time, though.'

Neither project happened, but after a gruelling task directing the western *The Claim*, released in 2000, Winterbottom wanted to make something closer to home. The initial plan was to make a Factory biopic and meetings took place with Tony to talk through the idea. It was then that the film-makers realised that here was someone far more interesting than any mere musician.

Frank Cottrell Boyce: 'Tony was a fan who couldn't just spectate. He was a perfect narrative device. I don't think he understood how central he was to the film. He was always talking.

He was usually wrong about things but often in a beguiling way. He was a good device for driving a movie forward. You have this idea when you're growing up that musicians are rock'n'roll and suits are boring. Tony was *massively* more interesting than any musicians he worked with. I know he worked with geniuses. I'm sure Ian Curtis was an amazingly charismatic person and Shaun Ryder as well, but utterly *boring* compared to Tony. Musicians become fossilised; Tony was always moving forward. He was alive in a way that most musicians aren't. And more romantic. He cared less about money than they did. He was incredibly generous. He was like a perverse St Francis, he gave everything away. He was psychotically generous.'

'When I became involved I thought it was a good idea when the film-maker said it's like a *Boogie Nights* concept,' Tony told me while the film was being filmed in Manchester in 2001. 'It's the dawn of punk to the death of acid, taking you through two revolutions on their up-and-down cycles. Hopefully the movie will have the feel of these moments and give that background, that cultural movement, although the film has resolved itself into being not really about the music. It's more a comedy about a bunch of idiots, which is me and my mates. A black comedy because quite a few people die in it. It's a comedy film but nevertheless Michael Winterbottom, Frank Cottrell Boyce and Andrew Eaton [producer] lived through these moments and they understand the importance of punk and the importance of acid house and how it works in terms of art and generation and expression.'

Both Cottrell Boyce and Winterbottom wanted Tony Wilson to be played by Steve Coogan, the north Manchester comedian and impressionist. 'I first encountered him when he came to a party my aunt threw at my parents' house,' Coogan later told *The Guardian*. 'I was ten years old and banished upstairs, but I caught a glimpse of him walking down our hallway, that slightly hippish bloke who presented the news. Twenty-five years later I got a phone call from Michael Winterbottom asking me to play Tony Wilson. I'd worked with Tony on a local television programme

[*Granada Up Front*], so I knew him from that. Also I'd grown up with him on television and I was aware of Factory and I bought Joy Division's records. I was slightly too young maybe to go and see them live but I remember that was what my older brother did [Mock Turtles' Martin Coogan] and that was a cool band to like. And I used to go to The Haçienda and hang out there, like any other young happening person in Manchester.'

Coogan had also played The Haçienda in the pre-acid house days, even slipping in his impression of Wilson for good measure. 'The subject matter was close to my heart and I felt very proprietary about it because I'm from Manchester. I'm proud to be from Manchester. Part of it was not necessarily that I wanted to play Tony but that I didn't want anyone else to play Tony Wilson.'

'We started talking to Steve about it before we even started writing the script,' Winterbottom told reporters at the press conference featured in the preface of this book. 'He always seemed to me to be the perfect person to play Tony. I just really like his work, so I really want to work with him.'

Not everyone was quite so keen on the Coogan for the role. New Order's Peter Hook described the casting as, 'The biggest cunt in Manchester being played by the second-biggest cunt in Manchester.'

From the start there were issues with the script. It seemed to cause upset or offence depending on who was the target of a particular scene. Lindsay Reade objected to an early section showing her having sex with Howard Devoto in a toilet. Devoto was concerned that Buzzcocks were not recognised in the early drafts for their part in the Sex Pistols' Lesser Free Trade Hall gigs. Tony was put out that the script made him appear to be the kind of person who boasted about going to Cambridge. Most of these problems were headed off at the pass by a deft tweak by Cottrell Boyce, often by a character turning to camera and pointing out that the scene you were currently watching never actually happened. There was one area, however, that was out of bounds.

Frank Cottrell Boyce: 'Hilary was a really difficult area. If it had been a biopic of Tony, Hilary would have been incredibly important. But he was quite sensitive about Hilary and the children. There was a basic thing that we're not talking about Hilary. It's a comedy film – no one should be hurt.'

Michael Winterbottom: 'We were really nervous at first. It's really difficult – you're talking about making a movie about real people, with their names and events in their lives.'

Cameos were given to the likes of Howard Devoto, Mark E Smith of The Fall and the Mondays' Paul Ryder. 'The first script I saw I thought this is going to be *fucking awful*,' remembers Ryder. 'But it turned out OK. Tony was portrayed as being a bit buffoonish and nothing could be further from the truth. I hope he wasn't upset about that. It made for a good film. The film is 60 per cent true and 40 per cent made up. For anyone reading this book he was no buffoon. Far from it. A very, very clever man.'

An early scene featuring Tony attending the Sex Pistols' first gig at the Lesser Free Trade Hall – yes, I know – was filmed in the real building, just before it was partially demolished to make way for a five-star hotel. 'That's quite an important moment in the movie and I hope they get it right,' Wilson told me on the day of filming. 'In the original screenplay it was everyone pogoing and jumping up and down and it was a riot. I said, "You can be unreal but the reality is, there was no pogoing." Pogoing really hadn't been invented at that point. The people who were in there were just sitting, sitting in these chairs just... gobsmacked, which I think was the phrase I passed on to Coogan.'

When I mentioned to Cottrell Boyce that Tony clearly wasn't at the Pistols' gig, his view is one that echoes through the film. 'Tony's attitude was, "Print the legend." He was mythologising Manchester. He wanted a big celebration.'

With The Haçienda already history, its scenes were shot in a replica club constructed in a warehouse in the Ancoats area of Manchester at a cost of £150,000. Wilson was taken to the set prior to filming, took a good look around... and burst into tears.

Former Haçienda DJ Dave Haslam was brought in to look after the ersatz club and ensure a heavy night was realistically recreated for filming. 'My job was to get a thousand extras in the room to make it like the 1989 glory days and pull the DJs together.'

Haslam's involvement prompted an extraordinary reaction from Tony Wilson. 'I had one massive row with Tony which was horrendous,' says Haslam today. Wilson believed that Haslam had done him a great disservice by writing about the demise of his ventures in the music press – one article entitled 'From Palatine Road to Skid Row' had particularly irked him – and he was livid when he heard of Haslam's involvement. Tony was known for his ability to brush off issues that would keep the rest of us awake at night, but here was a ticking time bomb waiting to explode.

'He held grudges against certain people he felt had done him over,' says Yvette Livesey when I asked her about Tony's temperament. 'He held them very well.'

'One morning I got a phone call at half nine in the morning,' says Haslam. 'It was Tony. I don't think I've had such an aggressive phone call with anyone in my life. He said, "You're not listening to me. I'm doing this event, not you. Gretton's dead, you're dealing with me."

'I said, "I don't know what you're talking about. I'm doing a job for Michael Winterbottom." He repeated what he said about Rob Gretton, then he said, "I'm going to kill you." He put the phone down.

'I immediately rang Michael Winterbottom and said, "You know the money you're paying me to do this event? I want you to double it because it's not worth it if I'm going to get this grief from Tony."'

An accord was reached whereby Tony was given a hundred tickets for the filmed event, which went off like clockwork. There was, however, one person missing on the night. 'Tony never even came,' says Haslam. 'He'd created this huge furore, fought battles and he didn't even come. I remember saying to him at the time, "Tony, someone's making a film of your life. Sit back. Enjoy."'

'Almost anyone who had a connection with the club was there,' Steve Coogan later wrote in a piece about Tony for *The Guardian*. 'The real New Order, the actors playing New Order, the Happy Mondays, the actors playing them, Dave Haslam, Mike Pickering. The party continued into the early hours, long after filming had stopped. Only one person didn't turn up: Anthony H Wilson. I never knew why. Did he not want to cramp my style? Did he not want to say "goodbye"? Or was he already moving forward on to the next thing?'

In fact, Yvette Livesey recalls that she and Tony fully intended to go to the filming, but changed their minds at the last minute and went out to dinner instead. 'Reasons for not going to the reconstruction? Neither of us were very big on harping on about the past. The place was going to be packed with everyone from the past. Way too much hassle.'

The Haçienda's real-life manager Leroy Richardson was there for the filming which turned into the Last Night of The Haçienda that the club never actually had. 'It was great,' says Richardson. 'When I walked in there were so many people there – it was emotional but not *sad* emotional. They'd done a really good job. It was the reaction of people outside afterwards: they were saying, "Is this going to be every week?" Let it go, it's gone. That's the last you're going to see of it. A lot of people were saying, "Let's get the set and make a club." No, it's gone, that's it. I'm glad The Haçienda's gone. It's more about people's experiences – and you're never going to forget them, are you?'

As the film was being put together, Tony was being slowly drawn back into Granada. His finances were not in a great state and he would ask for money from Granada colleagues to appear in their programmes – I gave him £150 for an interview in a documentary I produced in early 2001. The executive producer of Granada's regional programmes at this time was Eamonn O'Neal: 'Tony was on an unusual contract – a unique contract – with a retainer as "Mr Granada" but he wasn't actually being used onscreen. He still had this passion and was desperate to do more.'

Slowly, O'Neal began to use Tony, first as presenter of an arts series called *The Works* and then as a presenter of sports shows. Tony's 1970s researcher Don Jones was by now head of sport at Granada. 'He did *The Sport Exchange* – effectively a sports chat show. It was fantastic. It was Wilson talking to big names in sport. He was asking them questions they wouldn't normally be asked. Wilson was a real sports fan. He loved football. He loved Manchester United. He had a real knowledge of sport. Not just football – he loved *all* sport. He had a thing about American football. He had total recall. He never ever gave me a moment's grief in terms of being a prima donna or a smart arse. He was easy to work with, a joy compared to some of the wankers I've come across. 'He turned up, knew what he was talking about and did it. I never had a cross word with him. You'd think he'd be a pain in the arse but he wasn't. When I was head of sport they used to say Wilson's on a retainer. There were points where they said if you can use him, use him. He wasn't always in favour. There were periods when they didn't know what to do with him. If we could use him in sport then they loved it because it justified his retainer. That sounds harsh but that's true. There was a big period of time when people running the place didn't like the cut of his jib.'

Wilson was also asked to be the anchor of Granada's political programme *The Sunday Supplement*. Nearly 30 years after Tony had lost out on getting Granada's political show to Gordon Burns because he wasn't seen as a safe pair of hands, he achieved his ambition. The programme's producer was Peter Berry, Tony's former researcher on *Up Front*. 'He was brilliant on *Sunday Supplement*,' says Berry today. 'He did things off the top of his head. He didn't need a script. Everyone knew his politics, he wasn't neutral but he kept it even-handed. There were reservations high up because of his views. He executed it with professionalism. He *was* a safe pair of hands.'

As if by way of recognition that he was now 'safe', at the end of 2001 Tony was told that he was to be given a lifetime achievement award by the Royal Television Society. Eamonn

O'Neal, who had been instrumental in bringing Tony back into the Granada fold, says, 'I was chairman of the North West RTS. I suggested Tony Wilson should get the achievement award. Everyone said, why? I met with a fair amount with opposition – mainly from the BBC, who'd never worked with him. I managed to convince them. Tony was in the States doing some In the City work. He was able to come back on the day of the ceremony. Our guest speaker was Stuart Cosgrove, head of nations and regions at Channel 4. He and his wife were sat with me at our table. Tony arrived at the last minute, fresh from a transatlantic flight and worse the wear for substance entertainment on the plane.'

Tripping up the steps to stage, Tony shook the hand of the guest presenter – Noddy Holder of Slade, no less – and let rip. 'There is a subtext to this piece of shit,' he said, brandishing the hefty RTS award at the audience. 'This implies closure, old age and maturity.' Tony then set his sights on Stuart Cosgrove from Channel 4. 'In all these years, for me, my professional colleagues and my region, you've never done a fucking thing.'

Eamonn O'Neal: 'It was an amusing Tony Wilson speech but it was quite an embarrassing moment, insulting the invited guest and his wife. And he was pissed. For a moment or two I was quite hurt by that. I had quite a battle to get that award for him. It involved a crate of champagne from me to Stuart Cosgrove. The rest of the room said, "Well, that's Tony Wilson."'

Tony's old colleague Gordon Burns – now presenter of *North West Tonight*, the BBC's rival to *Granada Reports* – was in the audience. 'It was brilliant. You had this bloody Channel 4 commissioner that came up from London to make a speech about how great it was up north and what great talent we have and blah, blah, blah... and Tony got up and just picked on the guy – he just let fly. I could have stood up and cheered. That was Tony Wilson. That said it all. He didn't care who he upset. It was his love for the North West. Here was this guy who was coming out with all these bloody platitudes that were crap. And he was prepared to stand up and give him hell.'

Eamonn O'Neal: 'It was rude. It was inappropriate and unnecessary, I suppose. It showed a lack of gratitude for the industry marking his achievements. That wasn't the done thing. Everyone in that room recognised what he'd done for television and music and popular culture in the eyes of the country and the world. He should have accepted it with better grace. But he didn't. His excuse to me afterwards was that he was out of it. Those who were critical of me pushing the award through then came back and said, "We told you so. It was wasted on him." I'm still happy – he deserved it.'

Perhaps Tony's poor humour could be attributed to his run-in with the taxman. A mix-up saw him declared bankrupt in October. A £50,000 tax bill needed paying and Wilson offered to remortgage the Deansgate loft. But the bankruptcy petition had already been issued, slowing down the remortgage, making the payment late and putting Wilson in, as he put it, in a 'Kafka-esque nightmare'. Although a deal was struck and the order was overturned, it was a humiliation for Tony. He was not happy – and it showed. 'I am useless at filling in forms,' Tony told *The Guardian*, 'but the Inland Revenue are fucking idiots.'

It was probably time for someone to take Wilson down a peg or two, but it would take more than the Inland Revenue to do it. The job was finally done at the end of 2001 by his children, Oliver and Isabel. Granada broadcast a documentary about its wayward son called *That Tony Wilson*. It was the first programme actually about Wilson ever to be made.

Eamonn O'Neal: 'I found it unbelievable that we – his professional and personal buddies – had never made a documentary about him.' Among the archive clips and talking heads, Tony was skewered with ruthless efficiency by his kids, then aged 11 and 17, as they described what annoyed them about their dad.

'You can always hear people chatting,' Oliver told documentary maker Ged Clarke as he described what it was like going out and about with Tony Wilson. 'I like to hang back and listen to what people are saying. You can hear them saying, "That's Tony Wilson, he's a *twat*."'

Isabel twisted the knife a little more: 'When he swears in front of me I'm not bothered, but other people's dads don't do that. He's just a bit more open and... *childish*.'

Then Oliver went in for the kill. 'He likes to say, "Do you any of your friends have dads like me? That are *crazy*... and *wacky*. Wacky. That's his special word.'

*   *   *   *

As the interest and hype around *24 Hour Party People* began to swell, Tony travelled down the M62 to the Liverpool Institute for Performing Arts where he was being made a LIPA Companion in recognition of his contribution to the creative scene. The institute is based in Paul McCartney's old school and is the Scouse equivalent of a *Fame* school; it's bursting with singers, actors, performers and leg-warmers.

Tony had undergone something of a conversion in recent years and had begun talking up the city of Liverpool, claiming it was now superior to Manchester. In the City even moved there for a year in 1999. At the ceremony – where he would join the likes of singer Joan Armatrading and Sex Pistols' manager Malcolm McLaren in LIPA's list of companions – Tony was spotted by a familiar figure. As lanky and curly-haired as he had been in 1978, Andy McCluskey of Orchestral Manoeuvres in the Dark bounded over to Tony, determined to make good on a promise he'd made himself nearly 25 years earlier.

McCluskey was a record mogul himself by this stage, experiencing massive success with girl group Atomic Kitten. 'I went over to him and said, "I know this going to sound soppy but now I've been through the music industry I can completely and utterly see what you've done for me. I didn't know anything about the music industry. All I can say is, from the bottom of my heart, 'Thank you'. You went out of your way to spend your own time and money to make a record that would help us leave your record company. Totally fucking bonkers, but thank you very much."

'I think he found it rather difficult. I did feel that I'd generated an awkward moment but it needed to be said. Sometimes you go through life and in hindsight you often don't get a chance to thank them. I'm fortunate I did have the opportunity to say that to him.'

It can't have been a coincidence that Tony and Yvette put their loft apartment up for sale just as *24 Hour Party People* was about to come out. The film would put his profile at a higher level than ever before and was an obvious source of free publicity. The 3,200 square-foot apartment went on the market for a whopping £1.8m. It was judged to be the biggest and most expensive flat in the north of England. 'We couldn't replace it for less than £1.8m,' Tony told Manchester's *Metro News*. 'There is simply no other building in Manchester like it. Most apartments are just grey boxes, whereas our loft is something original, a complete one-off, a work of art.'

Prospective buyers were in the unusual position of being able to view not only the flat but a version of its co-owner being abused on posters across the city. *24 Hour Party People* was publicised by single images of its three principal characters, under each of which was a word: Sean Ryder got 'Poet', Ian Curtis got 'Genius' and Tony got... 'Twat'.

'People had been calling him that for a generation,' reasoned Frank Cottrell Boyce. 'He'd say that in Manchester "Twat" was a compliment.'

Prior to its release, the view in Manchester about *24 Hour Party People* was along the lines of, 'Who apart from people in this city will get this film?' When it was shown for the first time, it's fair to say the comment remained unchanged. Much the same as the man who provides its narrative thrust, *24 Hour Party People* is as entertaining as it is uneven. It's not a documentary – though it's shot on grainy digital video – so most of the events need to be taken with a large handful of salt. It's a comedy, but many people still took it very seriously indeed.

Coogan's Wilson – all adenoidal voice, dropped literary references and saintly, apologetic hand gestures – is in virtually every scene, so your opinion of the film is immediately coloured by your tolerance of the star's performance. The characterisation is, by turns, inspiring and tiring. He is an oblivious windmill-tilter, treading on toes by accident rather than by rebellious design. We follow him from daredevil Granada presenter to the owner of a worthless record label and it's constantly made clear to the audience that many events either didn't happen in the way they are being presented or didn't happen at all. Wilson/Coogan even paraphrases a line from *The Man Who Shot Liberty Valance* – John Ford's purist elegy for the passing of the Old West: 'Given the choice between the truth and legend, print the legend.'

This is a obviously a gloriously convenient cop-out which is both aimed at those Manc fusspots who complain the film bears no relation to what really happened and is a way to tie up any rewrites. Or as Cottrell Boyce puts it: 'If you want to have your cake and eat it, you bake two cakes.'

The film had premieres in London and Manchester and Dave Haslam DJ'd at both. He and Wilson managed to keep the peace. But shortly afterwards Tony's anger at Haslam surfaced again. Haslam: 'I was in Iceland, being interviewed on the radio in Reykjavik. The DJ was a big fan of The Haçienda and the whole Factory story. He'd interviewed Tony about *24 Hour Party People*. During my interview the DJ said he wanted to play a bit of Tony's interview to me. I said, "Wow, Tony, great man, good friend of mine."

'Live on air Tony's voice came on. He said, "In life you make friends and enemies. I've made enemies, everyone does. Dave Haslam – if I see him tomorrow, I'll kill him. I'll shoot him."'

'I got back to Manchester, phoned Tony, left a message on his mobile – "You know where I live, come and shoot me." Think that's the last conversation I had with him. It's part of the carnival, I suppose.'

Film reviewers at the time didn't quite know what to make of

24 Hour Party People. 'If Wilson hadn't existed, Steve Coogan, who impersonates him so engagingly, might well have invented him,' said *The Guardian,* judging the film to be 'affectionate although not always coherent.'

Empire's take was that the film 'leans too much towards the TonyWilson/Steve Coogan Show to really do justice to such a vibrant era; at times, particularly when the floppy-lapelled TV presenter is up there in grainy glory, it's like Eric Idle playing Steve Coogan playing Alan Partridge playing Tony Wilson. But there's no doubt that this is a brave and brilliant movie that bristles with energy and attitude.'

Time Out probably had it about right: 'A raucous unruly mob of a movie which pulls this way and that with drunken abandon, stepping on toes left and right, stumbling more than once, probably pissing all over the floor with the facts but always having a high old time.'

Tony had high hopes for the benefits he might reap from the release of *24 Hour Party People.* Frank Cottrell Boyce: 'He was still after another career. He said explicitly, "This is the re-launch, this is my remake." He thought the film would re-cool him and re-hip him.'

The reality was slightly different. He was offered a knowing, ironic quiz show on Channel 5 called *Topranko!* which he hosted with Yorkshire-born comedienne and presenter Charlotte Hudson. And he was offered his old job back as co-presenter of *Granada Reports.* Yvette Livesey: 'He needed money. However much he earned he spent it. So he went back to Granada.'

Granada Reports was co-presented by Tony's former *Up Front* colleague Lucy Meacock and the departing Tony Barnes. Granada's programme controller Kieron Collins: 'We had a meeting after I'd just gone into the job. I was sitting in my office wearing a suit wondering how this all happened and as he got up to leave he said, "Well, thanks, boss," and it completely threw me, because I had grown up with Tony Wilson, thinking he was all the things that television should be – completely uncontainable and completely of his own kind... and I absolutely loved him for it. So to find myself in the position of being his boss was completely strange. I think we both knew it was ludicrous but we went through the motions of it.'

Another of Tony's former *Up Front* researchers, Mark Alderton, was now head of news: 'You don't feel like you're the boss with Tony Wilson. Being Tony's boss was just making sure he turned up on time. That was as much as you could do. If he was going to fly to New York for the weekend you had to make sure that you rang him in New York on a Sunday to say, "Don't miss your flight," then you ring him at the airport to make sure he's landed. Then when he arrives and he hasn't slept, you say, "Go down to make-up early, Tony."'

Kieron Collins adds, 'I think he was brilliant, a genius. I think he was completely unpolished in the way that television presenters currently are and it's to his credit that he was like that. There are an awful lot who are glossy and have the right hairstyle and can turn from one camera to another – Tony was never like that. I think he was a complete natural as a television presenter. I don't think he was the best television presenter, but he was completely natural.'

Mark Alderton: 'He left Granada on a number of occasions, but he was always there or thereabouts. He may have left the building but he never left the area. It was odd but fairly enjoyable having him back. He *loved* television. He loved Granada. Granada had this immense place in Tony's heart – he was a Granada boy. Once Granada always Granada and that was it for Tony Wilson. It was as much his television station as it was the [Granada founders] Bernsteins'. I really do believe that. It had a call on him no matter where he was in the world – it called to him and he was there.'

Tony's arrival back on *Granada Reports* was marked by the traditional statement from the Quay Street press office regarding Tony's name: 'Anthony Wilson is to be known as Anthony Wilson or Anthony Howard Wilson, not Tony Wilson or Anthony H Wilson,' the statement read. Nice to have you back, Tony.

The day after he reappeared onscreen at *Granada Reports*, Tony headed to Cannes to see *24 Hour Party People* in competition, where he was spotted by Frank Cottrell Boyce. 'We were in a car on the Croisette heading towards the event. We saw Tony walking the opposite way. He was a bit phased.'

'I went up the red carpet and what suddenly starts booming out all over the fucking place across Cannes?' Tony later recalled. '"Atmosphere" by Joy Division. I began to get tearful. I realise I'm going to see this film about most of my friends who are dead and I slink into the bushes. I was dragged up the red carpet and slipped a French E.' Wilson decided that 'Atmosphere' would be the song that he would have played at his funeral.

The late journalist Shelley Rohde – a former colleague of Tony's at Granada – caught up with him in Cannes before he had to fly back for *Granada Reports*. Perceptively, she asked Tony if he thought the film would change him, his life, or people's perception of him. 'Not at all,' he said. 'I know I sacrificed my television career for The Haçienda and the music. But now, ironically, I don't think I'd have got a quiz show [*Topranko!*] if it had not been for this film.'

A quiz show and a return to a job he'd done 30 years earlier may not have been the re-launch that Tony Wilson was hoping for. Neither would last long. And it is hard to see how Coogan's characterisation of Tony – a vainglorious poseur seemingly oblivious to the harm and offence he causes – could have 're-cooled' him. Coogan's Wilson is no safe pair of hands. When I asked Frank Cottrell Boyce if he felt that the film had harmed Tony's fortunes, he was genuinely shocked.

'Tony never complained to me about the film,' he said. 'I don't think it's a damaging picture of him. It's never occurred to me that it could have harmed him – it's a pro-Tony film. He always said he was a minor player in his own story – Factory Records is the story of four heterosexual men who were in love with each other. He loved the film.'

In early 2003, Tony's focus was abruptly shifted away from the movie and his career to his health. Yvette Livesey: 'He had a mini-stroke. He went into Hope Hospital but we didn't tell anyone about it. A minor infarction. He was at lunch with Isabel. When he went to sign the bill his hand wouldn't work. He was fine but his blood pressure was through the roof and he was on tablets. It was a godsend he was fired from Granada.'

THIRTEEN

A PROVINCIAL
ACADEMIC

*It is better to entertain an idea than to take it home to live with you for
the rest of your life*
– RANDALL JARRELL

Tony's departure from Granada in the spring of 2003 and the
circumstances surrounding it go as close as anything thus
far to summing the man up. Professional yet sloppy, clever but
daft, a sweet way with words but he swore like a burning docker.

Tony was sometimes asked to read the short news bulletins
that peppered Granada's schedules during the day. Immediately
after the news at 3pm was CITV – ITV for children. Peter Berry
was news editor on Tuesday 18 March: 'I produced that bulletin.
All the kiddiwinks were lined up to watch CITV. He does his
first link into a package – "Elaine Wilcox reports" – then he
starts swearing...'

An essential rule of broadcasting – one that Tony would have
had drilled into him on his first day at ITN – is that every mike is
an open mike: you never swear near a microphone whether it's on
or off. Tony noticed that a 'tally light' – the red light on top of a
camera that tells you it's live – was broken. He pointed this out
to the gallery staff in a Wilson-esque fashion. 'If we had
rehearsed, I would have noticed that none of your fucking red
lights were working, guys. Camera one, you have no fucking red
light on.' The light was indeed broken, but the microphone was
live and Wilson's comments were broadcast.

Peter Berry: 'I was furiously typing an apology but I didn't need to. He knew and busked the apology at the end. He knew he'd broken a golden rule. I think he recommended his own suspension. Typical of him. He held his hands up. There was a lot of pressure on people at that time. His frustration came through. The red light wasn't working. The light was bust. He was right. But you should never ever swear in a studio whether you're on or off air. Golden rule.'

Mark Alderton: 'Part of me thought, *Ooh, Tony*. He came back upstairs and said, "Sorry, darling."

'I said to Tony, "You've landed me in it right up to my neck."

'"Sorry, darling."'

Tony went up through a series of managers to say 'Sorry, darling' to each of them. Eamonn O'Neal was next: 'I saw it on the TV in my office and I thought, Please tell me this is a rehearsal. Tony apologised on air but not before the phones started ringing. The one call that stuck in my mind was the guy who rang and said, "I'm sat here with my grandson waiting for Thomas the Tank Engine to come on and now he's running around shouting, 'Why is there no fucking red light on that camera?'"'

Kieron Collins' office was the last stop on the line. 'Every moment of my time being Tony Wilson's boss was totally enjoyable and utterly surreal. On a day-to-day basis it threw up something that you least expected – and that was one of them,' says Collins. 'He knew full well he shouldn't have done it. He was completely charming about the whole thing. The irony was that it's a word that you wouldn't blink about Tony saying in conversation. A word he used frequently in conversation becomes completely unacceptable when you put an afternoon television camera in front of him. But he made it utterly easy for me to say to him, "We have to suspend you..."

'The problem was, the fact that you suspend Tony for saying, "Fuck" actually creates more headlines and creates more furore than if you'd completely ignored it. And because he was his own man and this maverick character, you could never win. Waving your finger at Tony and telling him off just made you look like a bit of a dick. Because he was so different to anyone before or since in that role.'

Tony was suspended. Swearing on air can mean censure or even a fine from the TV regulators, so this was a serious matter. As he was a union member, the National Union of Journalists were informed and the Father of the Chapel was summoned by management to be told one of their members had been sent home. In 2003, I was the FOC, so I was brought in to be told the news. I immediately huffed and puffed as union officials are wont to do – until I was told what Tony had done. Then I kept my mouth shut and left.

Tony missed that night's *Granada Reports* and an apology was issued. 'Anthony Wilson and Granada Television wish to apologise unreservedly for any offence caused by viewers watching the 3pm bulletin. We would like to stress that it was entirely unintentional and Anthony did not realise that his remarks were being broadcast.'

Mark Alderton: 'That's Tony Wilson. When you buy Tony Wilson you get everything. That's the great complexity of the man. Within him are all these elements. Yes, he's great. Yes, he can win all these RTS awards and yes, he can say fuck on air. That's Tony Wilson. You have to accept what he's like.'

While Tony waited to see what the fallout would be, he travelled to London to record the first edition of a revamped and returned *After Dark*, being shown on the BBC's upmarket digital channel BBC4. 'A very good evening. It really is a joy to be back,' Tony said at just after 11pm on 23 March. 'For those of you new to the *After Dark* experience, it's live and it's open-ended. You know it's live because... it's about eight minutes past eleven.' Rather charmingly, as Tony checked the time, viewers may have noticed that he still wore his watch on the inside of his wrist, exactly the way he did in the 1980s version of the show. Tony presided over a relatively genteel edition on the subject of *What's*

Oil Got to Do With It? joined by a group of activists, oil men and Middle East experts.

Sebastian Cody came back on board as producer. 'In 2003 when we revived the show he did the first of the series and one of the BBC people – who was very pleased with the programme – asked why we'd invited this provincial academic to present the programme. By that point *24 Hour Party People* had happened so it was an extraordinary reflection of the box that this executive lived in, completely unaware of the Tony Wilson cult. I think he would have been terribly proud of that remark – that he was like some professor of media studies at some regional centre and that we'd given him this break. That would have greatly amused him. He liked putting on the half-moon specs and revealing that he actually had a very good education.'

Tony returned to the *Granada Reports*' sofa but it was to be a short-lived reprieve. There are those who say – when the biographer's tape recorder has been turned off – that the swearing incident was used as an excuse to end Wilson's return to Quay Street. Figures were down and he was seen by some as a nuisance. He stepped down; the reason given was that he wanted to spend more time campaigning for a devolved North West parliament. The government had recently announced that the issue of regions being allowed to make their own decisions would be put to a referendum in the autumn. Tony had been a founder member of the Necessary Group, formed to put pressure on the government to listen to the regionalists' arguments. 'It would be impossible to combine this commitment with my presenting role,' he told *The Daily Mail*.

'The people who were leading the regional campaign were a bit horrified when he started getting involved,' says Tony's friend and colleague Rob McLoughlin. 'They saw it as a mixed blessing. He didn't get on with some of the personalities. Maybe Tony had plans to become Prime Minister of the North West. A regional parliament was a very good idea when Labour was in opposition. When the landslide came in 1997, these authorities that had previously been marginalised suddenly had a direct link to Westminster. After that it was dead in the water.'

The Granada world that Tony thought he had been coming back to was, essentially, no longer there. In his day he was able to go out with a three-man crew, make up something potty on the spot and have the time and leeway to make it happen. The television world of 2003 was one of slashed budgets and single-man crews. Reporters and presenters were even starting to film and edit their own material. Very different to the freedom Tony had experienced in the past.

Mark Alderton: 'His heart was in it but the timing was wrong. Right person, wrong time. It had changed. The type of programming we were doing then wasn't the type of programming he'd made his name on with Bob Greaves. It was a different era of television news, with all the implications that has of resources and limitations.'

Tony was able to leave Quay Street with dignity relatively intact and a pay-off. Although he was never a fully-fledged member of staff at Granada he had continuous service stretching back to the day he walked in the door in 1973. Managers managed to argue that he was therefore entitled to a pseudo-redundancy package. As ever with Tony Wilson, the money came in handy and was gratefully received. Almost exactly 30 years since he walked through the door, Tony Wilson left the Granada building.

What followed was one of Tony's leanest periods. Having found himself back in favour, he had fallen out of it just as quickly. Rob McLoughlin: 'The sad thing about the industry was when it was announced he was ill, everyone came out of the woodwork to say what a brilliant broadcaster he was. But many people hadn't worked with him for donkey's years and weren't giving him breaks. I think that's a shame.'

In March 2004 Tony took to the stage of Manchester's Ritz club for a memorial event for Rob Gretton. And You Forgotten took its name from Christopher Gray's *Leaving the 20th Century* and featured Doves, Peter Hook and – separately – Bernard Sumner, A Certain Ratio and Haçienda DJs Mike Pickering and Graeme Park. Tony added a Situationist flourish by quoting Gray's work to open the proceedings: 'And you, forgotten, your memories ravaged by all the consternations of two hemispheres, stranded in the Red Cellars of Pali-Kao, without music and without geography, no longer setting out for The Haçienda where the roots think of the child and where the wine is finished off with fables from an old almanac. Now that's finished. You'll never see The Haçienda. It doesn't exist. The Haçienda must be built.' Peter Hook joined A Certain Ratio and took the opportunity to say a few words about Rob Gretton and other members of the Factory family who had passed away. He speculated that Tony Wilson 'might be next'.

Tony needed a job and as none was forthcoming, he essentially invented one for himself. Figuring that he had spent most of his life giving ideas away for nothing, he decided to start charging for them. He and Yvette began to spend more and more time in Livesey's native Lancashire and became involved in plans to regenerate what was known at the time as East Lancashire: essentially all the chewy, unfashionable areas of the county like Darwen, Rossendale, Accrington and Clitheroe, lumped together in one largely unloved package.

Regeneration agency Elevate was given the task– worth nearly £200 million – of preventing the collapse of the area's housing market and the haemorrhaging of people, money and resources. They needed someone to come up with some – not a pretty expression this – *imagineering*. Chief executive Max Steinberg: 'There was an issue about the image of the place. I am a north-westerner and I didn't know anything positive about the place. I went to see Anthony. He said he'd been doing lots of this kind of work before but no one had ever paid him. The first thing he said was, "Are you going to pay me?" I said, "It's entirely possible..."'

Elevate communications director Kathleen Houghton: 'We asked for a big idea, something that could improve the area's image. Probably the most unusual brief I've ever written. One big idea, please. He went to all these meeting with the council chief execs. Fairly boring, chicken-dinner type things. He was standing up and speaking uncensored and people were loving it. I think there was scepticism at first – over time they really captivated the local authorities. They were excited by the enthusiasm and the possibilities.'

The idea was to make the unappealing appealing to locals and outsiders, attract inward investment, beef up the image and make the area more attractive to a wider audience. Tony and Yvette drove around East Lancashire 'mining' ideas. 'He did his best work when he was driving around arguing with Yvette,' recalls Max Steinberg. 'They had a dynamic, interesting... *volatile* relationship. Tony made it clear that the creative spirit isn't something that can be easily managed by bureaucrats. There were times when I thought, Those people who said it's a risky business employing Tony Wilson, they might have been right. The issue for some was: "Why do we need this man up here? That rubbish is all right for Manchester but it won't work up here." But in fact what became clear was that we weren't going to get one idea. The danger was we were going to get hundreds of ideas. Because their creative juices were flowing.'

By the end of 2004, Tony's juices were flowing in a direction he'd tried 20 years earlier: film. He was asked to co-produce the big screen version of Deborah Curtis's book *Touching from a Distance*, about the life and death of Ian Curtis. Tony had been involved in a separate project to film the book that had not been optioned. The producers of the new project cannily got Tony onboard. 'My job was to see off the rebel movie and make sure it got made – and I did my bit,' Wilson told me in 2006. 'If another two people buy or are open to wonderful music like Joy Division, then it's worth it.'

Dutch photographer and music video director Anton Corbijn was given the job of directing the film in 2005. He'd moved to England from Holland back in 1980 on the basis that if Joy

Division were in the UK, that's where he needed to be. Twelve days later he was taking their photograph. 'I had my own memories of Ian and the memories of people who knew him,' he told *Record Collector* magazine in 2007, 'Debbie, Annik, the New Order guys.'

Corbijn appeared at a hastily arranged press conference to announce the project in Manchester the day after his appointment on 6 January. With no finished script, no actors and a director fresh from Manchester Airport, producers Todd Eckhart and Orian Williams, writer Matt Greenhalgh, Deborah Curtis and Tony could reveal little more than the film was underway. It's likely that this show of strength was a shot across the bows of those who had thoughts of making a rival movie.

Tony voiced his own concerns about the film: 'Movie people, by and large, when they touch our world of music, fuck up. All music films invariably are shite, with the exception of ones that come from an askance point of view. So for example *Easy Rider* or *Performance* are great music films but as soon as someone famous tries to do music, however clever it is, something's always terribly wrong. And the miracle of the last one, *24 Hour Party People*, was... can you imagine all the ways that it could've gone wrong? And it didn't. So that was kind of a triumph that made it work and that is the challenge again. And, in some ways to me, by involving Matt and by involving Anton, I think Orian has gone a long way down the road to making sure that it's not the usual movie-people-fucking-up-music.'

Anton Corbijn was asked if there was a title for the film. 'Not being English I like simple, so I thought the word *Control*. It's an obvious reference to the song "She's Lost Control" and also I think that Ian was somebody who wanted to control his life, his immediate surroundings and his destiny. And there was, of course, the other element of his life that he couldn't control, the epilepsy.'

The task then was to cast the film – and find someone willing to follow Steve Coogan's turn as Tony in *24 Hour Party People*.

Blackpool actor Craig Parkinson was offered the part: 'I was really nervous because he was someone I'd grown up with,' Parkinson told me. 'For a split second I thought I'm not sure if I can play this guy. And I'm not sure I want to. I knew that growing up in Granadaland he was seen by some people as a bit of a fool, a bit of a laughing stock. To some – not to everyone. I wanted to get rid of the humour. When I was young I used to sit down in front of the telly and watch him on *Granada Reports* while I had my tea. He had an answer for everything. I used to wonder why he changed his name, why one minute he was Tony Wilson, then Anthony then Anthony H. I never could understand why. Maybe I thought he was a bit of a pretentious character. My dad thought he was a smartarse.

'But of all the newsreaders he wasn't bland. Gordon Burns was really boring. Tony was rock'n'roll. I didn't know he actually *was* rock 'n' roll. *24 Hour Party People* – that was always in my head. It was pushed away – I tried to push it to the back as much as possible. There's a place for both films. What I wanted to do was bring something different to it. It was already different in the script. If you look at the other film, it's a huge comedy part. I wanted to get to his passion and the fact that sometimes his brain didn't connect with his mouth. He seemed a passionate man, a caring man, a slightly foolish man. They asked me if I wanted to meet him and I said, "No." It's a film not a documentary. But I watched everything I could find.'

Just over a week after the *Control* announcement came another: 'WILSON LAUNCHES FACTORY RECORDS MARK IV'. It would be Tony's last hurrah as a musical tastemaker. He had managed to hustle up £30,000 to get F4 rolling, and his spiel was that he wanted one more hit act to join Joy Division/New Order and Happy Mondays to make it a hat trick, thus proving he was no fluke merchant. His first signing – on the advice of son Oliver – was Moss Side collective Raw-T.

'I hate English kids rapping,' he told *The Guardian*, 'but these little MCs blew me away. Every major in London has looked at them.' Tony had clearly changed his Factory Too view that the best acts were those that nobody else were interested in. 'It's only when you work with them that you realise they are geniuses. I was amazed when they walked into the studio carrying reporters' notebooks. They spend all their time scribbling poetry.' Raw-T's publicity stills were taken by Tony's former office helper Natalie Curtis.

F4 had the usual playful accoutrements one would expect from a Tony Wilson label: a nice metal badge, stationery and a mission statement that promised further releases from The Durutti Column and ramshackle chav-rockers The Young Offenders Institute. 'And this is just the start. More digital signings, more great songs, more value for money; it's called disintermediation, you dummy,' ran their 'manifesto' statement. 'Official downloads at last – pay for the music, you bastards, you know it's worth it.'

Tony was making all the right noises but he was still essentially out of work. Then a bit of good luck came his way. He was invited onto the BBC's GMR (Greater Manchester Radio) to talk about his life on a slot featuring notable people in the city. The item was called Mr Manchester. Tony was interviewed about growing up in Salford, about his life and music by veteran broadcaster Mike Shaft. It was apparent from his tone that Wilson felt aggrieved that he was out of favour and without a broadcasting gig.

By coincidence GMR was about to be revamped as Radio Manchester. The BBC's head of regional and local programmes Leo Devine heard the interview – and in particular Wilson's gripe that he seemed untouchable – and within a matter of weeks Tony Wilson had joined the BBC. Yvette Livesey: 'When the BBC offered him work he found a family again – they loved him and what he did. With this and the label, with the East Lancashire work, he suddenly started to come in his own.' What's more, he was reunited with his old Granada mucker Gordon Burns, now presenter of the BBC's regional magazine show *North West Tonight*.

Tony quickly managed to build a neat little portfolio of

programmes at the BBC's North West headquarters on Oxford Road. He got a sports programme called *Ground Rules*. He presented a chat show called *Talk of the Town* from the cafe of Manchester's Cornerhouse art cinema, and he was being lined up as a replacement for veteran political journalist Jim Hancock, another ex-Granada man, to present the North West's section of the *Politics Show*, the BBC's Sunday lunchtime Westminster round-up. Yvette Livesey: 'Politics... sport... debate... Everything fed into who he was and the BBC *got* him and they weren't afraid of him.'

Meanwhile, Tony and Yvette delivered their East Lancashire report to Elevate. Max Steinberg: 'We wanted the report by a certain date. He'd say, "We're not ready – you can't fucking well have it."

'I said, "We're *paying* you." Sometimes we used Yvette as a conduit to talk to him.'

The result of their creative 'mining' was *Dreaming of a Pennine Lancashire*. It's florid, cheeky, self-aggrandising and self-deprecating. Not bad for an urban renewal strategy. The list of ideas – or 'Series of Consummations Devoutly to be Wished' – included a football theme park, a canal-side curry mile, free PA systems and lights for rock bands, free lessons for creative people on how to run a business, 'chic' allotment sheds and a 'fashion tower'. The key was an insistence on rebranding East Lancashire as Pennine Lancashire, pointing out that 'anything with a compass direction in the title is a bureaucratic concept, not a place.' What's more, they'd get Peter Saville to do the logo.

Elevate were delighted. Max Steinberg: 'He said to us that he regarded this as a major piece of work. This was something he became hugely passionate about. At the time we didn't know he was coming towards the end of his life.'

FOURTEEN
THIS THING

*Illness is the most heeded of doctors: to kindness and wisdom we make
 promises only; pain we obey*
– MARCEL PROUST

The year 2006 was one of the busiest periods of Tony's life. He had bedded into the BBC – a very different culture to life at Granada – doing two radio shows a week. He would get a third thanks to XFM Manchester, who put him on a Sunday lunchtime slot. He invariably used it to get friends or people he was interested in to come in, talk and choose some music, meaning he had to do very little. Dave Haslam was also working at the station: 'XFM listeners were like Tony's children – exactly the right audience.'

His work for what was soon to be known as Pennine Lancashire was continuing: Tony and Yvette were commissioned by Elevate to do more with the project and there was talk of further local media work. Then illness interrupted to slow the momentum. Cancer. But not his. Yvette Livesey: 'I got cancer that summer. I got breast cancer. I was very, very lucky. They caught it early.'

Principal filming also got underway for *Control,* although Tony's role was minimal now the rival project had been stopped in its tracks. He did however visit the set, to the horror of Craig Parkinson. 'I said, "If Tony's going to visit the set, don't tell me. I don't want to know,"' said the actor. 'Weeks go by and I figure maybe he's popped in and no one's noticed. Then I'm just about to do a huge scene where I, as Tony, introduce Joy Division on television for the first time. A huge long scene at Granada, one of my biggest days and who's there with his dog and his glasses at the end of his nose? I was wearing a brown velvet suit. I knew Tony wore velvet suits in the 1970s. We were filming in black and white: the colour didn't matter. I was introduced to him and he said, "Yeah... when I introduced Joy Division I was wearing a black velvet jacket, not brown." I think he was helping – in his way. I *knew* he was wearing a black velvet jacket.'

Even with new projects coming in thick and fast, Tony still found time to get embroiled in Manchester music scene argy-bargy. Former Happy Monday man Paul Ryder launched his band Big Arm with the revelation that he hadn't spoken to brother Shaun for five years and that he no longer had the energy to deal with him. 'You only have to look at our kid to see what drugs can do to you,' Paul told the *Manchester Evening News*. 'I mean, he's not the sharp wit he used to be. I do miss him but I don't really like seeing him the way he is.'

Tony wrote to the *Manchester Evening News*, slapping Paul Ryder down. Paul and Tony then mounted a row via the paper's letters pages, with missives pinging off between the two about Wilson's perceived support of Shaun's lifestyle and his role in the Mondays. 'I'd never had an argument with Tony in my life,' says Paul Ryder, 'but when he jumped down my throat... He was a clever man, he knew how to have a good argument and he always had facts on his side. Unfortunately, on this occasion his facts were wrong and that's why I felt the need to stand up and tell him what was what. I made sure my words were spelt correctly so he couldn't pull me up on that!

'Tony always believed everything Shaun said. Tony thought that Shaun was some kind of musical leader of the Mondays. He was a leader in being vocal and doing interviews, but certainly not in the musical department. Someone told Tony that's what Shaun did – orchestrate the music – and he didn't. That's why I wrote the letter. Later, he apologised and I apologised. Everyone had spats with Tony. But they always made up.'

Back at the BBC, Tony was preparing for a new programme, this time on television – Sunday lunchtime's *Politics Show*, previously presented by former Granada reporter Jim Hancock. 'Tony checked with Jim Hancock to see if it was OK by him if he did it,' remembers *Politics Show* producer Michelle Mayman. 'Tony's agent then laughed at me when I told her how much money we could pay, but he said, "Just ignore her, let's do it anyway." He was really up for doing it. He told me he felt like it was a bit like coming home. He loved telly. He wanted to be on telly. He loved the live debating. He loved politics.'

Before he made his September debut as a BBC political presenter – a step towards his dream of hosting *Question Time* perhaps? – words were had to make sure Tony was going to play it straight. 'It wasn't that he wasn't seen as a safe pair of hands,' says Michelle Mayman, 'it was more about making sure he was impartial. I did my homework to see if there was anything he was involved with where he would run into any impartiality problems – like Elevate – and steer him away. He was well known enough for everyone to know about his political history. People loved him or hated him. Some guests came on especially to lock horns with him. He was very good. I gave him his brief on a Friday night – he'd turn up and he knew it all. I'm not convinced he'd actually *read* it. Whether he had the knowledge already, I don't know.

'He wasn't half as difficult as I thought he'd be. I was prepared for a diva – he wasn't. He was lovely. He was good at his job. He'd instantly spot if we'd missed anything. Plus it all went in when you squawked in his ear. He never looked startled like some presenters do. When it was time to hand back to the network, he would sign off with, "Now back to my colleagues in... some city... I think it's called... *London*."'

Meanwhile, plans to bring back *The Tube* – the Channel 4 show that had broadcast from The Haçienda 23 years earlier – were finally coming together. It was now to be an online radio show recorded in Salford and the executive producer was Tony's former colleague Rob McLoughlin. 'When Channel 4 radio were pitching for digital space,' says McLoughlin, 'I had the idea of selling them back one of their own programmes: *The Tube*. I thought it would work on the radio. When the TV show started there were a number of presenters. It eventually settled on Jools Holland and Paula Yates. We thought we'd do the same thing, get a family of presenters, some known, some not, and see where it went. We ended up with Alex James of Blur, we got Konnie Huq – which was quite an eye-opener for some as she was still on kids' show *Blue Peter* at the time. We brought in Emily Rose who'd never done radio or TV before. And I wanted Wilson for it. I know he still had a passion for it. There were people at Channel 4 who thought he was too old. They though he was too Manchester. There was some discrepancy as to whether he was right for it.'

Konnie Huq: 'I was supposed to fill in the gaps. It was supposed to encompass all music. I'd done the *UK Top 40* and stuff like that – but I'd worked on *Q* magazine too. Emily was grime and garage, Alex was the indie guy, Tony was the bonkers gravitas one.'

Her view of Tony Wilson was different to that of the Factory/Haçienda generation. 'I'd seen him on *Remote Control* – absolutely bonkers programme. It was on when I came home from school. That was my first TV viewing of him. I just thought he was a music guru. I really liked him. I was really *scared* of him. I knew he could be a real diva. I was expecting him to say, "What are you doing on this show?" But I got on with him from the word go. I could be quite cheeky with him and have a laugh. He was really fun loving. We'd tease him and call him Uncle Tony. And Jerry Springer. I called him "Ledge", short for legend. I think he liked that. He loved the whole thing of being at the centre of something. He was a bluffer and a blagger. That's part of the Manchester thing. He was at the centre of *The Tube*. He had the right to be.'

Tony also made sure some things were kept within the Manchester 'family'. Natalie Curtis was the photographer in the studio.

Just before *The Tube* started, Tony and Yvette went to America on one of their regular trips. 'We'd gone to New York in November,' she told me. 'I knew Tony wasn't so good when I said, "Do you want to go to the cinema?" He said, "I'm a bit tired." That wasn't like him.'

Mark Alderton – Tony's former head of news at Granada – was also part of *The Tube* team: 'He missed the dry run because he was in America – that's Tony. He literally got off the plane for the first episode, walked in and it was great.' Then there was the time before one of the shows when Manchester United were playing and Tony went missing. 'I found him in this old Salford pub round the corner watching the match with the regulars. He was standing there in his suit shouting at the TV till the last minute.'

Thirty years earlier Tony had banged on the desks of colleagues haranguing them about the Sex Pistols; now he did the same about St Albans' techno-rockers Enter Shikari. Tony had apparently seen the band on the recommendation of his son Oliver at Manchester's Music Box. The venue is on the site of Rafters, where Wilson first saw Joy Division. Rob McLoughlin: 'He still had the feel for it. Having fallen in love with the Sex Pistols you could see why he'd fallen in love with Enter Shikari as well.'

Mark Alderton: 'Fearsome din but great musicians. Very structured songs and great live performers. He thought they were wonderful and he was *there*. It wasn't like, "They're on now – I'll go and have a coffee." There's the suspicion that this might have been part of the persona and actually he was at home listening to Burt Bacharach. He was there, he genuinely was interested and he was moved by the music.'

Enter Shikari bass player Chris Batten: 'Well, it was strange for us because we had never met Tony and all we kept hearing was news of him spreading our name in all kinds of ways. Aside from the fact he genuinely loved the music, I think Tony was always really good at taking notice of what was going on under the surface of what the radio and magazines tell people they should like. I think he saw us building this huge young following just from playing shows before the press and radio started and thought that there was something going on under the mainstream's radar.'

Tony took on yet another job that same year, this time at Manchester's Channel M. The digital TV station had been broadcasting since 2000 and after a slightly rough-and-ready start was encroaching into programming areas previously occupied by Granada. The last-ever Granada music programme had gone out in late 2004 and there were no plans to make any more. As ever, people who had been shown kindness by Tony in the past were instrumental in getting him back on screen.

Eamonn O'Neal was the executive producer: 'What Channel M wanted was Tony Wilson on screen emulating what he'd done 30 years earlier on Granada. Music that you wouldn't necessarily *want* to hear – bands that were edgy. Philosophically recreate Tony Wilson bringing you new music. It was called *The New Friday* – it went out on a Thursday. We did one show – a transmittable pilot – before Christmas, then it was going to run every week through 2007. The first one was pre-recorded the night before [broadcast].

'Tony wasn't very well and he was coughing a lot. I asked him if he was all right and he said, "I've got this flu and I can't shift it – I'll have to go to the doctors." His voice was weaker than normal.'

Researcher Jenny Winstone: 'He had a bit of a cough and we said, "Come on Tony, what's up with you? Trying to get a day off?"'

Looking pale and a little drawn on that Thursday night recording in the first week of December 2006, Tony essentially did what he had been doing since he began introducing jazz bands at De La Salle 40 years earlier. He told us how utterly *fantastic* everything they were about to hear *really* and *truly* was. He introduced singer songwriter Paul Steel, prog rockers Silent Parade and showed a video for Enter Shikari's single 'Sorry You're Not a Winner', leaving no one in any doubt about his feelings for the St Albans shouters. 'It's the most important pop video of the year. Screw that – the most important pop video of the *millennium* so far,' he said in his introduction. 'I've sat in front of cameras like this and said, "Here are the Sex Pistols," "Here are the Stone Roses," "Here are Joy Division." It's a privilege I'm well aware of. Ladies and gentlemen and young people... Here is Enter Shikari.'

'Tony really loved Paul Steel,' says Jenny Winstone. 'He wanted him on the show and that's why we booked him. I loved him too but Tony introduced me to him. Enter Shikari was also a must for Tony on the show. When the other researcher on the show played me the tape of the video Tony wanted us play I thought he'd gone mad. It was totally not what I'm into. But he was right – they were doing something different to anything else around at that time. He loved the whole vibe of it, and the kids loved it.'

'It was incredible seeing just how influential he was in the rise to success of so many bands,' says Enter Shikari's Chris Batten. 'From signing bands in his own blood, getting a venue, to promoting his bands through his TV show, he did anything he could to get the bands he loved in front of as many people as possible.'

Just before transmission it was decided to give Tony an on-camera foil to bounce off. Jenny Winstone stepped in after other candidates were deemed unsuitable. 'For the screen test I had to talk about a car in the car park as if it were a work of art. The next thing I know I'm on the sofa with Tony Wilson,' she says. 'He never talked down to me. He was an educated man, he'd been there and seen it, he knew so much. He was still totally enthusiastic about music. I fell in love with him straight away.'

At the end of the show, Tony Wilson thanked viewers for

watching and advised them to keep the faith. Eamonn O'Neal: 'The people who hadn't worked with him before – the runners through to the producer – grew ten feet. However arsey he got in the eyes of the public, he was always, *always* delightfully helpful and supportive of the staff he worked with. Everyone who worked with him just that once still talk about it now. Like Jenny Winstone – her ambition was always to work on music TV and there she was sitting next to Tony Wilson. She's never forgotten it. Tony Wilson's last TV music show. He did the show as only he can, we all went out afterwards, then we went our merry ways and we never did another one.'

While out Christmas shopping the next day, Tony's cough continued to bother him and Yvette insisted he have it checked out. 'We went to the doctor and she sent him immediately to the Manchester Royal Infirmary. He had fluid on his lung and they did more tests. I paid for him to go into the Alexandra [private hospital]. They found he had kidney cancer. I think they knew then it was an aggressive form of kidney cancer.'

Tony got in touch with those he'd been working with to tell them that he wasn't able to continue. Michelle Mayman at the BBC: 'He rang me just before Christmas to say he was going in. My radar went up: they're taking him in over *Christmas*?'

'He phoned me to say he wasn't very well and he couldn't do any more shows,' says *The Tube's* Mark Alderton. 'It was a very, "Hi, darling how are you?" kind of phone call. "Hi, darling, I'm not going to be able to continue, I'm not very well. I've got this... thing."'

Yvette Livesey: 'It was Christmas time – then on 2 January he went into the Manchester Royal Infirmary and they took his kidney out. Then he went to Christie's.'

The Christie Hospital is in Withington, south Manchester, just round the corner from Tony's old house on Old Broadway. It's a specialist cancer facility and they've been treating people there for more than a hundred years. There are those who say – with typically dark Mancunian humour – that if you are going to get cancer, you're better off getting it in Manchester because that's where Christie's is.

Professor Robert Hawkins treated Tony at the hospital. 'He was referred here to learn how to manage the cancer,' he told me. 'It had already spread by the time he was diagnosed. That's an unfortunate fact. For about a third of people with kidney cancer, by the time they are diagnosed it's already spread. It's a very difficult tumour to catch early enough to cure by surgery. Kidney cancer is rarer than you might expect. Nobody knows in the vast majority of cases why people get it. It's more common in men. The only clear things that cause it are smoking and exposure to certain industrial chemicals. In Tony's case it was quite extensive. It had spread to the lungs and parts of his stomach.'

As Tony recovered from the operation at home, friends came by to help in various ways. Durutti Column drummer Bruce Mitchell came to do some electrical work. 'I thought, What can we do to help him and be positive and not wind him up too much? I went round to fix some lights.'

In the New Year there was a knock at the door and an unexpected guest was on the other side: Alan Erasmus. A combination of the Factory deal going sour and Erasmus' disapproval of Yvette meant that two men had not spoken since the early 1990s. Now was the time to make peace.

Bruce Mitchell: 'He said to me, "Guess who was round today? Razzer!" Hadn't seen him for 15 years, the wonderment of him... Razzer was *dropping by*.'

Eamonn O'Neal: 'I went to see him at his apartment after his operation. I was shocked. He met me at the loft door in the kind of dressing gown you'd expect your dad to be in, not a trendy one. He was shuffling along but he was still thinking about work and music and let's set a date for *The New Friday* to come back in Easter.'

Paul Ryder: 'I remember him saying, "It's weird when you're dying – everyone phones up and says they love you." I was one of them. I left him a message saying, "I love you and my life wouldn't be what it is without you." Thank God I did that.'

Bob Greaves: 'I have one major regret. Strangely he'd rung me early in the New Year out of the blue to ask if I was still at the same address because he'd neglected to send me a Christmas card. I found that odd because I'm not sure he and I exchanged Christmas cards as a matter of course. He then sent me one, with no hint of illness attached. Two or three months after that he rang me on another pretext and said he'd not been too well as a result of a trip to America. He'd got a chest infection. Eventually it all fell into place. I realised he'd probably been feeling ill long before he told people. I think that's why he rang me after Christmas. To catch up, which for him was unusual. I rang him several times and I always caught him when he was just about to go to hospital or go in for a consultation. It's my fault – I never actually visited him when he was ill at home. I didn't *insist*. It's my regret I didn't catch up with him. I should have insisted.'

In February, Tony wrote what he called a 'love letter to the NHS' about the treatment he had received. In the piece, which was widely reproduced in newspapers, Tony lavished praise on the nurses and doctors who had helped him, but there was an angry, disbelieving undercurrent.

It's early February and on our first meeting Prof Robert explains to Yvette and I that I can have normal chemo, Interferon, but that there is an even better drug that's just come through tests and has proved even better in the short term at combating kidney cancer. But there's a problem, the NHS hasn't approved it yet and you'd have to pay and it's incredibly expensive. It's called Sutent. I don't know who's reading this but can someone get the NHS to get their act together on a drug that tests show saves lives. Now. It's called Sutent and people need it.

Sutent would prove to be Tony's last stand, the final row, the last time he would roll up the sleeves of his crumpled designer jacket and pick a fight. Sutent targets cell growth and 'starves' the cancer – it also has fewer of the heavy-duty side effects associated with other cancer treatments. If Tony had lived a few miles down the road, he would have been eligible to get the drug for free. In Manchester it wasn't routinely funded. Apart from his postcode, there was another issue that may have gone against Tony Wilson... he was *Tony Wilson*.

Professor Robert Hawkins: 'Quite a high proportion of patients had got it. It's possible that he was so high profile it could have counted against him. Somebody less well known might have got it. We didn't want to be seen to be giving priority treatments to people because they're well known. The principle is good. There are different priorities in different areas. The idea of allowing local decisions is a good one. But when it comes to the availability of cancer treatment it's almost indefensible that you can have different treatments available in different parts of the country. It's a *National* Health Service. It's a national tax that pays for it. Therefore the treatment should be available nationally. Tony went through an appeal process – he was very capable of doing that. The onus is on the patient. If the NHS has decided it's not an appropriate use of their resources, it's up to the patient to convince the NHS that they are an exception. Unfortunately, he was turned down.'

One of the most articulate men of his generation tried and failed to convince the service he so cherished to help him. If he wanted Sutent he would have to pay for it himself. He couldn't afford it. Tony Wilson once said that you can't put a price on irony. Professor Hawkins begs to differ. 'The National Institute for Health and Clinical Excellence [NICE] decides if treatment is cost effective. A year of life is worth approximately £30,000.'

Yvette Livesey: 'He was incredibly angry. He had suddenly found this life again that he was loving. He loved everything he was doing. He was running at full speed again.'

In April, Tony and Yvette flew to the Coachella music and arts festival in California to fulfil a long-standing promise to attend the event and introduce Happy Mondays. He and Yvette stayed at the Chateau Marmont hotel in Hollywood – the rock'n'roll hotel on Sunset Boulevard that has seen bad behaviour from the likes of Led Zeppelin, Jim Morrison of The Doors and comedian John Belushi. Tony took to the stage of Coachella with the help of a walking stick. 'They changed the world, they're still doing it... Ladies and gentlemen, Happy Mondays...'

Yvette Livesey: 'We did America twice. We went to Coachella and LA. We went to New York [for In the City] in June. How the hell he got there... He was sick all the way there and back but he was determined to do it. In New York he was sleeping a lot. He was struggling to climb stairs but he never showed how ill he was or his pain. It was almost him saying, "Goodbye" to his friends in America. You know how men are.'

Weak as he was, Tony was still creating ballyhoo, demanding people roll up, roll up and check out his favoured bands. He had become entranced by emo music – the catch-all term applied to amped up, soul-baring, emotional punk, preferably performed by boys in eyeliner. He was convinced of the stadium prospects of some of the bands that fell into the emo catchment, particularly Fall Out Boy, and he was still banging the drum for Enter Shikari.

'I found out he was poorly not long before we flew out to New York to play at In the City,' Chris Batten says. 'When we got there we went to a seminar he gave with a few other music industry folk. It was upsetting to see him looking fragile. Although it didn't seem to affect his personality and charisma in the slightest. It was also very overwhelming at the time – because we didn't realise until we arrived – that Tony basically based the whole seminar on us. It was strange for us knowing the history of bands he discovered, to hear him talking about us in the same vein.'

Back in Britain there would be moments of fun, if grimly tinged. Tony was still a visible presence around the city of Manchester where, for more than 30 years, he had been able to guarantee a very particular type of greeting about town: 'Oi Wilson – ya fuckin' wanker.' Now he had to get used to sympathy. People would approach him in the street and ask after his health. Sometimes the temptation to turn the tables after all those years of public abuse was too strong to resist. Yvette Livesey: 'When he walked around town, people would stop and say, "Tony, are you all right?" He'd say, "Fucking fuck off!" Not in a nasty way – it was just him wanting to be controversial and not be loved.'

At Elevate, the unveiling of the multi-coloured, contoured Peter Saville-designed logo for the new Pennine Lancashire brand was brought forward. Max Steinberg: 'When we unveiled the logo... He said it was so beautiful it made him cry. He was so pleased to see the fruition of one of his ideas. I remember hugging him and his suit collapsed. There was nothing there.'

Tony carried on presenting the BBC's *Politics Show* on a Sunday. Off air, he would quiz any visiting medical interviewee about his current situation. Unsurprisingly, sometimes his mind was elsewhere. On one occasion he forgot to turn his mobile off before going on air. During the live show, the familiar monophonic ringtone strains of the Eminem/Dido track 'Stan' cut across the studio floor. Michelle Mayman: 'He looked so sheepish. I just screamed at him. It's never happened before. He was totally in the wrong. I got home and my friend said, "That man's unwell and you shouted at him?" I had to! I felt really guilty.'

It was becoming clear that Tony couldn't carry on. 'He was very angry,' remembers Yvette Livesey. 'One day he was doing the *Politics Show* and I said to him, "In your eyes you look really angry. I know this is a really harsh thing to say, but if you're going to keep doing telly you can't look like that."'

Tony Wilson's television career ended on 26 July 2007. Looking desperately ill and with a rasp where his booming voice used to be, he presented the *Politics Show* with items on council tax bankruptcy and the Labour Party conference in Manchester. He gamely got through a live studio interview, before whispering the programme outro: 'Next week we'll be taking a deep breath and discussing smoking, or the lack of it. The ban [on smoking in enclosed public places in England] will be in place by then. Contact us through our website. Back to John Sopel in London.' The name of the capital city he so heartily and volubly despised was the last thing Tony ever said as a TV presenter.

Michelle Mayman: 'We saw him deteriorating week after week. I saw him getting more and more ill. It came to the point where one day I got him a taxi and sent him home. His eyes had turned a different colour. We had that conversation... "Just take the next few weeks off – we'll pay you, don't worry about the money. I want you to go home." I'd spoken to my boss about how ill he looked. We talked about the duty of care. It got to a point where I looked at him and said, "Tony you're too ill. He was battling on and on."'

Though Tony continued to battle for Sutent, the money to pay for it eventually came from friends in the music and television business rather than the NHS. 'I know who gave the money,' says Yvette Livesey, 'but he didn't want to know. There were some really large amounts given by people in his past. He was very well looked after by the music industry. And even some small amounts given by local people. A hundred quid here and there.'

Tony took his fight over Sutent to a wider audience, writing an article for the *Daily Mirror* and being interviewed by the *Daily Mail*, a newspaper he would not ordinarily have given the time of day to. 'When I turned 50 I remember thinking that if I died then I wouldn't mind at all,' he told the paper. 'I had had such a colourful, fulfilling life and had done just what I wanted to do. But now that mortality was staring me in the face, I realised what an idiot I had been to think like that. I had so many things still to do.'

Tony even appeared on the BBC's *North West Tonight*, where was interviewed live by his old friend and colleague Gordon Burns. 'I think I did the last television interview with him before he died,' Burns told me. 'It was a very difficult interview because he looked terrible. Although there was a hope – because he was taking Sutent – that his life would be considerably prolonged, he looked terrible. But as always he did a great interview, a powerful interview and he was really getting stuck in about Sutent.'

'It's not about me, Gordon,' Tony said. 'Rich friends of mine in the music industry are looking after me, which is very strange and very wonderful. This is for all those other people who are trashing their life savings, selling their homes to pay for this drug which the NHS should be paying for.'

Gordon Burns – always a slightly hesitant interviewer – then bowled Tony a very slow ball indeed. 'Without this drug, what's the prognosis?'

After a brief pause, Tony connected with the question and smashed it over the boundary. 'I think it's called death.'

'We had a chat at the end on the studio floor then off he went with his son,' Burns recalled. 'And that was the last time I saw him. Looking at him you knew he was in a bad way. If you have cancer and you look like that, chances are you're not going to come back. But I wasn't expecting his death in a couple of weeks. I'm not sure I thought, This is farewell, but I remember feeling emotional. Just the way he shuffled off with his son helping him, bravely carrying on. You remember Tony as the young, exciting guy who was running around everywhere and doing exciting things and here he is – he's younger than me – looking like an old man and very ill. It was really emotional but I was really shocked at how soon it came.'

Tony contacted Canon Denis Clinch of St Mary's church in Manchester – The Hidden Gem close to Granada TV, where he would go to say a prayer for Doris. He and Clinch had become friends and enjoyed nothing better than a theological argy-bargy. Tony asked Canon Clinch to take his confession. Clinch would later joke that he had thought about packing an overnight bag as it might take several days.

Professor Robert Hawkins: 'Tony was certainly fighting. He wanted to have any treatment that might help him. He was realistic. He knew the odds were against him. But he wanted try everything that was available. He was realistic but he wanted to battle. He was very well informed. He wanted to know the truth. We told him the truth. He managed to lead a reasonably normal life right up to the end. I remember phoning him once – he was clearly out somewhere very lively.'

Yvette Livesey: 'He fought all the way. Right to the last minute. He hated it. Hated the fact there was the thing inside him. He battled all the way.'

'His treatment was going OK,' recalled Professor Hawkins, 'but not as well as we would have liked. He was weaker than we would have liked. He was taken into hospital. It was obvious he wasn't going to survive more than a few days. We had to have a very frank conversation with him and Yvette and others.'

FIFTEEN
THE CHRISTIE

*Love gives naught but itself and takes naught but from itself. Love possesses
not nor would it be possessed; for love is sufficient unto love*
– KAHIL GIBRAIN

Yvette Livesey: 'In a funny way, it was so full on and we kept
so busy – we were going between hospitals, then going to
America and to London, then to hospital again, just keeping
running really – I had no idea how ill he was. You block it out,
don't you? It was my job to keep him going. "You're looking
skinny. For fuck's sake, eat something." I was driving him
through. Until the week that he died – I didn't think he was *going
to die*.

'He just said to me on the Sunday, "I think I need to go to
hospital."

'I said, "Don't be stupid, you just need to eat," and he said,
"No, I'd feel safer there." That was it really. There were a lot of
people who came to the Christie and just sat in the waiting room.

'I don't think you *know* really. If you've never seen anyone die
before, you've no idea, have you? But you see it in doctors' and
nurses' faces – because they know. You can see that they are
preparing someone.

'Throughout his whole illness there was a lot of black humour
going on. Oliver got very upset one day. He said, "My dad was
on the phone to someone and he was *laughing*. It's not a funny
matter, this."

"I said, "You've got to laugh. What else do you do?"

'On the final day [10 August 2007], Tony couldn't talk by the end of it. He was trying to get something out, trying to say something. I was saying, "Try, please make the effort." He couldn't, so I said, "Write it down." I gave him a book to write it down. He tried; it took him so long to write this thing down. Then he showed it to me. It said: *Have you sorted the season tickets out?* Typically Tony. He died two hours later.'

SIXTEEN
200250100807

Render therefore all their dues; tribute to whom tribute is due; custom to whom custom; fear to whom fear; honour to whom honour
— NEW TESTAMENT, ROMANS 13:7

By the evening of 10 August, word of Tony's death had begun to spread. The *Manchester Evening News* – the paper that had followed his every move, praising and mocking him in equal measure for the last 24 years – opened up on online book of remembrance for people to log their memories and thoughts. It was flooded by people from Manchester, Britain and around the world.

RIP Tony!! Madchester was a better place, thanks to you!!! You are a legend and will never be forgotten. Angie, New Zealand

After the first TV for the Sex Pistols, you gave us JD, New Order, Haçienda and the Mondays. You will always be here while there remain people that you put a smile on their faces and meant so much. Gary, Southampton

Thank you Mr Wilson for all you have done for music. You will be sorely missed. Our thoughts are with your family at this difficult time. Amanada, Indianapolis

YOU'RE ENTITLED TO AN OPINION...

Tony Wilson was, is and will remain Mr Manchester until forever never ends. Thank you, from my soul. Lee, Manchester

At Manchester's town hall, the union flag was flown at half-mast as a mark of respect. Yvette Livesey: 'Tony always created reactions in people. They either loved him or they hated him. But they felt very strongly about him. Pat Karney [councillor for Manchester city centre] rang me the day after he died and said, "We've *never* had this kind of reaction to anyone dying in the city – ever." I don't know why he got that kind of reaction. I know he was a catalyst for a lot of people. And music touches a lot of people. But I never believed that anyone understood his importance to the British music industry. So I was very surprised.'

Those involved in Tony's lives and times heard the news in very different ways but their reactions were very similar. Peter Hook had been DJing in Japan. 'It's a very, very, very sad day,' he wrote on his blog. 'I feel very lost out here. It's like my father dying all over again. I'm devastated. I'll be going back to England as soon as possible to pick up the pieces. My heart goes out to all his family – thinking of you all. My heart is broken. Say "Hello" to Rob, Ian and Martin for me, Tony.'

Bob Greaves: 'I was filming a show with the BBC in Australia. I got the news of his death on the seventh day of our filming. My fortnight in Australia was cut short. He still owes me the better part of £1,500 – that's what it cost me to get back under my own steam! I couldn't face the thought of meandering around Sydney with the thought of his death on my mind.'

The film *Control* was about to be released in a matter of weeks. Actor Craig Parkinson was telephoned by the film's producer Orian Williams and given the news. 'It was one of the oddest phone conversations I've ever had,' he says. 'Tony wasn't someone I knew – but I felt like I did. He's not a friend or mentor. But in a way he was. For a few days I felt very odd. I didn't know how to feel. I remember seeing the film at the

Edinburgh film festival. They dedicated it to Tony's memory. I filled up a bit.'

As family and friends circled their wagons and decided how best to give Tony a fitting send-off, the obituary writers tried to sum up his achievements, though it was difficult to pin down exactly what he did. Some of Tony's former associates added their thoughts. In *The Guardian*, Paul Morley described Tony as a 'compelling, unique hybrid of selfish visionary, TV hack, charming bully, generous tyrant, commissioning editor, playful philosopher, inconsistent genius and down-to-earth intellectual [who] regenerated a declining city both economically and culturally.'

In *The Independent*, Tony's former colleague and neighbour Richard Madeley recalled how Wilson was, 'known in the newsroom by the obscure soubriquet of Fat Willy [and] was cock-of-the-walk. Most television presenters have large egos which, despite their size, need stroking; Tony's was big enough to take care of itself. Once, in a conversation about the most efficient way of committing suicide, Tony said comfortably that should the worst ever happen he would simply hurl himself from the top of his own ego.'

Peter Saville wrote in the *Manchester Evening News*: 'He was the pivotal facilitator through whom the talented and visionary of a generation were empowered to build a new here-and-now as an alternative to packing up for somewhere seemingly brighter and better. His legacy is not merely Factory product and The Haçienda legend but the very idea and initiation of a spiritual renaissance of the former industrial city through life culture. His sacrifice was his professional career but his memorial is modern Manchester.'

Friends and associates scanned the papers to find out details of when and where Tony's funeral would be, but it wasn't advertised in traditional style. Bob Greaves: 'I got back to England [and] discovered that the funeral was by invitation only. Great style, Tony, as ever.' It was to be held on 20 August at St Mary's. 'We had to go and pick up a pass – great style – from the Midland

Hotel before going to The Hidden Gem round the corner. It was a special pass with lots of digits on it. None of us really looked at it. It's a play on the FAC numbers that Tony used to dole out. This green pass was very similar. We looked at the digits but didn't give two hoots about what it meant. Later in the day someone said, "200250100807, what is it?" It is, of course, his date of birth and his date of dying. Great style. A maverick. I'm sure he planned all that.

'Knowing Tony he would have had a say. He certainly chose The Hidden Gem and he would have known that it wouldn't have held the number of people who would want to come. I bumped into a cameraman outside the church from Granada. He couldn't get in. That was the sadness about that decision but I understood why they did it. It was sad that people who wanted to get into the funeral couldn't. But that's what happens with big funerals.'

Those who did attend included Richard Madeley, Judy Finnigan, Shaun Ryder, Peter Hook, Peter Saville and many of the people who've contributed to this book. Gordon Burns: 'I thought his family were terrific at the funeral. His kids were so dignified and so welcoming. They did him proud the way they carried themselves that day.'

Yvette Livesey: 'He would have *loved* his funeral. It was right. The coffin was black and had cool silver handles on. He had his best Yohji suit on. Peter Saville designed the invite – the happy piece of plastic – Tony would have loved it. We run gigs. That's what we do. Bruce [Mitchell] was the first person I rang to help me. Oliver was great. We stuck FAC 501 on the coffin. Tony would have wanted a cool funeral. He got a cool funeral.'

Many of the Knupfer family stayed away, fearing they wouldn't know anyone and might feel out of place. Tony's cousin Geoff Knupfer: 'It seems sad now. I was in Singapore when he died. I didn't even try to go to the funeral, because Yvette wouldn't know me if she tripped over me and vice versa.'

Canon Denis Clinch took the funeral service. Frank Cottrell Boyce recalls: 'The canon's sermon was amazing. He talked about taking Tony's confession: *Tony told me everything and a lot of the time he forgot to regret it.* Tony was curious and unafraid about where he was going. He wasn't scared and he found someone to challenge him.'

Although many of those present probably didn't notice, at Tony's request the funeral was a very traditional Catholic affair. Frank Cottrell Boyce certainly realised, as he was one of the few practising Catholics present. 'I was expecting eulogies and rock music – it was a very straight Catholic mass. No recorded music, just hymns like "Star of the Sea" – until the coffin was leaving. Then there was "Atmosphere" by Joy Division.'

As Tony's jet-black coffin left the church there was applause and polite cheers from the crowd. Later, as guests gathered to talk and raise a glass, there was a clear indication of how Tony's persona had merged with the story people had seen on screen in *24 Hour Party People.*

Frank Cottrell Boyce: 'There was a PowerPoint thing projected on the wall with pictures and quotes from Tony – and more or less none of those quotes were actually from Tony. They were from the film. Seeing me quoted as Tony at his funeral was weird. I found it very odd that I'd done this Vulcan mind-meld with him.'

Some guests spoke to reporters outside the church. 'He was absolutely charming,' said Richard Madeley. 'He had utter belief in himself. There was no petty jealousy with him, which was unusual for someone working in television. He was just a very decent man.'

'Since Tony died, there have been an awful lot of public tributes,' Peter Saville added. 'I only wanted to say "Thank you" to him for what he did for me and to thank him for what he did on behalf of the city. We shared an opinion that time on Earth is short and is not about making a lot of wealth but about making a difference. Anthony Wilson made an enormous difference.'

And then Tony was truly gone. There were flowers and messages tied to railings next to what used to be The Haçienda.

The funeral cortège stopped briefly outside the spot where the club once stood.

Stopped. Just for a moment. And then moved on.

That's what you have to do isn't it? With help, of course. Yvette Livesey: 'There's people who you'd think would be there for you and haven't been. Other people who I never thought would be there have been stunning and ring me once a week to see if I'm all right. Tony would be very proud of them. He had some good friends.'

*   *   *   *

In October, *Control* was released. Most people agreed that *24 Hour Party People* had a ramshackle charm – the extent you succumbed to it was a fair indicator of how much you liked the film. *Control* tended to divide people into two camps: those who thought it European in its sensibility, gently ambiguous in its reasoning and haunting in its conclusion – and those who thought it boring, self conscious and a borderline puff piece for the benefits of suicide. *The Guardian* was in the former camp: 'Ian Curtis's great and terrible prophecy, the one about love tearing us apart, is followed through to its fulfilment in Anton Corbijn's glorious movie. It is the best film of the year: a tender, bleakly funny and superbly acted biopic of Curtis.'

'More sombre and grounded and less playful than the comic spins we've come to expect,' was *Time Out*'s take. 'Watching the film, one is left with a sense of Ian Curtis as the subject for an intense photographic study as much as a figure ripe for probing drama.'

The Times: 'Most rock biopics fail to convey the mixture of exhilaration and tedium that band life entails. But Corbijn has done his research during 30 years as a photographer, striking a realistic balance between farce and tragedy. Crucially, *Control* feels authentic in its concert footage, a detail very few music films get right.'

Not everyone was quite so keen. 'Goes on so long,' said *The*

Daily Telegraph, 'you're almost glad he put himself out of his misery when he did.' Charming.

Craig Parkinson's Tony Wilson is no comic turn. He is a slightly baffled, out-of-place character, grabbing onto the coat tails of Ian Curtis (Sam Riley) and Joy Division like a would-be-trendy sociology teacher encouraging a group of sixth formers. In *Control*, Wilson is one of the few who show kindness towards Samantha Morton's Deborah Curtis, a character so wallflower-ish she appears to have been transported from a 1960s kitchen-sink drama. Inevitably, Parkinson's Wilson was compared with Steve Coogan's.

'I was fully prepared for it,' says Craig today. 'It's another actor doing another portrayal of what a man was. Or wasn't. I know for a fact that Oli his son was very pleased. I thought if you please the family it's a job well done. I'm very proud. I don't think Tony was a buffoon. I think Tony's a huge influence on people who don't even know he was a huge influence. The first time you see Tony in the film he's on television. He had great authority on the telly – he was the ringmaster. I'm proud to have spent a few months with this character – someone I grew up with – you carry it around with you. I was very proud of him. Even though I didn't really know him, if that makes any sense.'

Back in the real world, there was work to do for Yvette Livesey: 'In the City was a month after he died. The people who came, came to say, "Hello" and "We're supporting you."'

Over the years Oasis, Radiohead, The Chemical Brothers, Coldplay, The Darkness and The Arctic Monkeys had all played In the City. Among the bands that year vying to be the next big thing were The Courteeners, Scouting for Girls, The Wombats and Get Cape Wear Cape Fly. Across Manchester – albeit whispered – there was another 'next thing' question being asked. A pointless, insensitive one. A debate. A need to know. Not quite a clamour, but certainly some heavy-handed cultural jostling.

Yvette Livesey: 'It's just terrible. I'm getting on with my life. Immediately after he died there was all this, "Who's going to be the next Tony Wilson in Manchester?" Horrible. There's an awful lot of egos out there with not a lot of intelligence. It just doesn't work that way. Tony was very good at managing crazy and intelligent people. Now there's no Tony in the middle to manage them, they've all gone off in their own crazy ways.'

A few weeks after In the City, Tony was awarded two posthumous Royal Television Society awards. He was given the judges' award for special achievement, the same award he described as a 'piece of shit' six years earlier. It was collected on the night by his children Oliver and Isabel. He was also named best presenter for his work on the *Politics Show*. Producer Michelle Mayman accepted it in his absence. 'I did the entry tape the morning of the day he died,' she says. 'I didn't know he'd died when I did it. I collected the one for best regional presenter. I seem to remember saying I was very proud to have worked with him and I told the story of how I was convinced I wouldn't be able to afford him when I wanted a presenter for the *Politics Show*. But Tony said, "Darling, I'll do it for nothing." He didn't do it for nothing but the sentiment was there. Lovely man. It makes me sad. They are easy words to trot out, but my little heart would go when he walked in the room. He was a little star. No... a great big star.'

Many of the people in the room at the awards ceremony had been present when Tony was so ungracious at the same event just a few years earlier. His electric, anarchic presence was sorely missed. But they, like the rest of Manchester and the wider musical society that had embraced Tony Wilson, were going to have to get by without their pop-culture big brother – the one who had shown them how to do it... and how *not* to do it.

In a questionnaire for the *Manchester Evening News*, in April 2000, Anthony Howard Wilson was asked what he would like to have as his epitaph. His answer was uncharacteristically brief. He managed it in just three words: 'Made a difference.'

There will be those who will tell of the many and varied ways that Tony Wilson made a lasting and telling difference – I'm going to list some of them in the final chapter. But just for a moment let's put aside the obvious – *So It Goes*, Sex Pistols, Factory Records, Joy Division, The Haçienda and so on – and focus on one that's less well known. The person who will tell us about it is not a musician or a writer or pundit; he's a professor of medical oncology.

'One thing changed directly as a result of Tony,' says Professor Robert Hawkins of the Christie hospital. 'A company was doing a trial to see if their drug was effective when added to the standard treatment. They read about Tony and funded the drug in the UK for any patient. They're not a charity – I suppose it highlighted the issue. That helped 50 or 60 people in this country. I told Tony about this before he died. He seemed pleased.'

SEVENTEEN
SIZE 40 MILLION BOOTS

There is a strange charm in the thoughts of a good legacy, or the hopes of an estate, which wondrously removes or at least alleviates the sorrow that men would otherwise feel for the death of friends
– MIGUEL DE CERVANTES

There won't be another Tony Wilson. That's not sentiment talking – there are very straightforward reasons why we won't see his like again. Technically, politically, *digitally* the world has changed. 2009 will be the year that Tony's world – or at least the world he represented – was switched off. If metaphors are your thing then look no further than the Winter Hill transmitter in Chorley, Lancashire.

Standing at more than a thousand feet, it provides the analogue television signal for Manchester, Lancashire, Cheshire and Liverpool, but also takes in the lower half of the Cumbria, a bit of North Wales and small slices of Staffordshire and Derbyshire. It's the region that makes no sense – the North West of England. When the analogue is switched off at the end of 2009, so is the idea of the North West. Because Granadaland defined the North West rather than the other way around, the switchover to digital means the dissolving of the concept of regionality and identity through a TV service and the removal of the platform Tony used to launch his career, his bands, his musical aspirations... *himself*.

'Tony would have gone, "It's great that the transmitter's being switched off. It'll be a much better signal, it's great that Granadaland is disappearing, it stinks of the 1960s. Let's move on,"' says Frank Cottrell Boyce. 'But he was the face of analogue. He was an analogue person. He lived in an analogue universe. He had an analogue haircut and analogue suit.'

Tony's Granada colleague Bob Greaves: 'That world has gone. It was good times. But good times don't last forever. There isn't room for someone like him. There aren't the bosses who would indulge someone like Tony. That world has disappeared. I can't think of anyone else like him. He was literally a one-off. They go for safety.'

There are no more music shows on Granada. There's no space for a jumped-up reporter to put bands on at the end of the news. There probably won't be any ITV regional news soon and the iconic – now half empty – Granada building on Quay Street, with its distinctive red lettering across the top is likely to be sold off.

David Liddiment, former head of entertainment and director of channels at ITV: 'The notion that a broadcaster on the scale of Granada would ever rise again is unrealistic. But there are other ways now that the Wilsons of today or tomorrow will find their voice – there's easy accessibility for making films or expressing yourself through the internet. Wilson was about breaking boundaries. He didn't want to recreate – that's boring. He wanted to find the next new thing. He was excited by what's coming. I don't accept that the Tony Wilsons of now won't have a voice. It's different. In some senses there are more opportunities than ever before. People who are good at telling stories or have passions that they have to communicate to people will find their way.'

Tony's own story – even without the television shows, the music, the club and the films – was as unusual as the man himself. Through him shone his mother's forceful personality mixed with the innate showmanship of his father – nearly half his wife's age. Sydney Wilson's sexuality was something that everybody knew of but was rarely talked about. It's easy to compartmentalise this as some typically repressive, 1950s guilty secret – but perhaps the Wilson-Knupfers were a little more enlightened than their contemporaries. They certainly operated a family unit that was unlike that of their neighbours with Mum, much younger gay dad and bachelor uncle all taking care of one child: Anthony Howard Wilson.

Then there was his Salford upbringing. Tony would consistently cite his it as a cornerstone of who he was. Although he and his parents maintained the business links with the city and Tony spent seven years commuting to De La Salle, there's something deliciously *Marple* about him. Tony's one-upmanship, slightly superior attitude, its gentle and easily-deflated pretension could also be found in the gravelly, not-*quite*-poshness of the south Manchester suburb where he spent most of his youth.

Don't get me wrong: I like Marple. I live there. Tony Wilson had Marple written all over him, but he rarely mentioned the place because Salford was what he aspired to. Remember what he told his friends and family in the Cross Keys pub in Eccles on his 18th birthday? 'I wish I had been born in a terraced slum down by the docks. So that I could experience it first hand.' He never did.

But Tony would change from Salford to Marple when it suited his purposes, even to the point of which name he preferred. Tony's son Oliver Wilson: 'It depends if he's in a "I'm a middle-class boy from Marple" mood or "I'm a working-class boy from Salford" mood – he's Tony or Anthony.'

No one who watched Tony's brief flirtation with print journalism could have been in any doubt that he was never really a serious newspaperman, nor did network current affairs suit his default mode of tipping up and busking it. But there is no shortage of people to tell you how kind, professional and nurturing Tony was to people who worked with him in television.

After Dark producer Sebastian Cody: 'We all know presenters – who are horrible human beings held together by their production teams – who are the nation's sweethearts. We've all got our own lists of those people. Tony's real nature was that he was a *mensch* and that came over. What he presented to people wasn't a blank screen. What he presented them with was, "Look

– this is Tony here, please define yourself against me." He would emphasise and irritate in equal proportions.'

Tony ended up a big fish in a small pool. Maybe he wasn't up to the job of network? Perhaps regional telly was his limit? Former *World in Action* editor Ray Fitzwalter: 'He ought to have been on a bigger stage – maybe he had too many interests. I wonder if anyone would have stabilised him, or if they could, he wouldn't have been Tony any more? Or it is the case that you can stabilise him sufficiently to get him to realise his abilities?'

Tony's former Granada colleague Don Jones: 'The wider telly world never clasped him to their bosom. He should have been doing *The South Bank Show*. He'd have been brilliant but they couldn't see it. In TV terms he never fulfilled his potential because he wasn't allowed to.'

Gordon Burns: 'He never knuckled down to any area of TV. He had all these other interests. You could say he never took his TV career seriously. He enjoyed the bits he had but he never said I want to do *this* in television. And he was mad. Totally off-the-wall mad.'

Tony's attitude to television was a typically contrary one. He loved – *loved* – being on screen. He didn't seem to care whether it was Channel 4, *Granada Reports, After Dark* or Channel M – as long as he was on the telly that was enough. If he had been drawn up the ladder to being on network TV all the time, he wouldn't have had the time or opportunity to be the person he was or pursue the interests that excited him. It's hard to imagine David Dimbleby, the host of *Question Time,* running a record label. Or indeed having a comedy film made about his chaotic off-screen life.

For the best example of Tony's attitude to his 'day job' it's perhaps best to turn to another man who also loves being on television. 'Tony used to revel in the fact that there was graffiti [outside his house] saying *Tony Wilson is a wanker*,' Richard Madeley told *Sky* magazine. 'I said, "How can you not mind coming out of your door and seeing that?" He said, "'Cos I am a wanker and you're a wanker too, 'cos you're on television. Anybody who chooses to do this for a living is a wanker." And he was absolutely right.'

In purely commercial terms, Tony's other interests could not have been counted as wild successes. Factory Records' financial profile was dismal. After Joy Division/New Order and Happy Mondays, probably the label's most successful records were by Section 25 – but they were largely unknown to the general public. That left just a swathe of handsomely sleeved curios that would singularly fail to trouble chart compilers.

Musician Chris Lee, one-time member of Alberto y Lost Trios Paranoias: 'If you set yourself up as a member of the *avant garde*, you have to perpetually be at the forefront. A lot of the people Tony signed were wacky, weird and wonderful – that doesn't mean they were any good. Factory wouldn't have lasted more than a few years had it not been for Joy Division. Tony was Manchester's worst businessman. The enigma is that he's perceived of as this great success. Most of the success had very little to do with him: he just happened to be in the right place at the right time. Now perhaps we're getting to the negative image of the man. I really do think he ripped off a lot of ideas. But that's what movement is built on. I think he genuinely thought they *were* his ideas. I'd be in rooms with him when somebody would say something. Twenty minutes later he'd say it and it'd be hailed as "*Marvellous* idea, Tony."'

Factory's aesthetic and anti-philosophy philosophy was a template for doing things in a very particular, very Mancunian, very *Factory-esque* way. Designer Peter Saville: 'For the latter half of the 20th century Manchester has had a rather cool image, brokered around contemporary pop culture. That is the legacy of Factory and The Haçienda. By making that statement here and showing you could change your reality instead of going somewhere else, that inspired and informed other people to do the same thing. The whole club and bar culture, the whole 1980s/'90s cultural character of Manchester was defined by this sort of re-evaluation of pop in this industrial city. It gave people a pathway to then do their own projects and their own ideas.'

Many Factory acts went on to success – James and Orchestral Manoeuvres in the Dark being the most notable examples. Sitting in his rambling recording studio off Liverpool's Lark Lane, OMD's Andy McCluskey ponders what motivated the man who kick-started his career by releasing the band's single and helping them to get a big record deal: 'Part of the continuing allure is that different people have different handles on Tony. He certainly wasn't a buffoon. He wasn't a very good businessman. He was a catalyst. He wasn't particularly good at *anything*... apart from tying this thing to that thing, I'd respectfully suggest.

'He could make things *work* and would derive pleasure from that. Somewhat of a magpie. You wonder if he wasn't confident in himself that he was good enough at one thing, so he spread himself around. He had the overview. We all needed him. But probably he needed all of us too. He was lovely, charming, open and sweet and he did something for me that I can't imagine anyone else doing. The myth, legend and mystery – particularly around Ian Curtis and Joy Division and New Order – perhaps give Factory a credibility and a kudos beyond what they deserve. I can only say lovely things about Tony. He was wonderful and his company made the most selfless gesture imaginable.'

A recurring theme through all the interviews conducted for this book is Tony's attitude to money – particularly his attitude to money that *wasn't technically his*. If Ian Curtis hadn't died, Tony would probably never have made enough money to be careless with in the first place. 'I think he would have been quite happy with the label selling two thousand copies of each album,' says A Certain Ratio's Martin Moscrop. 'It was totally by accident that Joy Division took off. He loved the music but he didn't know they were going to take off. When Ian died they didn't know that New Order were going to get up there and do it again. Happy Mondays were this crappy little Manc band that he loved... they were never going to be commercial. Look what happened to them. So the success was totally by accident, not steered by Tony at all. Tony would have been happy with his label lasting 15 years, just putting out records by the left-field artists like Cabaret Voltaire that he so loved. Just having an underground label and not having to worry about pressing an extra 30,000 copies. He did like the success, but it was by accident. It wasn't orchestrated.'

'I think the great thing about Tony was that he used to put everything down to praxis,' Joy Division and New Order drummer Stephen Morris told BBC News at the time of Tony's death. 'We'll just go ahead and do it, steamroll along and afterwards we'll think about why we did it in the first place. It was that great sense of enthusiasm that let us put up with him for all those years.'

Tony Wilson always said it was better to make history rather than money. In March 2008 his will was published, revealing he left an estate valued at £484,747 after tax. Looks reasonable, until you realise it includes the value of the Deansgate loft, which was up for sale at one point for £1.8 million. Yvette Livesey was left the proceeds from the loft and Tony's share of six businesses, which included Livesey/Wilson Ideas Management. The remainder of the estate was left to his children Oliver and Isabel.

But Tony's legacy was never going to be measured in terms of money. There are those who point to the confidence found in Manchester in recent years and believe they know where it came from. 'Manchester's trendiness over the last 25 years can be traced back quite plainly to The Factory and The Haçienda,' says Peter Saville. 'There have been other groups from here – Oasis have come from here, Take That have come from here – but the important thing about Factory and Joy Division and New Order and the Mondays and obviously The Haçienda – they were actually *here*. They claimed Manchester as their place of origin and their place of activity. It didn't start here and go somewhere else – it started here stayed here and influenced here. It was the major export over the last 25 years.'

This image of Tony and his fellow Factory 'workers' as the

saviours of Manchester and its pop culture is a common one. Did they do extraordinary things? Absolutely. Is the legacy to there to see the moment you leave the city's shiny, cosmopolitan train station? Yes. Go to any regional city in Britain and they all look like Manchester now. But the ballyhoo about the wonders of the new Manchester has often been at the expense of the old Manchester.

Everything was shit until Tony Wilson and friends came along and saved us. The music, the nightlife, the venues, the architecture, the ambition, the coffee. Sorry, darlings... *all shit*. That's not the old Manchester I recognise or remember. This is a city that has throbbed with clubs, gangs, beer houses, beat groups, punks and poseurs long before Factory and The Haçienda – a nocturnal economy that has fizzed with aspiration, glamour and magnetic seediness from all shades of the spectrum for 200 years.

What Tony Wilson provided was a focal point, doling out encouragement, ideas, bluff and bluster – whether or not it was deserved or asked for. Without him, there is something of the heritage park about the Manchester music scene. There's even an annual Tony Wilson Experience now: 24 hours of 'chain-chatting and binge-thinking' where musicians, writers and creative types can get pissed and heckled – usually in that order – in Tony's name. The likes of Steve Coogan, Irvine Walsh and Peter Saville featured on talking-head panels in the first year, but the most entertaining moment was when Stella Grundy, former singer with local dance-rock act Intastella, got into a row with Shaun Ryder and Bez of Happy Mondays that ended in pitchers of water being chucked and security being called. It's supposed to be an annual event but with a Wilson-esque flourish, 2009's was cancelled – because there wasn't time to organise it.

Elsewhere though, it's all getting a bit... chicken in the basket. You can go to a wine bar and pay for An Evening With Peter Hook or Bez (with meal). There are rock history exhibitions in the museums. You can pick up a tourist map from the local libraries that will show you where The Ting Tings rehearsed and where Tony Wilson went to school – I can hold my hand up here, because I made that last one. We're all at it. I think Tony Wilson would have been aghast. Here was a man who made a feature out of wilful bridge-burning, snubbing what had gone before in favour of the future, even if the future wasn't worthy of his patronage. It would be a shame if Manchester's best known export turns out to be nostalgia. There's a word for a city that lives in its cultural past – that word is 'Liverpool'.

The 2002 revolution never came according to Tony's 13-year cycle – Teddy Boys (1950) Beatles (1963), punk (1976) and acid house (1989) – but it didn't stop him hoping. 'I've had to hold my hands up and say I was utterly wrong. If I thought all the revolutions and changes and new surges of creativity were over, I'd probably slit my throat – or I'd slit my throat if it happened and I missed out on it. What I expected in the early 2000s was British kids to absorb nu metal, churn it out with British irony and take the world by storm. That didn't happen.'

Such was Tony's skill at articulating the wonders of rock'n'roll that he became synonymous with it to a greater extent than those who actually made it. He talked the talk and others were supposed to be walking the walk, but as *24 Hour Party People* showed, Tony was often far more interesting than the musicians he represented. He was omnipresent; you could be forgiven for thinking that he had invented *everything*.

DJ and writer Dave Haslam: 'I hear Tony being described as a club promoter. He wasn't a club promoter. I hear Tony being described as, "Wasn't Tony clever the way he helped instigate indie-dance music and the way he helped bring house music to Britain?" I understand he had a part to play in the process but it wasn't as the instigator. Even though he's one of the most celebrated people I've shared space with, he actually failed. Or at least wasted golden opportunities. Maybe that's what it's like when you're successful.

'Tony was never full of regret as far as I know. That's one of the paradoxes. Look at the music industry – led by a bunch of morons, shadows compared to Tony. He never thought he'd made mistakes. That's how he was right to the end. He believed in it all. For all the bluster and the ambition and the conceitedness and the bullying that were parts of Tony's personality, there was also a man very interested in ideas, very interested in how culture works, very restless, very challenging, very inspiring and amusing. If it hadn't been for Tony I probably wouldn't have felt confident that you can be interested in ideas and culture and still be off your head in a nightclub late at night. That the two worlds aren't incompatible. If only more people thought like that. That was a part of Tony's personality that I felt energised by.'

Just as he did at De La Salle as a teenager, in later life Tony managed to avoid performing or creating in a traditional sense in favour of enthusing. The Manchester music scene is a self-supporting, complex structure that has a higher regard for itself than you find elsewhere in the country, generating a higher number of films, documentaries and books. Even the London scene looks shy and retiring by comparison. Bands who are serious about 'making it' flock from all over the country to Manchester rather than the capital. It's an interconnected series of well-travelled routes, favoured stop-offs and regular pick-ups like a like a vast train set – and Tony Wilson became its pop culture controller, making the right connections and keeping the juice flowing. Without him, the trains now seem to have difficulty getting started – or just go round and round.

Photographer Kevin Cummins: 'I think a lot of people got so used to having Tony around. He was the catalyst for things in Manchester. Suddenly there's this huge vacuum there and people don't know how to get round it, because you always went through him. Suddenly they realised he was a big loss. Tony touched a lot of people's lives. He was a dream-maker and he helped a lot of people fulfil their dreams. No matter how foolish he may have seemed he gave people something to look forward to. He made people believe in themselves because he believed in them. You just have to be the man who says, "You're great and I believe in you" – and that's what he did.'

A Certain Ratio's Martin Moscrop: 'Tony used to annoy lots of people. Rob Gretton would get pissed off with Tony. *Everyone* would get pissed off with Tony. Everyone thought he was a knobhead. Until he died. Then people looked back at him and thought this guy wasn't a knobhead at all. He was just a really good guy. People used to take the piss out of him – the "wanker Wilson" thing – it's very true.'

Everyone is entitled to an opinion about Tony Wilson. I thought I would wait until now to offer mine. There's no more typical example of what Dave Haslam has called 'Tony's Children' than me. I grew up in south Manchester and Tony was my newsreader – the Nolans were very much ITV people; we were *Magpie* not *Blue Peter*, *Tiswas* not *Multi-Coloured Swap Shop*. I was 14 when *A Factory Sampler* came out and I bought a copy from Street's Ahead records in Altrincham. I was nearly 18 when The Haçienda opened and went every week from 1982 to 1985. I was 24 when acid house kicked in. Like Tony, I had no feeling for dance music and I swerved it in favour of more guitar-based fayre. There's loads of us, 'Tony's Children', practically a generation.

Where my experience differs slightly from the rest of the generation is that I ended up working at Granada Television, somehow became a producer for *Granada Reports,* made lots of music programmes for the company and found myself working in the same open plan office as Tony Wilson. I found him a bit baffling. Unless you talked football (I don't) he seemed unable to make small talk of any description. His dreadful mobile phone with its dreadful ring tone ('It's not Dido – it's Eminem!') would ring across the office with dreadful regularity. Then he would answer it and swear a lot. He seemed able to make everyone around him swear a lot too. It was infectious. Women who would normally speak like nuns would suddenly start 'cunt'-ing this and 'cunt'-ing that in his presence.

He was really tall, surprisingly broad and he seemed unable to keep his glasses from slipping to the end of his nose. All the better for glaring at you. I found him intimidating, to be frank. I interviewed him several times – the last was in December 2006, a few days before he recorded *The New Friday* and went into hospital. He was always good copy but would often play safe and say the same killer quotes over and over again. He preferred to quote others. He loved a good quote. He could string them together like slightly pretentious pearls; I don't know what he would have made of the contents of this book, but I'm sure he would have approved of the quotes at the head of each chapter.

'It was always someone else's words,' recalls Kevin Cummins about the Wilson way with a quote. 'It was almost like he didn't have the confidence to say it himself. He'd attribute things to people even if they hadn't actually said it in the first place. I remember walking to his car with him. When we got there was a big scratch down the side of it. He said, "Well, as Jimmy Savile said, His Majesty the general public paid for it, His Majesty the general public can do what the fuck they like with it."'

His Majesty the general public was greatly moved when Tony Wilson died. Here was a man who'd lived life at greater pace than many of the rock stars in his charge, had a fuck-off attitude to money and took bold chances with large chunks of it, who had stayed in a city that most people leave when the first royalty cheque appears. He also staged a heroic fight against a health service he believed in almost entirely for the benefit of those who would come after him because his own fight was lost. Manchester was red raw when Tony Wilson died. But this is the same man who was essentially unemployed before his Indian summer because he seen as yesterday's man.

'We underestimated him when he was alive,' says Frank Cottrell Boyce. 'It's time to start overestimating him. I thought he was a clown, a windbag, I thought he was pretentious when he was alive. Now that he's dead I can see that he was unstintingly generous, fantastically energetic, visionary, unembarrassable and cool. I think he was great.'

In the past, people would shout at Tony Wilson in the streets of Manchester, informing him that they thought he was a wanker. Now, the streets are his. In 2008 he was made an honorary freeman of the city of Manchester, the first person to receive the status posthumously. You get your name carved into a wall of honour at the town hall when you're made a freeman with a brief description of what you've done; Tony's was 'Broadcaster and Cultural Catalyst'. Not bad. Not the easiest thing to do, sum up Tony Wilson in few words.

'One day I was looking at the *Rochdale Observer*," remembers Tony's Granada colleague Rob McLoughlin. 'There was a picture of Tony handing out awards at a girls' school. The caption read: "Anthony H Wilson: TV presenter, entrepreneur, capitalist, Marxist and Christian." He'd obviously dictated it to the young reporter. In that mix was Tony.'

One of the keenest descriptions of Tony Wilson was by Happy Mondays' Paul Ryder: he believed Tony had 'Size 40 million boots' and the worry was who would fill them after he'd gone. 'He did have some big boots,' says Ryder today. 'I'm hoping there's some kid in a bedroom now in Salford, preparing a speech before a local band is about to come on at their school. He could be the next Tony. There's got to be someone. Salford's got to carry on that spirit. I'm sure there's someone out there slowly growing into those size 40 million boots.'

In the meantime, life without Anthony Howard Wilson – television presenter, record label boss, nightclub entrepreneur, professional pop culture enthusiast and a man who believed that you were very much entitled to an opinion, even though it was shit – continues. Many feel his loss, none more so than the woman who shared his life for 17 years.

Yvette Livesey: 'I get on with my life. I don't know what the future holds – but I'm quite interested. Tony was a huge part of my life. We were intertwined in so many ways. I am incredibly grateful for having met him because he changed my life in the sense that he made me believe in myself. I have my own life now, but I want to phone him ten times a day – because that's what we did – and talk to him. I have no one to replace that intellectual quality in my life. But because Tony isn't here, there are a lot of friends I've got much closer to. He was the most honest person I ever knew. He had his faults. He could be incredibly selfish – emotionally underdeveloped! But he was an incredibly good man.'

EIGHTEEN
CAST OF CHARACTERS

Here are the key players in the lives and times of Tony Wilson – and where they are now.

MARK ALDERTON
Former Up Front *researcher who went on to become head of news at Granada. He was in charge the day Tony swore twice during a bulletin. He's now a media consultant in reputational management and crisis communications. 'It was never dull with Tony Wilson. People fall into two camps. You either liked him or you loathed him. I liked him.'*

CHRIS BATTEN
Bass player with Enter Shikari, the last band to benefit from Tony's patronage. Now two albums into their career.

PETER BERRY
The ex-Granada researcher and news editor is now a team leader in the media department of Edge Hill University, Lancashire. 'I miss the old days. But I wouldn't want to be back there now. The fun's gone out of it. You go back into the newsroom now and everyone looks like an extra from a Kraftwerk concert glued to computer screens.'

FRANK COTTRELL BOYCE

The man who created Tony's on-screen persona with his script for 24 Hour Party People *is now a children's writer. 'We were very un-dewy-eyed about Tony when he was alive. So it's right that we get dewy-eyed now.'*

GORDON BURNS

Tony's friend and colleague at Granada went on to present TV quiz The Krypton Factor *for 17 years. He now works at the BBC as the presenter of* North West Tonight, *the rival show to* Granada Reports. *'There's a big picture of Tony on the outside of the BBC building,' he says. 'It makes me gulp every time I look at it. I come in the back way so I don't have to see it.'*

LARRY CASSIDY

Still touring and recording with Factory band Section 25 with his brother Vin.

VIN CASSIDY

In 2008, Vin and Larry joined forces with Peter Hook to tour a set of Section 25/Joy Division songs. The venture is known in some circles, rather charmingly, as Hooktion 25. 'Peter seems keen to work with us. He still likes doing it... strutting his stuff, treading the boards. And being paid for it.'

SEBASTIAN CODY

The producer of After Dark *is now an associate fellow of the Rothermere American Institute at the University of Oxford and special advisor to the director of the International Institute for Applied Systems Analysis (IIASA) an international science research organisation. Cody knew nothing about Tony's music background when he worked with him in the 1980s. He now has a music career of his own: Sebastian was behind the million-selling 2008 album* Chant: Music for Paradise *by The Cistercian Monks of Stift Heiligenkreuz.*

KIERON COLLINS

Kieron was head of regional programmes at Granada when Tony returned. He is now an executive producer at the BBC and has recently completed a series for BBC2 that aimed to find Britain's best young public speakers.

STEVE COOGAN

The man who played Tony in 24 Hour Party People *has since appeared in a slew of Hollywood films. Recently toured the UK with a stand-up show and was booed in Liverpool.*

KEVIN CUMMINS

The former De La Salle schoolboy became a photographer famed for his pictures of Manchester musicians and has published a book compiling these images called Manchester – Looking for the Light through the Pouring Rain. *'I am very grateful to Tony. He made you feel good about yourself. I've had a great career and I couldn't have done it without him. He did it with all his bands – even if they were crap he'd tell you they were great and made them feel good about themselves.'*

IAN CURTIS

The late Joy Division singer and subject of the film Control *died by his own hand in 1980. In 2008 his memorial stone was stolen from Macclesfield cemetery. It read 'Love Will Tear Us Apart'.*

HOWARD DEVOTO

The lead singer of Buzzcocks and Magazine, and the man who organised the famed Sex Pistols' gig at Manchester's Lesser Free Trade Hall, reformed Magazine in 2009.

PAT DILIBERO

Tony's cousin now lives in Marple Bridge, Stockport, close to the Wilsons' family home.

ALAN ERASMUS

The actor turned Factory Records partner now lives in Wales.

JUDY FINNIGAN

Tony's colleague on Granada Reports *and neighbour in Withington, south Manchester. In May 2009 it was announced that the digital show she presented on* Watch TV *with husband Richard Madeley was to be dropped.*

RAY FITZWALTER

The former editor of World in Action *and independent programme maker has written a book about the decline of Granada and ITV called* The Dream That Died. *Now a visiting professor at Salford University.*

BOB GREAVES

*The ex-*Granada Reports *presenter is now retired. 'What do I do now? Social and domestic. Quite happy. I worked for 50 years. No one should work for more than 50 years.'*

PROFESSOR ROBERT HAWKINS

Director of medical oncology at Christie Hospital. In February 2009 it was announced that Sutent – the drug that Tony was refused by the NHS – would be made available in Manchester.

MARTIN HANNETT

The Factory producer died in 1991. His grave now has a headstone thanks to a campaign led by Tony's ex-wife Lindsay Reade.

DAVE HASLAM

The former NME writer and Haçienda DJ is now an author and has his own show on XFM Manchester. 'I absolutely liked him – absolutely,' he says of Tony Wilson. 'Especially on the occasions when he'd just relax and not try too hard to be Tony Wilson.'

ALAN HEMPSALL

Lead singer of Factory band Crispy Ambulance. 'Tony hated our name. He said he'd never sign another band with a stupid name. Then he signed a band called Thick Pigeon.'

PETER HOOK

The Joy Division and New Order bassist is now a DJ for hire. He also does spoken word events and appeared at Orlando's cafe bar in Chorlton, Manchester in 2008 for 'An Evening with Peter Hook' at £27 a head (with food) or £22 (without).

KATHLEEN HOUGHTON

Communications director for Elevate, the recipient of Tony's imagineering for east Lancashire, now known as Pennine Lancashire.

KONNIE HUQ

Konnie left Blue Peter *in 2008 – the programme's longest-serving female presenter. 'It seems like a dream that I knew Tony. When you watch* Control *and* 24 Hour Party People *– you realise those are films about him.'*

DON JONES

Tony's former TV researcher became head of sport at Granada. He's now executive producer at LFCTV – the Liverpool team's own TV channel.

GEOFF KNUPFER

After a distinguished career as a police detective and Special Branch officer, Tony's cousin is now a consultant forensic scientist, heavily involved with the Disappeared, the ongoing search for people killed by the IRA and INLA whose bodies have never been found. Geoff took Moors Murderer Myra Hyndley's confession over the killings of Keith Bennett and Pauline Reade. In 1987 Geoff and officers from Greater Manchester Police were searching for their bodies on a wind-

whipped Saddleworth Moor. 'This TV journalist approached me in the middle of the moor, whispered, "Tony says hi" and walked off.'

TADEUSZ KASA

Tony Wilson's school friend at De La Salle in Salford now lives in London. 'I'm a graphic designer. If I'd stayed in touch with Tony I could have been Factory's graphic designer– Peter Saville might have been nothing! Instead, I worked for sensible companies.'

HOWARD KINGSTON

The former lead singer of Gentlemen – the band that nearly came to blows with the Sex Pistols on So It Goes *– now lives in Montana, USA. He's an actor and singer. 'I wouldn't want to go back to Manchester. Too grey. I'm an American now.'*

CHRIS LEE

Also known as CP Lee, the man who organised Tony's stag night is now an author and lecturer and still plays music with the Salford Sheiks.

DAVID LIDDIMENT

Tony's old boss at ITV is now an independent TV producer and is also involved with The Old Vic theatre and the BBC Trust.

YVETTE LIVESEY

Tony's partner of 17 years lives in Manchester and East Lancashire – now known as Pennine Lancashire, thanks to them. She still runs the In The City festival, which she created in 1991.

RICHARD MADELEY

The man on the receiving end of Tony's advice that everyone who appears on TV is a wanker has said he believes his onscreen partnership with wife Judy Finnigan is close to its end. 'I think we both feel we have done pretty much all we can do as a partnership in terms of the talk shows,' he told the BBC in March 2009. 'It has been over 20 years doing the same kind of thing and there are tantalising possibilities in terms of solo projects or doing one-off projects together. I am not saying we will never work together again – I'm sure we will.'

MICHELLE MAYMAN
Now head of the North West arm of the BBC's Inside Out *series. The BBC is getting ready to move out of Oxford Road to Media City, the new super-site in Salford. Some London departments have already moved there. 'The BBC moving from London to Salford? Tony would have loved that.'*

PETER MCNAMARA
Tony's school friend is now a virtual school head teacher for looked-after children in Salford, providing online mentoring for teenagers who have been in care. 'We try to improve outcomes for children in care – education is a route out.'

ANDY MCCLUSKEY
The Orchestral Manoeuvres in the Dark singer has reformed the group with Paul Humphreys. 'For the last 30 years people have asked me, "How do you make it in the music industry?" I say, "Don't fucking ask me. I was leaning on the back door, somebody opened it and I fell in."'

ROB MCLOUGHLIN
Tony's colleague in the Granada newsroom during the 1980s and executive producer of The Tube *radio show. 'I'm a broadcaster and a businessman,' he says today. 'I'm doing what Tony did.'*

LUCY MEACOCK
The presenter of Granada Reports *and now also a newsreader on ITN.*

BRUCE MITCHELL
Tony's friend is still drummer with The Durutti Column.

MARTIN MOSCROP
Now touring and recording with a revitalised A Certain Ratio.

DESSIE NOONAN
The former Manchester nightclub security enforcer was stabbed and killed in 2005, just days before the scheduled screening of a documentary by Donal MacIntyre about his life of crime.

EAMONN O'NEAL
The former executive producer at Granada is now a radio presenter and runs an independent TV production company with his stepson, actor Chris Bisson. 'We mourn the loss of the world Tony inhabited. There won't be another Tony Wilson. He was very generous with his talent and had a finger in every pie. Some of those fingers got burnt...'

STEVE PANTER
Former crime reporter on the Manchester Evening News. *Now lectures in journalism at Salford University.*

GRAEME PARK
Graeme DJ'd at The Haçienda for nearly ten years. '2009 is my 25th anniversary as a DJ. That's another excuse for a tour. I'm also a university lecturer. You can't put a price on bringing up stories about Tony Wilson during a lecture.'

CRAIG PARKINSON
The actor who played Tony in Control *has since filmed a drama about northern soul. 'Am I happy with my portrayal of Tony Wilson? Yes, I am happy. His son was happy with it – that's where it ends for me.'*

LINDSAY READE

Tony's first wife has co-written a book about Joy Division's Ian Curtis. Now in a relationship with Tosh Ryan, creator of Rabid Records.

VINI REILLY

Still recording and touring as The Durutti Column.

TOSH RYAN

The man behind Rabid Records – some say it was the model for Factory – now lives in Anglesey, North Wales.

PAUL RYDER

The founder member of Happy Mondays formed Big Arm in 2006. He now lives in California.

SHAUN RYDER

The Happy Mondays' singer is still estranged from brother Paul. In February 2009 he had a cameo appearance on TV show Shameless. 'I don't really like doing owt like that,' he told the Daily Mirror. 'But the part was cool because I didn't have to speak or anything. I tried, I can't do it.'

PETER SAVILLE

In 2004 the Factory co-founder was made creative director of the city of Manchester and led a rebranding exercise named 'Manchester – original modern'. In 2009 he collaborated with OMD's Andy McCluskey on an art installation called The Energy Suite, *based on images from five power stations.*

CHRIS SIEVEY

Former Rabid Records employee and creator of Frank Sidebottom. Work is currently underway on a film of Frank's life. 'If I live till I'm 104 I'd do about four per cent of the things I want to do.'

YOU'RE ENTITLED TO AN OPINION...

MAX STEINBERG
Chief executive of regeneration organisation Elevate. 'Tony's simple idea of Pennine Lancashire has caught fire. It's now the kernel for the transformation of the entire area.'

BERNARD SUMNER
The Joy Division guitarist and New Order singer has been recording with a new project, Bad Lieutenant.

PETER TROLLOPE
The former crime reporter on the Liverpool Post & Echo *is now a producer at the BBC.*

HILARY WILSON
Tony's second wife still lives in Didsbury, south Manchester, close to the former of site of the Factory 'offices' on Palatine Road.

ISABEL WILSON
Tony's daughter is at Cambridge University.

OLIVER WILSON
Tony's son is now a music promoter based in London. In March 2009 he presented a TV piece for the BBC's Inside Out *programme about drug availability on the NHS.*

JENNY WINSTONE
The last person to present a TV show with Tony Wilson is still involved in the industry as a freelance researcher. 'Anything to avoid reality,' she says.

DICK WITTS
The musician and former Granada presenter is now a music lecturer at Edinburgh University.

REFERENCES

I'd recommend the following books for more on some of the people and events involved in the lives and times of Tony Wilson:

Life With My Sister Madonna – Christopher Ciccone
Touching From A Distance – Deborah Curtis
The Dream That Died – Ray Fitzwalter
1 Top Class Manager – Rob Gretton/Lesley Gretton
Manchester England – Dave Haslam
Shake, Rattle and Rain – CP Lee
And Finally... The News From ITN – Richard Lindley
Richard and Judy: The Autobiography – Richard Madeley and
    Judy Finnigan
Bernard Sumner: Confusion – David Nolan
I Swear I Was There: The Gig That Changed the World –
    David Nolan
Gang War: The Inside Story of the Manchester Gangs – Peter
    Walsh
Hallelujah! – John Warburton
24 Hour Party People – Tony Wilson
Mersey: The River That Changed The World – Ian Wray/Colin
    McPherson

And finally, should you wish to develop a *Wilson-esque* persona...
The New Penguin Dictionary of Quotations – Editor:
    Robert Andrews

NINETEEN
JUST THE FACS

THE FACTORY CATALOGUE

Factory's cataloging system was almost an extension of Tony Wilson's personality – posters, records, dental bills and even Tony's funeral form part of this pop culture collage. For more about all things Factory, go to www.cerysmaticfactory.info
Many thanks to Steven Hankinson and John Cooper.

FACTORY COMMUNICATIONS LIMITED

FAC 1: The Factory (event/poster)
Gigs in May to June 1978 at The Factory club, including Joy Division, The Durutti Column, The Tiller Boys, Cabaret Voltaire, Jilted John, Big in Japan and Manicured Noise.

FAC 2: 'A Factory Sample' (single x 2)
First Factory record release with Joy Division, The Durutti Column, Cabaret Voltaire and John Dowie.

FAC 3: The Factory (event/poster)
Gigs at The Factory club, including Cabaret Voltaire, Joy Division and The Tiller Boys.

FAC 4: The Factory (event/poster)
Gigs at The Factory club, including The Distractions, Human League, Magazine, Manicured Noise and The Undertones.

FAC 5: A Certain Ratio – 'All Night Party' (single)
Debut ACR single.

FAC 6: Orchestral Manoeuvres in the Dark – 'Electricity' (single)
Debut OMD single.

FAC 7: Factory Notepaper (stationery)

Letterhead, envelopes and visiting cards.

FAC 8: Linder Sterling – Factory Egg Timer (concept)

Prototype-only, menstrual egg timer in the shape of an abacus.

FAC 9: Various Artists – The Factory Flick (event)

Film exhibition held at Scala Cinema, London September 1979 featuring footage of Joy Division, A Certain Ratio and Ludus.

FACT 10: Joy Division – *Unknown Pleasures* (album)

Debut album.

FACT 10+4: Posters

Promotion for Unknown Pleasures *along with A Certain Ratio, OMD, X-O-Dus and The Distractions, hence the '+4'.*

FAC 11: X-O-Dus: 'English Black Boys' (single)

Produced by Dennis Bovell.

FAC 12: The Distractions – 'Time Goes By So Slow' (single)

Debut single.

FAC 13: Joy Division – 'Transmission' (single)

FACT 14: The Durutti Column – *The Return of the Durutti Column* (album)

Debut Durutti Column album in sandpaper sleeve that damaged any album it was racked with.

FAC 15: Leigh Festival/Zoo Meets Factory Halfway (event/poster)

Festival in August 1979, featuring The Distractions, Echo and the Bunnymen, X-O-Dus, OMD, Elti-Fits, Crawling Chaos, Lori and the Chameleons, A Certain Ratio, The Teardrop Explodes and Joy Division.

FACT 16: A Certain Ratio – *The Graveyard and the Ballroom* (album)

Half-studio, half-live cassette album available in a variety of coloured plastic pouches.

FAC 17: Crawling Chaos – 'Sex Machine' (single)

FAC 18: Section 25 – 'Girls Don't Count' (single)

Produced by Ian Curtis and Rob Gretton.

FAC 19: John Dowie – 'It's Hard to be an Egg' (single)

White vinyl, 'egg-yolk' label, with a chicken feather in clear sleeve.

FAC 20: A Certain Ratio – Too Young to Know, Too Wild to Care (concept)

A film script with A Certain Ratio and The Distractions attempting various forms of terrorism around Manchester, including kidnapping Ian Curtis and blowing up Joy Division.

FAC 21: F logo (badge)

The logo for Fractured Music, Joy Division's publishing arm.

FAC 22: A Certain Ratio – 'Flight' (single)

FAC 23: Joy Division – 'Love Will Tear Us Apart' (single)

FACT 24: Various Artists – A *Factory Quartet* (album x 2)

2 albums x 4 Artists = 24, Durutti Column, Kevin Hewick, Blurt and Royal Family and the Poor.

FACT 25: Joy Division – *Closer* (album)

Second Joy Division album.

FAC 26: Durutti in Paris (event/poster)

Cancelled Durutti Column gig. Only seven posters printed.

FAC 27: Sex Machine Alternative Sleeve (concept)

Cancelled Peter Saville/Rob Gretton 'revenge programme' for alternative FAC 17 sleeve.

FAC 28: Joy Division – 'Komakino' (flexi-single)

FAC 29: The Names – 'Night Shift' (single)

FACT 30: Sex Pistols – The Heyday (cassette)

Judy Vermorel interviews the Pistols. Comes in custom plastic pouch.

FAC 31: Minny Pops – 'Dolphin Spurt' (single)

FAC 32: Crispy Ambulance – 'Unsightly and Serene' (EP)

FAC 33: New Order – 'Ceremony' (single)

First New Order single.

FAC 34: ESG – 'You're No Good' (single)

FACT 35: A Certain Ratio – *To Each...* (album)

FAC 36: The US *Closer* campaign (advertisement)

Print advertising campaign for Joy Division's Closer *album in the United States, including* Billboard *and* Rolling Stone *ads.*

FACT 37: Joy Division – *Here are the Young Men* (video)

Live footage filmed at the Apollo, Manchester in October 1979 and Eindhoven, Netherlands in January 1980, plus 'Love Will Tear Us Apart' promo video.

FACT 38: A Certain Ratio – *Below the Canal* (video concept)

Never completed. Live and promo videos.

FAC 39: Tunnelvision – 'Watching the Hydroplanes' (single)

FACT 40: Joy Division – *Still* (album x 2)

FAC 41: Stockholm Monsters – 'Fairy Tales' (single)

FACT 42: A Certain Ratio – 'The Double 12"' (single x 2)

Combines FAC 22 'Flight' and FACUS 4 'Do The Du'.

FAC 43: Royal Family and the Poor – 'Art Dream Dominion' (single)

FACT 44: The Durutti Column – LC (album)

FACT 45: Section 25 – *Always Now* (album)

FACT 46: Various Artists – *The Video Circus* (video screenings)

Umbrella title given to previews of work in progress – forthcoming videos, etc.

FAC 47: Factory Anvil (logo)

Designed by Peter Saville and first used on FACT 45 (but also appeared on the 'Factory Game Plan' release schedule sticker)

FAC 48: Kevin Hewick – 'Ophelia's Drinking Song' (single)

FAC 49: Swamp Children – 'Little Voices' (single)

FACT 50: New Order – *Movement* (album)

FAC 51: The Haçienda (building)

FAC 51b: New Order – 'Christmas at the Haçienda' (flexidisc)

Given away at The Haçienda, Christmas Eve 1982.

FAC 52: A Certain Ratio – 'Waterline' (single)

FAC 53: New Order – 'Procession' (single)

Available in nine different sleeve colours.

FAC 54: Haçienda Construction (video)

Footage of the Haçienda being built.

FACT 55: A Certain Ratio: *Sextet* (album)

FACT 56: Various Artists – *A Factory Video* (video)

Promo video compilation including Section 25, New Order, A Certain Ratio, OMD, Cabaret Voltaire, The Durutti Column, The Names, Crispy Ambulance and Stockholm Monsters.

FAC 57: Minny Pops – 'Secret Story' (single)

FAC 58: Stockholm Monsters – 'Happy Ever After' (single)

FAC 59: 52nd Street – 'Look into my Eyes' (single)

FACT 60: The Wake – *Harmony* (album)

FAC 61: FCL vs Hannett (lawsuit)

A lawsuit brought by Martin Hannett, requesting that either Factory Communications be 'wound up', with all profits and capital distributed proportionately to each of the Factory directors, or that Hannett's shares in the company be bought out by FCL and/or the directors.

FAC 62: A Certain Ratio – 'Knife Slits Water' (single)

FAC 63: New Order – 'Temptation' (single)

FAC 64: The Durutti Column – 'I Get Along Without You Very Well' (single)

Female vocalist is Lindsay Reade, ex-wife of Tony Wilson.

FACT 65: A Certain Ratio – *I'd Like to See You Again* (album)

FAC 66: Section 25 – 'The Beast' (single)

FAC 67: Quando Quango – 'Go Exciting/Tingle' (single)

FAC 68: Section 25 – 'Back to Wonder' (single)

FAC 69: There is no FAC 69

FACT 70: Swamp Children – *So Hot* (album)

FAC 71: Various Artists – *A Factory Outing* (video)

All tracks live at The Haçienda Club, Manchester, thus '51/71' cover graphic, includes New Order, James, Stockholm Monsters, 52nd Street, A Certain Ratio, Swamp Children, The Durutti Column, The Wake, Section 25 and Quando Quango.

FAC 72: A Certain Ratio – 'I Need Someone Tonight' (single)

FAC 73: New Order – 'Blue Monday' (single)

FACT 74: The Durutti Column – *Another Setting* (album)

FACT 75: New Order – *Power, Corruption and Lies* (album)

FACT 76: Jazz Defektors – *The Movie* (video)

Eight-minute video; never released.

FACT 77: New Order – *Taras Shevchenko* (video)

Live at the Ukrainian National Home, New York, 18 November 1981.

FAC 78: James – 'Jimone' (single)

FAC 79: Quando Quango – 'Love Tempo' (single)

FACx 79: Christmas Present

Factory's first Christmas present; a set of ear–plugs.

FACT 80: Stockholm Monsters – *Alma Mater* (album)

FAC 81: Factory First International Congress/notepaper (event/stationery)

10 September 1983, 6.15pm, The Connaught Building, Manchester.

FAC 82: Cabaret Voltaire – 'Yashar' (single)

FAC 83: Haçienda 1 Year (event/poster)

The Haçienda's first birthday party, 20-21 May 1983.

FACT 84: The Durutti Column – *Without Mercy* (album)

FACT 85: Thick Pigeon – *Too Crazy Cowboys* (album)

FAC 86: Christmas 1983, The Haçienda

Pop-up Haçienda model kit.

FAC 87: Kalima – 'The Smiling Hour' (single)

FAC 88: The Wake – 'Talk About the Past' (single)

FACT 89: John Dowie – *Dowie* (video)

Live comedy video filmed at the Edinburgh Festival Fringe.

FACT 90: Section 25 – *From the Hip* (album)

FAC 91: Facsoft computer program (concept)

Never finished.

FAC 92: Marcel King – 'Reach for Love' (single)

FAC 93: New Order – 'Confusion' (single)

FAC 94: F-Dot (logo/badge)

FACT 95: Royal Family and the Poor – *The Project – Phase 1* (album)

FAC 96: Ad Infinitum – 'Telstar' (single)

Stockholm Monsters and Peter Hook.

FAC 97: Streetlife – 'Act on Instinct' (single)

FAC 98: Swing (hairdressers)

Salon located in the basement of The Haçienda.

FAC 99: Molar Reconstruction (event)

A dentist bill paid for by Factory for 'Robert Leo Gretton's mouth'.

FACT 100: New Order – *Low Life* (album)

FAC 101: (Tony Wilson's) lofts (concept)

Disused warehouses in Manchester. Tony Wilson wanted to convert them into flats. Never happened.

FAC 102: Quando Quango – 'Atom Rock' (single)

FAC 103: New Order – 'Thieves Like Us' (single)

FAC 104: *The Tube* from The Haçienda (event)

An edition of Channel 4's The Tube *partially broadcast from The Haçienda on January 27 1984, featuring Madonna's first UK performance.*

FACT 105: Biting Tongues – *Feverhouse – The Soundtrack* (album)

FACT 105: Howard Walmsley – *Feverhouse* (video)

FAC 106: Life – 'Tell Me' (single)

FAC 107: Stockholm Monsters – 'National Pastime' (single)

FAC 108: Section 25 – 'Looking From a Hilltop' (single)

FAC 109: Caroline Lavelle – 'Untitled and Undone' (single)

A 12" slated for release by the Durutti Column cellist. Not issued.

FACT 110: Quando Quango – *Pigs & Battleships* (album)

FAC 111: Shark Vegas – 'You Hurt Me' (single)

FAC 112: A Certain Ratio – 'Life's a Scream' (single)

FAC 113: The Wake – 'Of the Matter' (single)

FAC 114: The Durutti Column: 'Say What You Mean, Mean What You Say' (single)

FAC 115: Second Generation Notepaper (Stationery)

Onion skin paper with red and black thermographic printing.

FAC 116: Red Turns To… – 'Deep Sleep' (single)

FAC 117: Abecedarians – 'Smiling Monarchs' (single)

FAC 118: 52nd Street – 'Can't Afford (To Let You Go)' (single)

FAC 119: James – 'James' (single)

FAC 120: Factory Silhouette (Logo/Badge)

Two badges – crimson and black – 200 of each issued.

FAC 121: Riverside Exhibition & Performances (event/poster)

A series of London premieres and live performances over a five-day residence at the Riverside Studios, Hammersmith, London.

FAC 122: Life – 'Optimism' (single)

FAC 123: New Order – 'The Perfect Kiss' (single)

FAC 124: Streetlife – 'No More Silence' (single)

FACT 125: Various Artists – *Bessy Talks Turkey* (video)

Christmas video of Factory acts, discussed and presented by Claude Bessy. Short video clips and some of Bessy's work.

FAC 126: Alan Goes To Moscow (event/poster)

Alan Erasmus's trip to the USSR; Factory's first attempted move into the field of classical music.

FAC 127: Kalima – 'Four Songs' (EP)

FAC 128: A Certain Ratio – 'Wild Party' (single)

FAC 129: Happy Mondays – 'Delightful' (single)

Debut single.

FACT 130: The Wake – *Here Comes Everybody* (album)

FAC 131: 'It Isn't Only Low-Life Who Record For Factory' (poster)

Poster listing six future Factory releases.

FAC 132: Section 25 – 'Crazy Dancing' (single)

Unreleased single.

FAC 133: New Order – 'Subculture' (single)

Saville hated the remix and refused to design a sleeve for this release, thus the generic black sleeve.

FAC 134: Biting Tongues – 'Trouble Hand' (single)

FACT 135: A Certain Ratio – *The Old & The New* (album)

Compilation.

FAC 136: Factory Gaffer Tape (Item)

Custom sellotape.

FAC 137: Quando Quango – 'Genius' (single)

FACT 137: Various Artists – *Shorts* **(video)**
Promo videos from The Durutti Column, Stockholm Monsters, The Wake, Royal Family & The Poor, Section 25, Jazz Defektors, Quando Quango, 52nd Street and New Order.

FAC 138: James – *Village Fire, Five Offerings From...* **(EP)**
Combines the two earlier James 7" singles FAC 78 and FAC 113.

FAC 139: Royal Family and the Poor – 'We Love the Moon' (single)
Picture disc single.

FACT 140: Royal Family and the Poor – *The Project – Phase 2* **(album)**

FAC 141: Third Generation Logo (Stationery)
Waxed white paper, envelopes, visiting cards and additional stationery with thermographic black printing and embossed logo. Designed by Peter Saville.

FAC 142: Happy Mondays – 'Freaky Dancing' (single)

FAC 143: New Order – 'Shellshock' (single)

FACT 144: The Durutti Column – *Domo Arigato* **(album)**
Factory's first CD release.

FAC 145: Christmas 1985 (XMAS)
Cardboard (non-playable) "CD" in sleeve.

FAC 146: Stockholm Monsters – 'Party Line' (single)

FAC 147: Kalima – 'Whispered Words' (single)

FAC 148: Styal Mill Bucket (sponsorship)
A watermill blade/bucket donated to a rebuilt mill in Cheshire with plaque.

FAC 149: Little Big Band – *First Project* **(album)**
Aborted album.

FACT 150: New Order – *Brotherhood* **(album)**

FAC 151: Festival of the 10th Summer (event/posters/merchandise)
A festival celebrating 10 years of punk, organised by Factory, 12–20 July 1986.

FAC 152: 'With Love From Manchester' (t-shirt)
Produced for a New Order benefit gig at the Royal Court Theatre in Liverpool, 8 February 1986, in aid of Militant Tendency.

FAC 153: New Order – 'State of the Nation' (single)

FACD 154: The Durutti Column – *Circuses & Bread* **(album)**

FACT 155: Kalima – *Night Time Shadows* **(album)**

FAC 156: Quando Quango – 'Bad Blood' (single)
A 12" that was never released, because the band had split up.

FAC 157: Section 25 – 'Bad News Week' (single)

FAC 158: Anna Domino – 'Summer' (single)

Licensed from Les Disques Du Crepuscule (TWI 641).

FAC 159: Fac Facts (book)

Sent out to retailers and distributors. Included short band bios and discographies.

FACT 160: Section 25 – *Love and Hate* (album)

FAC 161: Out Promotion/Dave & Nicki (contract)

Refers to a deal with London-based agency Out Promotion, run by Nicki Kefalas.

FAC 162: The Railway Children – 'A Gentle Sound' (single)

FAC 163: New Order – 'Bizarre Love Triangle' (single)

FACT 164: The Durutti Column – *Valuable Passages* (album x 2)

Compilation for US release.

FACT 165: Anna Domino – *Anna Domino* (album)

Licensed from Les Disques Du Crepuscule (TWI 600).

FACT 166: A Certain Ratio – *Force* (album)

Final ACR Factory album.

FAC 167: The Railway Children – 'Brighter' (single)

FAC 168: A Certain Ratio – 'Mickey Way The Candy Bar' (single)

FAC 169: Pleasure Crew – 'I Could Be So Good For You' (single)

FACT 170: Happy Mondays: *Squirrel and G-man...* (album)

Produced by John Cale.

FAC 171: White Columns NY (event)

US release celebration of FACT 150 with a video/sculpture/installation Compact designed by Peter Saville.

FAC 172: The Railway Children – *Overseas* (album)

Unreleased singles collection. Refers to the remixed version of FACT 185 that was released by Virgin America in November 1987.

FAC 173: New Order – *Bizarre Love Triangle* (video)

Shot by Robert Longo.

FAC 174: The Durutti Column – 'Valuable' Press Pack (item)

Clear vinyl press pack for US release of FACT 164, consisting of press clippings, band biog and US tour dates.

FAC 175: Christmas Gift 1986 (XMAS)

'Origami' Factory logo and Thick Pigeon cassette.

FAC 176: Happy Mondays – 'Tart Tart' (single)

FACT 177: New Order – *Pumped Full of Drugs* (video)

Recorded at the Shinjuku Kosei Nenkin Hall, Tokyo, Japan.

FAC 178: The Wake – 'Something That No One Else Could Bring' (single)

YOU'RE ENTITLED TO AN OPINION...

FAC 179: Miaow – 'When It All Comes Down' (single)

FACT 180: Various Artists – *Factory Instore Tape No.1* (video)

Promo videos.

FACT 181: Bailey Brothers – *Mad Fuckers!* (film)

Bailey Brothers (Keith Jobling and Phil Shotton) 'youth exploitation' movie. Production started July 1987 and was aborted in 1992. Tony Wilson even went to Hollywood (see FAC 221) to raise money for the film.

FAC 182: The Hood – 'Salvation' / Jumpin' Jesus – 'You Can't Blackmail Jesus' (single)

Licensed from Les Disques Du Crepuscule (TWI 823) who never released the 12".

FAC 183: New Order – 'True Faith' (single)

FAC 184: The Durutti Column – 'The City of Our Lady' (single)

FACT 185: The Railway Children – *Reunion Wilderness* (album)

FACT 186: Various Artists – Festival of the 10th Summer (album and video)

Commemorating the FAC 151 G-Mex festival. Never released due to publishing problems with some of the non-Factory bands' labels.

FAC 187: Kalima – 'Weird Feelings' (single)

FAC 188: Biting Tongues – 'Compressor' (single)

FAC 189: Miaow – 'Break The Code' (single)

FACT 190: Wim Mertens – *Educes Me* (album)

Licensed from Les Disques Du Crepuscule (TWI 808).

FAC 191: The Haçienda Cat (cat)

FAC 192: Happy Mondays – '24 Hour Party People' (single)

FAC 193: New Order – 'Touched by the Hand of God' (single)

To accompany the single, 30 Adidas Aztec Maya soccer balls were made with the TBTHOG graphic design printed on them, inspired by Diego Maradona and his 'hand of God' goal.

FAC 194: The Durutti Column – 'When The World' (single)

FACT 195: Wim Mertens and Glenn Branca – *The Belly of an Architect* (Original Soundtrack) (album)

FAC 196: Meat Mouth – 'Meat Mouth is Murder' (single)

FAC 197: Fadela – 'N'Sel Fik' (single)

Licensed from Attitude Records.

FAC 198: Vermorel – 'Stereo/Porno' (single)

Labels state "Specially commissioned for the BPI awards 1988."

FAC 199: Vermorel – Bums for BPI (poster)

Part of Fred and Judy Vermorel's tactical campaign against the BPI (British Phonographic Industry).

FACT 200: New Order – *Substance* (album x 2)

Singles compilation.

FAC 201: Dry (bar)

Bar at 28–30 Oldham Street, Manchester, opened July 1989. Its official name is 'FAC 201'.

FAC 202: Dream Flight Balloons (sponsorship)

A British Airways charity event in London's Hyde Park.

FAC 203: '12 Inches of New Order' (item)

Factory promotional gift ruler.

FACT 204: The Durutti Column – *The Guitar and Other Machines* (album)

FACT 205: Jazz Defektors – *Jazz Defektors* (album)

FACT 206: Kalima – Kalima! (album)

FACD 207: Little Big Band: 'Little Big Band' (EP)

FAC 207 *number also allocated to unrealised Little Big Band: 'Digital Buskingomo video' 1/88.*

FAC 208: Disorder Post G-Mex Haçienda Party (event)

17 December 1988. Party after New Order's and Happy Mondays' gig at G-Mex.

FAC 209: Happy Mondays – Film Shoot (event)

Shootings of the 'Wrote For Luck' and 'W.F.L.' videos, at Legends Disco, Manchester, 27 October 1988.

FACT 210: Cath Carroll – *England Made Me* (album)

Number also allocated to a MIAOW LP titled Priceless Innuendos, *which was recorded but never released.*

FAC 211: Wired Joy Division feature (video)

An 18-minute Channel 4 TV documentary, broadcast 1 July 1988.

FAC 212: Happy Mondays – 'Wrote For Luck' (single)

FAC 213: Joy Division – 'Atmosphere' (single)

FAC 214: The Durutti Column – 'The Guitar and Other Marketing Devices' (flexidisc)

A free promo record containing excerpts from FACT 204.

FAC 215: Haçienda House Wine (White) 'Vin D'Usine Blanc' (item)

200-bottle edition. (Flyers/table cards also produced.)

FAC 216: Haçienda House Wine (Red) 'Vin D'Usine Rouge' (item)

Not produced.

FACT 217: To Hell With Burgundy – *Earthbound* (album)

FACD 218: To Hell With Burgundy – 'Who Wants to Change the World?' (single)

FACD 219: Kalima – *Flyaway* (album)

CD-only "Best Of" compilation, including tracks from The Swamp Children.

FACT 220: Happy Mondays – *Bummed* (album)

Produced by Martin Hannett.

FAC 221: Factory Goes to Hollywood (event/badge)

A badge with the Factory US logo, issued at the same time Tony Wilson went to LA to raise funds for FACT 181.

FAC 221: Factory Contract (item)

Factory forgot about having allocated the number already and also assigned it to their contract binders from mid-1990, starting with Cath Carroll (who allegedly signed an eight-album deal). Two clear perspex plates held with 4 metal bolts.

FAC 222: Happy Mondays / Karl Denver – 'Lazyitis' (single)

FAC 223: New Order – 'Fine Time' (single)

FACD 224: The Durutti Column – The First Four Albums (album x 4)

FACT 225 New Order – *Substance* (video)

Video compilation.

FACT 226: Kreisler String Orchestra – *Kreisler String Orchestra* (album)

Factory Classical release.

FAC 227: 'Fred Fac' NME Feature Page (Item)

A three-part catalogue feature published by NME *(13 May 89, 20 May 89, 27 May 89) in 'Fred Fact'.*

FAC 228: Karl Denver – 'Wimoweh 89' (single)

FAC 229: Fac 229! – The Music Week Factorial (advertisement)

Twenty-four-page booklet celebrating 10 years of Factory (1979–1989) containing a label chronology and articles by (or interviews with) various staff members. Free with 'Music Week' 15 July 1989.

FACT 230: Revenge – *One True Passion* (album)

FAC 231: Yo John (advertisement)

Factory ad in Music Week *for John Peel's 50th birthday.*

FAC 232: Happy Mondays – 'W.F.L.' (single)

Vince Clarke and Paul Oakenfold remixes of 'Wrote for Luck'.

FAC 233: New Order / Joy Division Accounts (corporate)

"Substantial Matters 1986–1988 between Joy Division, New Order and Factory Communications Ltd (The Summer of Love)."

FACD 234: The Durutti Column – 'WOMAD 88 (Live)' (EP)

FAC 235: New Order – Blue Monday 88 Flickbook (item)

Xmas gift. First designed for the 'Blue Monday 1988' video clip.

FACT 236: Robin Williams – *Oboe and Piano* (album)

Factory Classical release.

FAC 237: New Order – Here Are the Old Men (video)

Unreleased video concept.

FAC 238 Haçienda '96: 'Citius Altius Fortius' (t-shirt)

Issued to celebrate Manchester's bid for the 1996 Olympic Games.

FAC 239: Halcyon Daze – Happy Mondays Fanzine (publication)

FAC 240: Factory (10th Anniversary) Wall Planner (item)

Issued to celebrate Factory's 10th anniversary.

FAC 241: 'Just Say No To London' (t-shirt)

A Bailey Brothers (and Tony Wilson) idea to go with FACT 181. Never manufactured.

FAC 242: Happy Mondays – 'Madchester Rave On' (single)

FAC 243: Steve Mason – *Technique* Bronze Cherub (item)

Cherub as used on cover of FACT 275.

FACT 244: The Durutti Column – *Vini Reilly* (album)

FACT 244+: Vincent Gerrard / Stephen Patrick – 'I Know Very Well How…' (single)

An out-take from the recording sessions for (Stephen Patrick) Morrissey's 'Viva Hate' LP sessions with Vini (Vincent Gerard) Reilly.

FAC 245: Madchester Christmas 1989 (XMAS)

Pictures from 'Madchester'. A sequence of five (retouched) photo cards purporting a Madchester roadsign, Madchester 1996 The British Olympic Bid (picture of the town hall), Madchester Piccadilly (railway station), University of Madchester and Madchester United (picture of Old Trafford stadium). Original photos by Vini Reilly, concept by Tony Wilson.

FACT 246: Duke String Quartet – *Duke String Quartet* (album)

Factory Classical release.

FAC 247: Revenge – *Revenge* (album)

FAC 248: 'On CD At Last, On DAT Already' (advertisement)

This was a full page ad in NME and Music Week 17 March 1990 for FACD 40 and FACD 170, as well as the Factory DAT back catalogue and the Factory Classical DAT titles… except the Factory Classical DATs were never issued.

FACT 249: Kalima – *Feeling Fine* (album)

FACT 250: Joy Division: *Substance* (1977–1980) (album)

Compilation.

FAC 251: New Factory (building)

The new Factory headquarters. The building was acquired in October 1988, officially opened on 29 September 1990 and closed November 1992.

FACD 251: Steve and Gillian – 'Loved It (The New Factory)' (single)

CD given away to those attending the FAC 251 opening party.

FAC 252: Happy Mondays – 'Hallelujah Radio-Only CD' (single)

Another identification for FACD 242+, not actually another release.

FAC 253: Chairman Resigns (event)

This was a bet between Tony Wilson and Rob Gretton regarding FAC 263 going Top 5 in the UK charts. If it didn't, Wilson was to resign. It didn't. Bet not upheld.

FACT 254: The Durutti Column – *Guitar One* – House (album)

Not released.

FAC 255: Cath Carroll – 'Beast' (single)

FACT 256: Rolf Hind – *Rolf Hind* (album)

Factory Classical release.

FAC 257: Electronic: 'Getting Away With It' (single)

Bernard Sumner, Johnny Marr and Neil Tennant, with drums by David Palmer (ABC) and strings by Anne Dudley (The Art Of Noise).

FAC 258: 'Fac Off' (t-shirt)

FAC 259: Staff Christmas Party (event)

A staff party and Tony Wilson's 40th birthday party held 19 February 1990 at The Green Room and Lazerquest on Whitworth Street West, for Factory, Dry and Haçienda staff. (Also included a live performance from Northside.)

FACT 260: Happy Mondays – *Hallelujah* (album)

Compilation issued outside the UK.

FAC 261 'Madchester' (t-shirt)

Logo used on FAC 242 (various formats) and FAC 262 among others.

FACT 262 Happy Mondays – *Madchester* – *Rave On* (video)

Video compilation issued through Virgin.

FAC 263: New Order – 'Round & Round' (single)

FACT 264: The Durutti Column – *Guitar Two* – *Acoustic* (album)

Never issued.

FAC 265: From Manchester With Love (artwork)

A heart-shaped stars and stripes image used on information sheets, shirts and banners during Factory's campaign at the New Music Seminar in New York, July 1990.

FACT 266: Steve Martland – *Steve Martland* (album)

Factory Classical release.

FAC 267: Revenge – 'Pineapple Face' (single)

FAC 268: Northside: 'Shall We Take a Trip' (single)

FAC 269: Kalima – 'Shine (Remix)' (single)

FAC 270: Various Artists – *Our Dance Days* (album)

A planned 1990 release to consist of Marcel King, 52nd Street, Section 25, and Quando Quango 'house remixes' organised by Mike Pickering. Not released.

FAC 271: Technique Advertising (promotion)

A billboard campaign at 150 sites around Great Britain for FACT 275 as well as four (15-second) TV ads for the album.

FAC 272: Happy Mondays – 'Step On' (single)

FAC 273: New Order – 'Run 2' (single)

The release had to be retracted due to "compositional sampling" problems with the John Denver song 'Leaving on a Jet Plane'

FACT 274: The Durutti Column – *Obey the Time* (album)

FACT 275: New Order – *Technique* (album)

FACD 276: Various Artists – 'Factory Classical CD Sampler' (EP)

Promotional-only Factory Classical release.

FAC 277: Joy Division – *Substance* (album)

Never officially released compilation of videos, live footage and interviews, but Qwest US released some promo editions (which were subsequently recalled).

FAC 278: Indambinigi – 'Zimba' (single)

Karl Denver and Steve Lima. The name was meant to be "Indamaningi", but Factory got the spelling wrong.

FAC 279: Revenge – 'Slave' (single)

FAC 280: The Wendys – 'More Than Enough' (single)

Promo given away to DJs and independent record stores mainly in Edinburgh, Manchester, and London.

FAC 281: The Area (shop)

Factory's memorabilia shop on the second floor of Affleck's Palace, 35–43 Oldham Street (across the road from FAC 201).

FAC 282: Flowers for Horse's Wedding (event)

Horse is Paul Ryder from Happy Mondays.

FAC 283: 'World in Motion' (t-shirt)

A white shirt with gold and blue printing, with the FAC 293 cover design. (A cap and shorts with the same design were also issued.)

FAC 284: The Durutti Column – 'The Together Mix' (single)

FACT 285: The Wendys – *Gobbledygook* (album)

FAC 286: Bloomsbury Classical Showcase (event)

The 'Classics in Motion' FAC 318 concerts.

FAC 287: Electronic – 'Get The Message' (single)

FAC 288: 'Shaun on One' (t-shirt)

FAC 289: New Order – 'Campaign Technique' (promotion notepaper)

A set of four (size A4) paper sheets in white, red, green and yellow, with 'FAC 289' at bottom.

FAC 289: The Wendys – 'The Sun's Going to Shine For Me Soon' (single)

FACT 290: Electronic – *Electronic* (album)

FAC 291: Factory Classical Notepaper (stationery)

Typography matches that of Classical releases. ('FAC 291' appears on the business cards only.)

FAC 292: Shaun Ryder – 'Colours' (single)

Unreleased solo single; cover of the Donovan song. Backing music was recorded by Electronic, but the song was never finished.

FAC 293: ENGLANDneworder – 'World in Motion' (single)

FAC 294: Durutti Column Jazz FM Radio advert (promotion)

FAC 295: Christmas 1990 Photo-Print (XMAS)

A3 photo-print of FAC 251 by night, on heavy stock paper.

FACD 296: Various Artists – *Factory Classical* 5-CD Set (album x5)

FAC 297: The Wendys – 'Pulling My Fingers Off' (single)

FAC 298: Northside – 'My Rising Star' (single)

FAC 299: Factory (logo/t-shirt)

A navy-blue shirt (long-sleeve and short-sleeve versions) with the new Factory logo in silver, and a small label at the bottom of the shirt with FAC 299.

FACT 300: New Order – *{Untitled}* (album)

Unreleased. Ended up as Republic *on London Records.*

FAC 301: Factory Conference 'Think About the Future' (event)

Held at Mottram Hall, Cheshire, 5 July 1990.

FAC 301: *First 50* (book)

Never realised. A book to be written about the first 50 numbers in the Factory catalogue.

FAC 302: Happy Mondays – 'Kinky Afro' (single)

FAC 303: Various Artists – *Palatine Lane* (album)

Given away to new subscribers of Les Inrockuptibles *music magazine.*

FAC 304: Various Artists – 'Palatine (The Single)' (single)

FAC 305C: Various Artists – *Select* Factory Sampler (cassette)

Given away free as part of Select *magazine March 1991 issue.*

FAC 306: Steve Martland – 'Glad Day' (single)

Factory Classical release.

FAC 307: Cath Carroll – 'Moves Like You' (single)

FAC 308: Northside – 'Take 5' (single)

FAC 309: Hi–Nek (Second Generation) (t–shirt)

FACT 310: Northside – *Chicken Rhythms* (album)

FAC 311: Fourth Generation Notepaper (stationery)

New Factory logo typeset from the custom Factis 90 font (based on Otl Aicher's Rotis typeface). Stationery pieces included letterhead, continuation, comp, sticker, envelopes, white waxed paper, envelopes, and visiting cards.

FAC 312: Happy Mondays – 'Loose Fit' (single)

FAC 313: Joy Division – *Transmission* (video)

Black and white version of Joy Division performing 'Transmission' on BBC2's Something Else. (Number allocated to the actual clip. Released to TV stations as FAC 400.)

FACT 314: Various Artists – *Palatine – The Factory Story / Vol. 1* (album)

FAC 315: Cath Carroll – Promo Package (promotion)

Promoting a Cath Carroll concert at Ronnie Scott's, 1 August 1991. Contained video, CD, cassette, photographs and invitation.

FACT 316: I Fagiolini – *The Art of Monteverdi* (album)

Factory Classical release.

FAC 317: Cath Carroll – 'England Made Me' (badge)

Promotional badge for FACT 210. 2cm x 1cm, black and gold enamel.

FAC 318: Classics in Motion (event)

Classical showcase event to launch FACT 316 / 326 / 336 / 346 / 356 at London's Bloomsbury Theatre, 29/30/31 October 1990.

FAC 318: Flying Start Exhibition Stand (event)

A Factory artwork exhibition.

FAC 319: Adventure Babies – 'Camper Van' (single)

FACT 320: Happy Mondays – *Pills 'N' Thrills and Bellyaches* (album)

FAC 321: Jonathan Demme – *The Perfect Kiss* (video)

The video-clip as seen on FACT 225.

FACT 322: Happy Mondays – *Live* (album x 2)

This release is the official version of the 'Baby Bighead' bootleg.

FAC 323: New Order – '*{Untitled}*' (single)

Unreleased.

FACT 324: Various Artists – *Palatine – The Factory Story / Vol. 2* (album)

FACT 325: Various Artists – *Martin, The Work of Martin Hannett* **(album)**
A tribute compilation.

FACT 326: Rolf Hind – *Country Music* **(album)**
Factory Classical release.

FAC 327: Revenge – 'Gun World Porn' (EP)

FAC 328: Electronic – 'Feel Every Beat' (single)

FAC 329: The Other Two – 'Tasty Fish' (single)

FACT 330: The Other Two – *{Untitled}* **(album)**
Unreleased. The album was finally issued as Other Two & You *on London Records.*

FAC 331: The Temporary Contemporary Table (item)
Factory boardroom table. Designed by Andy Woodcock & Ed Jackson. Broken by the Happy Mondays.

FAC 332: Happy Mondays – 'Judge Fudge' (single)

FACT 334: Various Artists – *Palatine – The Factory Story / Vol. 3* **(album)**

FACT 335: Adventure Babies – *Laugh* **(album)**

FACT 336: Red Byrd – *Songs of Love and Death* **(album)**
Factory Classical release.

FACT 337: The Wendys – 'I Instruct' (single)

FAC 338: Northside – 'Want A Virgin' (single)
Unreleased. Demo only. Intended for the second album.

FAC 339: MTV Special History of Factory (video)
A 27-minute documentary featuring various Factory artists and interviews. First broadcast 26 January 1992 on MTV's 120 Minutes, later shown on MTV Europe.

FAC 341: Pills 'N' Thrills and Bellyaches Launch (event)
A meal, organised by Factory/London at the London Zoo Aquarium.

FAC 342: Happy Mondays Charter Clinic (concept)

FACT 344: Various Artists – *Palatine – The Factory Story / Vol. 4* **(album)**

FAC 345: Palatine Sleeve (item)
A wrap-around sleeve for the booklet included with the Palatine *boxed set (FACT 400). The booklet in this sleeve was Factory's Christmas gift.*

FACT 346: Graham Fitkin – *Flak* **(album)**
Factory Classical release.

FAC 347: Adventure Babies – 'Barking Mad' (single)

FAC 348: Electronic – '{Untitled' (single)
Nothing released under this number.

FAC 349: The Other Two – 'Movin' On' (single)
Unreleased.

FAC 351: Jon Savage – *The Haçienda Must Be Built* (book)

FAC 352: Happy Mondays – 'Staying Alive' (single)

Unreleased as a single, 'Staying Alive' was later released on FAC 372. Its intended B–side 'Baby Bighead' was later released on FAC 362.

FAC 354: Palatine Celebrations (event)

FACT 356: Erik Satie – *Socrate* (album)

Factory Classical release.

FAC 357: Adventure Babies – 'Laugh' (single)

Unreleased. Cassettes of this forthcoming CD single went out to licensees and other parties, just before Factory collapsed.

FAC 362: Happy Mondays – 'Stinkin Thinkin' (single)

FAC 366: Steve Martland – *Crossing the Border* (album)

Factory Classical release.

FAC 372: Happy Mondays – 'Sunshine and Love' (single)

This was the last (chronological, not numerical) original Factory release.

FACD 376: Piers Adams – *Handel Recorder Sonatas* (album)

Factory Classical release.

FAC 383: The Vikings (fan club)

New Order "hardcore" fan club.

FACD 386: Walter Hus – *Muurwerk* (album)

Factory Classical release.

FAC 396: Two Guitarists – *Still Life* (album)

Unreleased.

FACT 400: Various Artists – *Palatine – The Factory Story / 1979–1990* (album x 4)

Boxed set consisting of FACT/D 314 + 324 + 334 + 344 + 36-page booklet.

FACT 400v: Various Artists – *Palatine – The Free Vid* (video)

Free with initial copies of FACT 400 bought from HMV.

FAC 401: *24 Hour Party People* (movie)

Allocated to the Michael Winterbottom-directed film. The number appears on the press releases and stationery.

FACT 406: Steve Martland – *Wolfgang* (album)

Factory Classical release.

FAC 413: *Jack* – January 2003 edition (magazine)

FACT 420: Happy Mondays – *Yes Please!* (album)

FAC 421: 'factoryrecords.net' (website)

Factory fan site.

FAC 424 Anthony H Wilson – *24 Hour Party People* (book)
Novelisation of the FAC 401 film.

FACDVD 424: *24 Hour Party People* (DVD)
DVD release of FAC 401.

FAC 433: '24 Hour Party People' (website)
Website for FAC 401.

FAC 441: 'worldinmotion.net' (Website)
New Order fan site.

FAC 451: Jane Stanton – *Love Will Tear Us Apart – A History of The Haçienda* (video)
Thirty-minute documentary for Granada TV.

FAC 451: Haçienda (film set/event)
The 24 Hour Party People *film's reconstructed Haçienda set and filming party/session.*

FAC 461: Matthew Robertson – *Factory Records – The Complete Graphic Album* (book)

FAC 471: 'Hot' – A Celebration of The Haçienda (events)
An official series of one-off, single-night club events presented by 'Wilson House' (Oliver Wilson, son of Tony).

FAC 473: Les Paul FAC 473 (Item)
Ten-foot, free–standing fibreglass Gibson Les Paul guitar, designed by Peter Saville incorporating his colour-wheel coding from FAC 73. Part of a music and art campaign for three charities: The Prince's Trust, Nordoff-Robbins Music Therapy and Teenage Cancer Trust.

FAC 481: Building – 27 January 2006 issue (magazine)
'Oh Manchester!' issue edited by Tony Wilson and Yvette Livesey. "...Starring Britain's Most Dynamic City".

FAC 491: Haçienda 25 (exhibition/event)
Haçienda 25th anniversary exhibition at Urbis, Manchester and opening party launch event.

FACT 500: Happy Mondays – *Uncle Dysfunktional* (album)
Factory in number only; released on the Sequel label.

FAC 501: Anthony H Wilson (man/event/plaque)
2/20/1950 – 8/10/07. Anthony H Wilson's coffin bore the plaque 'FAC 501', but the number refers to his funeral and the man himself.

FAC 511 'And You Forgotten' (event)
Rob Gretton memorial concert held at The Ritz, Manchester, 5 May 2004; benefiting Manchester Kids.

OBSCURE FACS

Tony Wilson's indefatigable enthusiasm for music meant that other outlets were needed for artists he believed in. What's more, when Factory collapsed in 1992, he continued the brand with several more incarnations.

FACTORY BENELUX

FAC BN 1–004: A Certain Ratio – 'Shack Up' (single)
The first and last Factory Benelux records were Crepuscule releases at the same time: FAC BN 1 = TWI 004, FBN 839 = TWI 839. FAC BN 1 originally was planned to be a mini-album by Joy Division.
FBN 2: The Durutti Column – *Lips That Would Kiss* (album)
FAC BN 3–006: Section 25 – 'Charnel Ground' (single)
FAC BN 4: Crispy Ambulance – 'Live on a Hot August Night' (single)
Number originally allocated by a Factory Shareholder Analysis to "Manhattan Project or Nicky". (Manhattan Project was Jane & Jeff Hudson.)
FAC BN 5: Section 25 – 'Je Veux Ton Amour' (single)
FAC BN 5 was originally allocated to an eight-song Blurt 10". It was also allocated to a Crispy Ambulance single.
FAC BN 6: Crawling Chaos – *The Gas Chair* (album)
Original album title: The Gas Chair Clown. *This number also allocated to a 'Manhattan Project' (see FBN 4).*
FAC BN 7: Various Artists – *A Factory Complication* (video)
Compilation of promo videos and live performance tracks including A Certain Ratio, Section 25, New Order, Cabaret Voltaire, The Durutti Column, Crispy Ambulance and OMD.
FBN 8: New Order – 'Everything's Gone Green' (single)
Originally allocated to an ACR 12".
FBN 9: The Names – 'Calcutta / Swimming' (single)
Originally allocated to a Durutti Column release.
FBN 10: The Durutti Column – 'Deux Triangles' (single)
Original 12" (with completely different tracklist) was to have been released a year earlier.
FBN 11: Minny Pops – 'Time' (single)
A 12" version was also planned but was never released.
FBN 12: Crispy Ambulance – *The Plateau Phase* (album)
Debut album.

FBN 13: Various Artists – *Vinyl* magazine flexi (flexi)

Included with the Dutch magazine Vinyl *(Issue 8, November 1981).*

FBN 14: Section 25 – *The Key of Dreams* (album)

FAC BN 15: Minny Pops – *Sparks in a Dark Room* (album)

FBN 16: Swamp Children – *Taste What's Rhythm* (album)

FBN 17: A Certain Ratio – 'Guess Who?' (single)

FBN 18: Crispy Ambulance – 'Sexus' (single)

FBN 19: Stockholm Monsters – 'Miss Moonlight' (single)

FBN 20: 52nd Street – 'Cool as Ice' (single)

FBN 21: Swamp Children – *So Hot* (album)

Released before UK FACT 70 version; different sleeve.

FBN 22: New Order – 'Murder' (single)

Parallel release to 'Thieves Like Us'.

FBN 23: Quando Quango – 'Love Tempo' (single)

FBN 24: The Wake – 'Something Outside' (single)

FBN 25: Cabaret Voltaire – 'Yashar' (single)

Artwork unique to this issue.

FBN 26: Surprize – 'In Movimento' (single)

Italian band based in Bologna; recorded in Manchester by Donald Johnson and Bernard Sumner.

FBN 27: Various Artists – *FBN Greatest Hits* (album)

12" remix compilation.

FBN 28: Nyam Nyam – 'Fate/Hate' (single)

Produced by Peter Hook.

FBN 29: The Wake – *Harmony* (album)

FBN 30: The Durutti Column – *Another Setting* (album)

Japan-only release.

FBN 31: Stockholm Monsters – *Alma Mater* (album)

Unreleased FBN issue of FACT 80. Number also allocated to a proposed Thick Pigeon release ('Jess & Bart') and a mini-LP from James.

FBN 32: A Certain Ratio – 'Brazilia' (single)

FBN 33: Section 25 – *From the Hip* (album)

Unreleased issue of UK album.

FBN 34: Lavolta Lakota – 'Prayer' (single)

Produced by Peter Hook.

FBN 35: The Wake – 'Talk About the Past' (single)

Unreleased FBN issue of FAC 88.

FBN 36: The Durutti Column – *Circuses and Bread* **(album)**

FBN 36 was originally to have been another Durutti Column album, Short Stories for Pauline, *which was not released due to Factory UK pressure. They didn't want it to interfere with the release of FACT 144, Factory's first CD. SSFP was ultimately shelved as Vini Reilly had recorded a new album in the meantime. SSFP tracks retitled and released on other DC records.*

FBN 37: Life – 'Dites Moi' (single)

FBN 38: Life – 'Dites Moi' (single)

Unreleased 7" of FBN 37.

FBN 39: La Cosa Nostra – 'Coming Closer' (single)

7" version.

FBN 40: La Cosa Nostra – 'Coming Closer' (single)

12" version.

FBN 41: Simon Topping – 'Prospect Park' (single)

FBN 42: Life – 'Better' (single)

FBN 43: Marcel King – 'Reach for Love' (single)

FBN 44: Stanton Miranda – 'Wheels Over Indian Trails' (single)

FBN 45: Section 25 – 'Crazy Wisdom' (single)

A 7" was almost released (but wasn't) on Factory UK as FAC 132.

FBN 46: Stockholm Monsters – 'How Corrupt is Rough Trade?' (single)

FBN 47: The Executioner – 'Executioner's Theme' (single)

Unreleased collaboration on 7" between Paul Haig and Cabaret Voltaire. One mix can be found on Paul Haig's European Sun *compilation LP/CD. Another mix can be found on the cassette version of* The Quick Neat Job *Crepuscule compilation.*

FBN 48: The Executioner – 'Executioner's Theme' (single)

Unreleased collaboration on 12" between Paul Haig and Cabaret Voltaire.

FBN 49: Playgroup – 'Euphoria' (single)

12" version.

FBN 50: Playgroup – 'Euphoria' (single)

7" version.

FBN 51: The Durutti Column – 'Tomorrow' (single)

FBN 52: Various Artists – *The Factory Complication 1* **(album)**

Unreleased compilation LP, announced early 1986 but never finished. No track listing available.

FBN 55: Various Artists – *The Factory Complication 2* **(album)**

Unreleased compilation LP, announced early 1986 but never finished. No track listing available.

FBN 100: The Durutti Column – 'For Patti' (single)

Meant to be included with a limited edition of FBN 10. Only 100 pressed.

FBN 100: New Order – *Low-Life* (album)

FBN 123: New Order – 'Perfect Kiss' (single)

Alternate 7" artwork.

FBN 839: New Order – 'Touched by the Hand of God' (single)

FACTORY AMERICA

FA1: New Order Gig – Ukrainian National Home (event)

The show as featured on FACT 77.

FA2: Ike Yard – *Ike Yard* (album)

The first FACT A (Factory America) release. The title is Ike Yard; *the sleeve graphics ("A FACT A SECOND") reflect its catalogue designation – FACTA 2(nd).*

FA4: A Certain Ratio – 'Knife Slits Water'

Same release as OFNY 4 (see below).

OF FACTORY NEW YORK

OFNY release numbers were spelled out as an ordinal (i.e. FIRST, SECOND, THIRD, etc) and/or given ordinal endings (i.e. 1st, 2nd, 3rd, etc.)

OF-1 (I/OF-1): The Birthday Party – *Pleasureheads Must Burn* (video)

Two live performances (July 1982 and February 1983) and the Nick the Stripper *promo film.*

OF-2 (I/OF-2): The Fall – *Perverted by Language Bis* (video)

Live, promotional and interview material.

OFNY 3: Cabaret Voltaire – 'Yashar' (single)

Alternate artwork to UK release.

OFNY 4: A Certain Ratio – 'Knife Slits Water' (single)

Through Mango Records. Alternate artwork to UK release.

OFNY 5: Quando Quango – 'Love Tempo' (single)

Alternate artwork to UK release.

OFNY 9: New Order – 'Confusion' (single)

Through Streetwise Records. Alternate artwork to UK release.

OFNY 10: Streetlife – 'Act On Instinct' (single)

Released by Blackmarket Records NYC with alternate artwork to UK release.

OFNY P1: New Order – Paradise Garage (poster)

By Lawrence Weiner for New Order's 1983 Paradise Garage show in NYC.

OFNY P2: Section 25/Quando Quango – The Ritz (poster)

By Lawrence Weiner for the 1985 Section 25/Quando Quango show at The Ritz in NYC.

OFNY P3: New Order – The Perfect Kiss (poster)

"Film poster" by Barbara Kruger for the Jonathan Demme video-clip of 'Perfect Kiss' as seen on FACT 225. (Also see FAC 321.)

OFNY P4: The film and video poster (poster)

Blue Factory US logo on white background.

OFNY P34: New Order – 1987 Substance (promo poster)

Four b/w photos, blue and pink artwork, by Lawrence Weiner.

(OFNY) 52nd Street – 'Cool As Ice' (single)

Released via A&M Records (U.S.)

(OFNY) Marcel King – 'Reach for Love' (single)

Released via A&M Records (U.S.)

(OFNY) New Order – Club 1018 (poster)

By Lawrence Weiner for the New Order's show at Club 1018 in NYC (5 December 1986).

FACTORY US

FACTUS 1: Joy Division – *Unknown Pleasures* (album)

FACTUS 2: Joy Division – 'She's Lost Control' (single)

Pressed for US and UK releases. (UK version has 'Atmosphere' as A-side.)

FACUS 4: A Certain Ratio – 'Do the Du (casse)' (EP)

Tracks including selections from FACT 16, FBN 1.

FACTUS 5: *From Manchester to New York Direct* (video)

Video show intended for use in NYC clubs.

FACTUS 6: Joy Division – *Closer* (album)

FACTUS 7: *Closer* billboard ad (concept)

Idea for billboard advertising on Sunset Boulevard, L.A.; not pursued.

FACTUS 8: New Order – *1981–1982* (album)

Compilation of 'Temptation', 'Everything's Gone Green' singles; A– and B–sides.

FACTUS 9: Section 25 – *Live in America* (album)

Proposed album from material recorded live in New York, February 1982. Never released on Factory; material subsequently surfaced on the LTM-issued album.

FACUS 10: New Order – 'Blue Monday' (single)

On Factory/Rough Trade US.

FACTUS 12: New Order – *Power Corruption & Lies* (album)

On Factory/Rough Trade US.

FACTUS 14: Section 25 – *From the Hip* (album)

On Factory/Rough Trade US.

FACTUS 16 Thick Pigeon – *Too Crazy Cowboys* (album)

FACTUS 17: Various Artists – *Young, Popular and Sexy* (album)

Compilation including Happy Mondays, Durutti Column, Stanton Miranda, Stockholm Monsters, A Certain Ratio, Shark Vegas, The Railway Children and Miaow.

FACTUS 19: Of Factory New York notepaper (stationery)

Paper and envelopes, using the 1984 Factory US logo.

FACUS 21: Factory US Logo (logo/badge)

Issued with FAC 120. Two versions, red and blue, both with the 1984 Factory US logo.

FACTUS 23: Joy Division – 'Love Will Tear Us Apart' (single)

Includes American 7" 'jukebox' pressing.

FACTUS 25: Various Artists – *Four + One* (video)

Promo videos (UK versions) from Fadela, Durutti Column, Happy Mondays, Biting Tongues and Stanton Miranda.

FACUS 28: Joy Division – 'Komakino' (flexi)

Came with The Other Sound *fanzine. Officially commissioned release. Also used promotionally by Rough Trade US.*

FACTUS 46: A Certain Ratio – Ratio > The Circus (event/sticker)

"FACT/US 46, RATIO > THE CIRCUS. On Stage, A Certain Ratio, Final New York Performance. On Screen, THE FACTORY VIDEO CIRCUS (3/4"), ACR, Cabs, Durutti Column, Joy Division, New Order, Omitd, Section 25 amongst others. CHASE PARK, 599 Broadway, Wednesday, October 14th, 1981. VIDIO [sic] 9 p.m. > 12:30, RATIO 1 a.m. Factus 46"

FACTUS 50: New Order – *Movement* (album)

Artwork has different colour scheme from UK release. Sleeve is white with black and burgundy typography.

FACUS 53 New Order – 'Procession' (single)

Actually UK release with sticker: 'A FACTORY US PROJECT, Mfg & Dist by ROUGH TRADE inc. SAN FRANCISCO, 415 621 4307'

FACTUS 164: The Durutti Column – Valuable Passages (poster)

US-only promo poster for FACT 164.

FACTORY TOO

FACD 2.01: The Durutti Column – *Sex and Death* **(album)**

FAC 2.02: Various Artists – 'A Factory Sample Too' (single x 2)

Four-band sampler.

FAC 2.03: Factory Too Bouncer's Hat / Christmas Present 1994 (XMAS)

Black wool knit cap with woven 'Too' logo.

FAC 2.04: HOPPER – 'On Peel' (single)

Live session from John Peel show on BBC Radio 1, first transmitted 15 October 1994. Originally allocated 2.01.

FAC 2.05: HOPPER – 'Wasted' (single)

FACD 2.06: The 6ths – *Wasps' Nests* **(album)**

Stephin Merritt (AKA The Magnetic Fields, Future Bible Heroes and The Gothic Archies) with guest vocalists.

FAC 2.07: Factory Internet Home Page v1 (website)

Official website, now gone.

FAC 2.08: The Demo Cassette Box

Details unknown.

FAC 2.09: Walks On Water (event/poster)

In The City '95 event, on two boats, featuring Hopper, Vini Reilly, The Space Monkeys and Khalique. Sunday 3 September 1995.

FACT 2.10: Hopper – *English and French* **(album)**

Produced by Suede's Bernard Butler.

FACDR 2.11: The Durutti Column – *Sex and Death* **(CD-ROM)**

Interactive version of Sex and Death *in sandpaper sleeve.*

FAC 2.12: Hopper – 'Oh My Heartless' (single)

Factory Too/London's last joint release.

FAC 2.13: Space Monkeys – 'Keep On Tripping On' (single)

FAC 2.14: The Factory Bag / Christmas Present 1995 (XMAS)

"Soft black leathery-plastic ruck sack with XXXL straps". The first 130 (of 170) had their straps snap shortly after manufacturing.

FAC 2.15: Space Monkeys – *Splinters* **(album)**

US-only release planned for 1997 cancelled due to 'licensing problems'.

FAC 2.16: 'Pornucopia'

An unreleased audionovel/CD Fred Vermorel project commissioned by Tony Wilson for Factory Too: "A recording of Obsessions created by the obsessed themselves". Originally was referred to as 'Starlust' (a book by Fred & Judy

Vermorel, published in 1985) but became 'Pornucopia' (aka 'The Pornucopia Experiment'), a website (www.pornucopia.org, existing from 1995 until 1998).

FAC 2.19: Space Monkeys / AHW – T*he Ineluctable Modality of Life* (video)

Interview video calling card to introduce the band to Interscope (USA).

FACT 2.20: Space Monkeys (album)

Planned release. Later changed to FAC 2.25.

FAC 2.21: The Durutti Column – 'Sing To Me' (single)

This was to have been a Trade 2 singles Club 7"/CD-single release, but it was cancelled due to publishing/licensing problems with London Records.

FAC 2.22: Hopper – 'Bad Kid' (single)

FAC 2.23: Space Monkeys – Signing On (event)

Video made on the day of the Space Monkeys signing to Factory Too. "Adventures in the tower of the Refuge Building in Manchester; starring the lawyers."

FAC 2.24: Space Monkeys – Christmas Present 1996 (item)

Twenty-page Xmas card, including a one-track promo CD single.

FACT 2.25: Space Monkeys – *The Daddy of Them All* (album)

The Factory web page v1 originally suggested that 2.25 was to be a release by Khalique titled Asian Man, *including the track 'Sids Tune'. Apparently completed ("Production by Jed and Martin, the vegans out of Black Grape"), but never released.*

FAC 2.26: Unofficial Durutti Column Internet Activities (website)

Relates to Rob Stanzel's unofficial Durutti Column website, a mailing list and donated audio tracks (available from the website).

FAC 2.28: Factory Too lapel badge / Christmas gift 1997 (XMAS/badge)

Enamel badge and Xmas card.

FAC 2.29: Space Monkeys – demo tape (cassette)

Promo-only cassette of new songs.

FAC 2.31: The Durutti Column – *Time Was Gigantic...When We Were Kids* (album)

FAC 2.32: Hopper – 'Ridiculous Day' (single)

FAC 2.33: Space Monkeys – 'Blowing Down The Stylus / Dear Dhinus' (single)

FAC 2.34 Website promo / Christmas gift 1998 (item)

A small case, with 'FAC 2.34' in gold on the cover, containing a paper insert printed with 'www.factoryrecords.com'.

FAC 2.35: FACD 2.60 Preview (event)

Preview of FACD 2.60 held on 24/5/99.

FAC 2.37: Factory Internet Home Page v2 (website)

Official website.

FAC 2.39: Space Monkeys – *Who's the Daddy Now?* (album)

Japan-only remix compilation.

FACT 2.40: Various Artists – *Different Colours, Different Shades* (album)

Re-issue compilation of Factory (Version 1) artists.

FACDR 2.41 The Durutti Column – *Time Was Gigantic / Reissued Experiment* (album x 2)

Limited edition double CDR promo featuring Time Was Gigantic... When We Were Kids *together with* Reissued Experiments, *a selection of some of the rare and previously unreleased material issued as extra tracks on the second phase of Durutti Column reissues.*

FAC 2.43: Space Monkeys – 'Acid House Killed Rock and Roll' (single)

FAC 2.53: Space Monkeys – 'Sugar Cane' (single)

FACD 2.60: Joy Division – *Preston The Warehouse 28/2/80* (album)

Not a Factory release, but the NMC label used approved FAC numbering.

FACD 2.61: Joy Division – *Les Bains Douches* (album)

Not a Factory release, but the NMC label used approved FAC numbering.

FACD 2.63: Space Monkeys – 'March of the Scarecrows' (single)

FAC 3.01: The Durutti Column – 'Sex and Death' (item)

A fan survey/info response card included in the initial release of FACD 2.01, with an offer for a free Vini Reilly plectrum or a Durutti Column 'The Return of...' *poster.*

FAC 3.11: The Durutti Column – Sex and Death (poster)

Promotional Durutti Column poster based on The Return of the Durutti Column – *a 1967 Situationist poster with cartoon imagery. (See FAC 3.01)*

FACTORY ONCE

Factory re-issue label. All Durutti Column releases have new artwork and additional tracks.

FACDO 14: The Durutti Column – *The Return Of The Durutti Column* (album)

FACDO 44: The Durutti Column – LC (album)

FACDO 74: The Durutti Column – *Another Setting* (album)

FACDO 84: The Durutti Column – *Without Mercy* (album)

FACDO 144: The Durutti Column – *Domo Arigato* (album)

FACDO 204: The Durutti Column – *The Guitar and Other Machines* (album)

FACDO 244: The Durutti Column – *Vini Reilly* (album)

FACDO 274: The Durutti Column – *Obey the Time* (album)

(ONCE) The Durutti Column – *The Third Member of the Durutti Column* (video)

Promo-only video for DC re-issues; film about Martin Hannett by Tosh Ryan; also titled Absolute Zero.

(ONCE) Happy Mondays – *Loads* (album)

"*Greatest Hits*" *compilation.*

(ONCE) Various Artists – *Too Young To Know, Too Wild To Care* (album)

Re-issued compilation of Factory (Version 1) artists.

F4 RECORDS

R1–M15: Raw-T – 'Switch/Ego' (single)

The first release on F4. (Touted as "promo only".)

R2–M15: Raw-T – 'Where We Live' (single)

R4–M15: Raw-T – 'Realise and Witness' (album)

R6–M40: The Young Offenders Institute – 'We're the Young Offenders' (single)

(F4) f4records.co.uk (website)

Nominal website for F4 digital releases.

(F4) F4 (logo/badge)

(F4) The Durutti Column – Heaven Sent (It Was Digital…It Was Heaven Sent) (album)

Download-only.